Jonathan C. Smith

Relaxation
Dynamics

NINE WORLD
APPROACHES TO
SELF-RELAXATION

Research Press

2612 North Mattis Avenue
Champaign, Illinois 61821

Advisory Editor, Frederick H. Kanfer

To my mother, father, sister, and friends

Contents

List of Exercises

List of Worksheets

Foreword

Dr. Thomas D. Borkovec
Dr. Douglas A. Bernstein

Relaxation techniques have been taught and learned for centuries. They encompass many different theoretical and philosophical traditions and an astonishing array of specific strategies. Edmund Jacobson's work in the early 1900s brought relaxation to the attention of modern Western practitioners and scientists; Joseph Wolpe's use of Jacobson's approach in the 1950s in systematic desensitization popularized the technique within the rapidly growing area of behavior therapy. Both as an adjunct to other forms of therapy and a useful coping strategy in its own right, relaxation training has received considerable research attention and clinical application. Its popularity has remained undiminished over the last 20 years. Indeed, as behavior therapy has increasingly emphasized self-control approaches to behavior change, interest in providing clients with such a practical skill has continued to grow.

Because Wolpe had chosen progressive muscle relaxation as the form of relaxation to be employed in his procedures, most early behavior therapists selected this technique, or a close variant, for their scientific and clinical applications. In the past few years, however, other relaxation traditions such as meditation, guided imagery, and autogenic relaxation have been incorporated into clinical practice and research. For the most part, research findings suggest that the type of technique employed really does not matter; all of the strategies result in rather similar outcomes when groups of subjects are compared. These results do not, however, correspond with the experience of clinicians who use relaxation approaches with their clients. They have found that there are marked individual differences in the effects of different techniques on clients' symptoms and general feeling states. Group outcome research, in which the average effects of one relaxation strategy on several people are compared to the average effects on people treated by a different technique, obscures what is happening to any given individual. Information about those who respond to a particular strategy either not at all or exceptionally well is lost.

As clinicians, we have been very aware of such individual differences. Relaxation training with a new client is never exactly the same as it was with a previous client, and must be modified according to the client's symptoms, personal characteristics, and lifestyle. Most of these technique decisions are made on the basis of clinical experience and clients' preferences. As of now there is little in the scientific literature on the issue of matching certain techniques to certain types of clients. That situation is beginning to change as investigation into behavior therapy moves toward identification of factors that can predict the ideal match between individual and technique. Meanwhile, we can learn from the clinical experience and thoughtful wisdom of those who have specialized in relaxation training.

Dr. Jonathan Smith, drawing upon his considerable clinical experience, has written a book that provides extremely useful guidelines for self-relaxation training. It is predicated on the very notion that relaxation techniques have different effects on different people. Several aspects of this fine book deserve comment.

First, Dr. Smith has included specific instructions for several types of relaxation procedures. The procedures he selected are among the most commonly used and most easily defined. While perhaps not every possible technique has been presented, the techniques offered, as a whole, cover nearly every dimension of relaxation currently considered important. Instructions for each technique are very carefully detailed. In a step-by-step fashion, Dr. Smith leads the reader through each aspect of 9 relaxation traditions, covering 58 specific exercises. Frequent demonstration exercises and analogies from everyday life make concepts easier to grasp and more familiar, and every training session has a script with instructions. Indeed, Dr. Smith encourages readers to tape the scripts and to include specific phrases or directions that will maximize their relaxation experience. We know of no other resource that presents so much useful material on such a wide range of relaxation strategies in such detail and clarity.

Second, the book has been written both for experienced clinicians who wish to train their clients in relaxation techniques and for those who wish to learn relaxation for their own use. The writing style appeals to a wide audience. It is exceptionally readable, and is systematically structured to foster rapid learning of each technique. Even more important, it clearly communicates Dr. Smith's desire to help readers achieve their goals while being sensitive to their individuality.

Third, the book reflects an awareness of clinical issues. For instance, Dr. Smith does not present relaxation as a panacea. He warns that relaxation strategies are best viewed within a total therapeutic context; that training by a mental health professional is usually superior to learning a technique solely on one's own; and that self-relaxation is of little or no value for severe adjustment problems. In addition, a rationale and historical background is always provided for each relaxation procedure, and areas where problems may occur, with suggested solutions, are outlined.

The next feature is the one that impressed us the most. The central assumption of the book is that relaxation is best learned through an adventurous, personal, experimental approach. Conforming to his view that relaxation involves a letting go of effortful striving toward a goal, Dr. Smith repeatedly suggests that the reader have fun and use those techniques that feel most pleasant. The wide range of relaxation strategies offered allows the reader to experiment, to determine what works best under what conditions. It is a decidedly empirical approach. Worksheets are provided to assist the reader in identifying the specific effects that accompany each technique. For example, comparisons of feelings before and after a procedure are made using checklists of possible feeling states, which aids in pinpointing changes. He encourages readers to recognize the diversity of possible goals for relaxation, helps them identify personal goals, and provides problem-solving methods for reaching those goals.

The structure of the program as a whole is conducive to rapid and successful learning. One can focus intensively on one or two techniques, or sample each of the traditions and later choose those that are most suitable for particular purposes. The entire program is presented in a hierarchical order, beginning with techniques that are more active, physical, and easy to attend to and progressing to those that are more passive, cognitive, and difficult to concentrate on. Other alternative sequences are offered as well. Readers are encouraged to find, through sampling, experimenting, evaluating, and choosing, that combination of procedures best suited to their personal goals and circumstances. Methods for applying techniques to daily situations are often mentioned to help bridge the gap between home practice and application elsewhere.

Throughout the book, Dr. Smith conveys a sense of trust and confidence in the reader's decisions and choices. He gives the reader a sense of realistic optimism, a feeling that there are things that can be done to achieve a more relaxed and satisfying lifestyle.

Foreword

Dr. Frederick H. Kanfer

Relaxation methods have been among the most widely used procedures in behavioral therapy. They have enabled clients with a variety of psychological problems to control their tensions, intrusive thoughts, and anxieties or to prepare for other forms of treatment. Many different methods, such as autogenic training, progressive muscle relaxation, or meditation, have been described in detail either as central or auxiliary therapy techniques. Yet most presentations have been limited to one specific procedure. *Relaxation Dynamics* is the first truly inclusive relaxation training manual written from a cognitive-behavioral perspective. In a field in which the use of relaxation and meditation techniques has been as diverse and as great as the use of aspirin in medicine, it is comforting to read a book that treats the topic as a theme in its own right.

The integrated conceptual framework of *Relaxation Dynamics* permits comparison of the requirements and potential applications of the different methods while providing the historical background and relevant research needed to view them in context. The richness of information presented here holds the promise for a prescriptive individualized approach. An appreciation of the many clinical aspects of relaxation training—differing intensities, varying difficulties in attaining the intended goal, differing effects on physical and psychological processes—will increase clinicians' awareness of the alternatives and their sensitivity for matching method and client. With this book clinicians can sample and choose various relaxation techniques with full regard for the individual needs of their clients and the compatibility of the techniques with a therapeutic program.

Dr. Smith presents the material in a spirited and highly readable style, tempting the reader to explore and experience the procedures, judge their utility, and enjoy as well as evaluate their effects. Presenting relaxation in such a manner, with so many options, may prove to be the best way to accommodate individual differences in clients and enhance motivation for therapy.

There are many excellent relaxation training manuals, but until now none have accomplished what is achieved in *Relaxation Dynamics*. In terms of scholarship, usefulness, and breadth of coverage, this manual has no equal.

Acknowledgments

Let me begin by thanking Ann Wendel for helping me through the growing pains of a first book. Ann, I want you to know that your warm, sincere, and enthusiastic support—not to mention our weekly phone talks—have meant much to me. It's been fun working with you.

With equal warmth, I would like to thank Pat Sammann, who with prodigious editorial patience read and checked every instance of error, inconsistency, and bad writing. Pat was more than an editor. Her deep understanding of this project helped at every step. In addition, I want to thank Bob Lange and the rest of the team at Research Press. I have been gratified by their energy, creativity, and commitment to quality.

I would like to thank three colleagues in particular for their special contributions. The work of Fred Kanfer, Doug Bernstein, and Tom Borkovec inspired and provided a solid empirical and conceptual foundation for much of Relaxation Dynamics. I deeply appreciate their encouragement and comments.

Finally, thanks to a number of friends who each played a part: Gerry Piorkowski, who in a sense planted the idea; Richard G. Mills, who was the first to insist that the idea was a book; and Reverend Kenneth Heavey, who in long conversations in a local tavern helped me to see that the scope of this book could indeed extend to each horizon.

HOW TO USE THIS BOOK

This book on relaxation training can be used by therapists, clients, students, and the general public. It is divided into two large sections. If you wish to learn self-relaxation, read Section I. It provides instructions, explanations, and guidelines for nine world approaches to self-relaxation. This section is written in nontechnical language appropriate for beginners. It also provides professionals with a model of how instructions can be simply and interestingly presented. If you are a qualified health professional and want to teach self-relaxation to others, read Sections I and II. Section II outlines a variety of training programs and presents important historical and technical information.

Section I

Relaxation Dynamics

Part I

Learning About
Relaxation Dynamics

Lesson 1

An Invitation to
Relaxation Dynamics

Welcome to Relaxation Dynamics, a comprehensive new approach to self-relaxation training. It is a system with many uses, ranging from clinical stress management to personal self-exploration. It is both rigorous and practical, appropriate for health professionals as well as the general public. But above all, it is an approach that is designed to be fun.

Relaxation Dynamics takes a new perspective on relaxation. Most world cultures have a relaxation-based discipline such as yoga, transcendental meditation, Zen, prayer, imagery, progressive relaxation—a complete list would fill pages. Relaxation Dynamics defines a path into the varied worlds of rest-related states. It is a discipline for exploring the rewards that can come from quieting the tensions of body and mind.

Relaxation Dynamics is based on six ideas:

Relaxation Dynamics is self-relaxation. Some approaches to relaxation training emphasize the importance of external help. Hypnosis, for example, relies on suggestions provided by a hypnotist. Biofeedback relies initially on electromechanical equipment. But Relaxation Dynamics emphasizes exercises that can be practiced alone, with a minimum of outside help. It is an approach to *self*-relaxation. It permits each of us to independently explore and learn from rest-related states.

Relaxation Dynamics integrates nine major world approaches. Traditions as diverse as Zen, Christianity, and yoga all have something important to offer concerning relaxation. Each proposes ways of reducing tension and fostering inner calm and relaxation. Taken together, thousands of specific exercises have been proposed. However, most can be reduced to nine fundamental world approaches to self-relaxation:

1. Isometric Squeeze Relaxation
2. Yogaform Stretching
3. Integrative Breathing
4. Somatic Focusing (Beginning Exercises)
5. Somatic Focusing (Advanced Exercises)
6. Thematic Imagery
7. Contemplation
8. Centered Focus Meditation
9. Open Focus Meditation

Each approach is by itself incomplete. Each is only part of what relaxation is all about. Relaxation Dynamics incorporates all nine major world approaches to relaxation in a grand total of 58 specific exercises.

Different approaches to self-relaxation have different effects. Some argue that although there are many different self-relaxation exercises, they all have the same end: a single "relaxation response" or general overall relaxation state (Benson, 1975). Relaxation Dynamics is based on the idea that different approaches have quite different effects. Some are easier than others. Some are physical, others mental. Some are simple, while others are complex. Some are active, while others are relatively passive. Most important, no two people react to the same exercise in the same way.

Different techniques seem to work better for different people. Some people are "natural meditators." They seem to learn meditation quickly and enjoy it greatly. Others prefer exercises that are more active and physical, for example, yogaform stretching. While very few people enjoy and benefit from all approaches to relaxation, just about everyone finds at least one approach that is rewarding. Often people have to explore many approaches before finding what's best for them.

Relaxation Dynamics emphasizes growth, change, and the interaction of all approaches to relaxation. It does *not* present a single, static, and unchanging technique. Basic exercises can be preparation for those that are more advanced; advanced exercises can provide a deeper appreciation of basic exercises. As training proceeds, skills are developed and insights emerge. Relaxation Dynamics is a path of discovery. It is an approach that is *dynamic* in every sense.

Relaxation Dynamics encourages experimentation and exploration. Relaxation training is often presented as a tranquilizer substitute, a tension-reducer, or a health chore for keeping fit (Woolfolk & Lehrer, 1984).

In contrast, Relaxation Dynamics is an adventure, a discipline of personal development. As such it is not unlike dance, sports, or music. By mastering different techniques we can acquire a fundamental skill, the skill of exploring, choosing, and developing a personal approach to self-relaxation. Through Relaxation Dynamics we can learn to explore the rewards that can come from quieting the tensions of body and mind. This, not the imposition of an "expert-prescribed" technique, is the proper goal of relaxation training.

Once mastered, self-relaxation can become an important part of other programs, including cognitive behavior therapy (Ellis & Harper, 1979; Meichenbaum, 1977), stress inoculation training (Meichenbaum & Jaremko, 1982), assertion training (Jakubowski & Lange, 1978), classical desensitization (Wolpe, 1958), pain management (Turk, Meichenbaum, & Genest, 1983), and anger management (Novaco, 1978). Relaxation-based programs can be targeted to a wide range of specific goals, including:

1. Preparing for and tolerating stressful activity
2. Recovering from stressful activity
3. Minimizing occupational burnout
4. Minimizing test-taking anxiety and performance stress
5. Reducing susceptibility to certain illnesses
6. Reducing pain
7. Waking up refreshed, alert, and ready for work
8. Recovering from a hard day of work
9. Preparing for sleep and combating insomnia
10. Preparing for sports, study, or work
11. Increasing creativity and productivity
12. Enriching pleasurable activity (music, reading, sex, etc.)
13. Enriching spiritual exploration and growth

Learning to relax is not unlike learning to swim. For both, the mastery of basic skills can be rewarding in and of itself. And for both, basic skills can be put to a variety of uses. For instance, we can swim for pleasure, or put swimming to use in sports, commercial deep sea diving, or lifeguard work. However, it is best not to approach Relaxation Dynamics with an urgent purpose or goal. Relaxation Dynamics should be done for the joy of self-mastery, self-expression, and self-discovery. Like the pursuit of dance, sports, or music, it should be done for the simple fun of it.

Lesson 2

A Grand Tour of the Worlds of Relaxation

In this lesson we're going to have some fun. We will be taking a tour of the world's approaches to self-relaxation. Our goal is not to master any one approach, but to become acquainted with them all, to develop an inner map of the worlds of Relaxation Dynamics.

First you need to get ready. Find a place that is quiet and free from interruption. Then sit down, preferably in a soft, comfortable chair. Now, place your hands in your lap and rest your feet flat on the floor. Let yourself settle into a position that is comfortable. We are ready to begin.

The next 30 minutes will be your time alone, a time to put aside the busy pressures of the day. You will have an opportunity to sample and enjoy relaxation systems that have evolved through the centuries from every corner of the world.

Relaxation Dynamics Tour Guide

Approach 1: Isometric Squeeze Relaxation

We will begin in America. In the 1930s a Chicago researcher, Edmund Jacobson, published a set of relaxation exercises that eventually became the most popular approach in the country. Although this approach has many versions, all involve simply tightening up or "squeezing" major muscle groups, and then letting go. Here we will call this approach isometric squeeze relaxation. The full Relaxation Dynamics program teaches 11 isometric squeeze exercises. Let's try one that most people find very easy and enjoyable. We will focus on a set of muscles in which many people feel tension, the shoulders and back of the neck. Here's how to do it:

> While keeping the rest of the body loose and relaxed, gently squeeze your shoulders up and together, as if you were shrugging. Tilt your head back, so your shoulder and neck back muscles all squeeze together. Now, create a nice good squeeze, as if you were giving your back a massage or squeezing the tensions out. Keep squeezing for from 5 to 10 seconds. Then let go. Let your shoulders hang loose, and let your tensions dissolve and flow away for about 30 seconds. If you want, try squeezing and letting go a few more times.

How did that feel? Many people find this approach very pleasurable (if it hurt, you did it too hard). Imagine how you would feel if you squeezed *all* of your muscles—from your fingers to your face to your toes—in the same way. It can be a deeply satisfying and relaxing experience.

Approach 2: Yogaform Stretching

We now move from a relatively recent Western approach to an ancient approach from the East. It too is among the most popular schools of self-relaxation. We will call this approach yogaform stretching since it is derived from yoga (Eliade, 1969; Iyengar, 1965; Kriyananda, 1967; Rama, Ballentine, & Ajaya, 1976). In a sense, yogaform stretching is the opposite of isometric squeeze relaxation. Instead of squeezing and letting go, we slowly, smoothly, and gently stretch and unstretch. Relaxation Dynamics teaches 11 stretching exercises. Let's focus again on the same muscles we relaxed with isometric squeeze relaxation, the neck and shoulders. Here's what to do:

> Are you still seated comfortably in an upright position? Are your feet flat on the floor? Let yourself settle into a position that feels comfortable. And focus your attention again on your shoulders and the back of your neck. Now let both arms hang to your sides and gently bow your head. Without exerting any effort, let gravity pull the heavy weight of your head down farther and farther toward your chest. Let gravity pull the heavy weight of your arms. Notice how the neck and shoulder muscles slowly stretch as the weight of your head and arms pulls farther and farther. Let the muscles stretch farther and farther, stretching out the feelings of tension. Take your time, until you feel a good complete stretch. Then gently and easily raise your head and return to your original upright position. If you wish, for the next 30 seconds you

may try this stretch again, or simply attend to the pleasant feelings of relaxation.

How did that feel? Did you notice any differences between isometric squeeze relaxation and yogaform stretching? Which seemed easier? Which was more active?

Approach 3: Integrative Breathing

The next approach is called integrative breathing. It is an approach that developed both in the East and the West (Iyengar, 1981; Jencks, 1977). In fact, breathing is an important part of virtually all relaxation exercises. Integrative breathing exercises are designed to help us breathe in a way that is easy and relaxed, that is, slow and even and full. They can be wonderfully restful and invigorating at the same time. Relaxation Dynamics includes 12 breathing exercises. We will try two of them, one that is active and one that is relatively quiet.

> In the first exercise we will slowly bow down and breathe out, and then sit up and reach up while breathing in. First, let your arms hang limply to each side. Take a deep breath, filling your chest and abdomen. Then slowly and easily let the air out through your nose and slowly, smoothly, and gently bow over in your chair. Let gravity pull your chest and head toward your knees, squeezing out all the air as you bow farther and farther. Do this as smoothly and gently as possible. Then, when you are ready to inhale, slowly, smoothly, and gently sit up while raising your arms higher and higher in front of you. Reach up to the sky and stretch as you take a good complete breath. Then, when you are ready, again slowly, smoothly, and gently lower your arms and bow over while breathing out. At your own unhurried pace try this again. Do this for about a minute.

What was that like? Did it resemble yogaform stretching? How was it different?

Our second breathing exercise is much more quiet. All you need to do is passively attend to how you are breathing. Often this is a very powerful way of calming down.

> How are you breathing at this moment? Notice the air as it flows easily in through your nose, filling your lungs with refreshing energy. There is nothing for you to do but observe the quiet flow of air. And when you breathe out, gently open your lips, and let the air flow out as if you were gently blowing on a candle flame just enough to make it flicker. Continue

breathing this way, easily and effortlessly in through your nose, and then easily out through your lips as you let go. Let the flow of air be comfortable and unforced. There is nothing for you to do but notice the relaxed movement in and out. Try this approach for about a minute.

We have just completed three types of exercises—squeezing, stretching, and breathing. Notice that they all involve physical movement. However, each is relaxing in a different way. Isometric relaxation is quite active. Breathing is very passive. Stretching is somewhere in between. We are now ready to sample exercises that are even more passive; in fact, they involve no physical movement whatsoever. We are going to try relaxing simply by using our minds in a special way.

Approach 4: Somatic Focusing
(Beginning Exercises)

Just about every world culture has developed a form of mental relaxation. Relaxation Dynamics teaches six approaches. The first three place relatively few restrictions on what can be done and as such somewhat resemble fantasy and daydreaming. We will start with an approach called somatic focusing.

When you are deeply relaxed, how does your body feel? How did your shoulders feel after squeezing and stretching? How did your breathing feel after doing the breathing exercises? Certain body sensations seem to go with relaxation. For example, many people feel physical sensations of warmth, heaviness, sinking, or tingling when relaxing. Such sensations are normal and simply indicate that physical relaxation is taking place. People using hypnosis (Bower, 1976) and a European relaxation system called autogenic training (Luthe, 1965) report that quietly thinking about such body sensations can actually help them physically and mentally relax. This approach appears to work because of the strong connection between the mind and the body, a connection demonstrated just about every day of our lives. For instance, imagine it is late in the day. You haven't eaten for hours. A friend has been preparing a meal and starts describing what's cooking. It's your favorite, perhaps steak. You begin thinking about what the meal is going to be like. You picture the steak and imagine its flavor, aroma, texture, color, and so on. You can almost taste and feel the steak in your mouth. Suddenly, you notice two distinct bodily changes: your mouth is beginning to water and your stomach is growling in eager anticipation. All this just because of a few simple thoughts.

In somatic focusing we entertain thoughts, not about eating, but about relaxation. Just as simply letting the mind dwell on words and images about eating stirred the body's digestive system, so quietly attending to thoughts about relaxation can bring about relaxation. Let's try it and see what happens:

> Let both of your hands fall to your sides. Let them become as relaxed as possible. Give yourself a while to settle into a position that feels very comfortable. Let your breathing be calm and even. Now, focus your attention on your hands. Simply repeat to yourself the phrase "My hands are warm and heavy." Let these words go over and over like an echo. There is nothing for you to try to do. Do not try to force your hands to feel warm and heavy. Simply let the words go over and over in your mind, like the words of a simple song or nursery rhyme. You might want to imagine your hands in warm water, or in the warm sun.

What was this exercise like? Some people who do this exercise actually feel their hands and arms getting heavy and warm, and very relaxed. Some even sink into a deep and comfortable slumber. However, somatic focusing takes time and practice. Don't worry if you didn't feel much during this brief demonstration. Our goal is to take a tour of approaches rather than to master them.

Approach 5: Somatic Focusing (Advanced Exercises)

In beginning somatic focusing exercises we attend to sensations associated with the body's surface, the skin and muscles ("My hands and fingers are warm and heavy"). Advanced somatic exercises are found in yoga (Rama et al., 1976), autogenic training (Luthe, 1965), hypnosis (Bower, 1976), and some approaches to Zen (Kapleau, 1965). They involve attending to a deeper set of body sensations. When happy and relaxed, have you ever noticed a warm glow in your heart, or a warmth deep in the pit of your stomach (as if you had just drunk a cup of hot chocolate)? These are sensations associated with parts of the body deep within. In advanced somatic focusing we actually attend to such sensations, just as we attended to sensations of warmth and heaviness. However, because of the time it takes to master advanced somatic focusing, we will simply note it here.

Approach 6: Thematic Imagery

As you can see, somatic focusing involves attending to physical sensations. As such, it is an approach that is both mental and physical. The next approach, thematic imagery, is entirely mental. This approach is found in just about every world culture (Kroger & Fezler, 1976; Masters & Houston, 1972; McCaffery, 1979; Samuels & Samuels, 1975). Let's start right out with a demonstration:

> Can you think of a theme, a scene or setting, that would be very relaxing to think about? How about a spring meadow? You might want to picture a cool and refreshing breeze. The sun is warm and comfortable. You can hear the grass and trees rustling and the birds singing. Or you might want to think of a quiet sunny beach. The ocean waves softly splash against the shore. You can smell the breeze. The sand feels warm and good. What relaxing scene comes to your mind? Don't try to analyze or figure things out. Try to experience your scene as a participant. What do you see? What do you hear? Are there any fragrances, tastes, or physical sensations? Imagine the scene with all your senses. Try this for about a minute.

Most people find thematic imagery an easy and enjoyable approach, something like taking a quiet vacation in the mind. Thematic imagery is also a rich and varied approach. It can be used for mastering a challenge, or just having fun. The topics of imagery can range from reminiscence to self-exploration and discovery. With thematic imagery you can be as creative and expressive as you desire.

Approach 7: Contemplation

In the previous three approaches, you had considerable leeway in what you attended to. You could construct and attend to images of considerable variety and complexity. We end our Grand Tour with a set of more restrictive approaches. In contemplation and meditation, what you attend to is simply and carefully defined. Your role is to simply observe. You are not in the driver's seat, steering wherever you want; what you experience is determined by processes outside of your direct influence. We will begin with a type of contemplation.

Many of us spend more time than necessary thinking about our short-comings. In the contemplation exercise that follows, you are asked to consider all of your good points, all of the positive things that realistically should make you feel somewhat contented and accepting of yourself. The instructions for this contemplation are simple.

> Quietly and easily direct your attention to the question "What are my good points?" and without trying to deliberately figure out an answer, simply and quietly wait. See what comes to mind, what ideas this question stirs. However,

whenever a thought does come to mind, do not pursue it. Simply note it (without evaluating or rejecting it) and return to quietly and easily attending to the question "What are my good points?" Your role is that of a passive observer, quietly noting thoughts and ideas that come to mind. Do not dwell upon or stay with any particular thoughts or ideas. Note them and let them float away, like clouds in the sky or echoes. This is contemplation. It's a way of letting yourself appreciate the subtleties and nuances of a pleasing object of your attention. Try this approach for a few minutes.

How did that feel? How was that different from how you ordinarily think? Did anything new come to mind? It is possible to contemplate virtually anything. You can quietly and passively look at a work of art and appreciate it more deeply. Listening to music can be a form of contemplation, especially when you let the music stir feelings in you. If you were to scrutinize a piece of art, trying to figure out if it were an original or a copy, you would not be contemplating. If while singing a song you were struggling to remember the lines, you wouldn't be contemplating either. In contemplation we do not deliberately try to figure something out. We simply attend and appreciate. We let the object of our contemplation reveal itself to us.

Approaches 8 and 9: Centered and Open Focus Meditation

Meditation is both the simplest and most advanced form of relaxation. It is hard to demonstrate in a brief exercise. However, it can be said what meditation is not. Meditation does not involve active or deliberate thought. Thinking about a problem or trying to analyze it is not meditating. Also, meditation is not fantasy or daydreaming. It does not involve letting the mind wander wherever it wants. Meditation is not quite the same as contemplation. When we meditate we do not even try to understand the object of our attention more deeply.

Meditation is doing nothing while attending to something very simple. Imagine you are on a vacation at a distant lake. You are quietly watching a beautiful sunset and doing or thinking nothing else. You haven't a care in the world. There is nothing that has to be done. You are completely satisfied and content. You feel deeply peaceful. This is a moment that approaches meditation. It is a moment in which you are doing nothing while attending to something very simple. Many people have such quiet moments without even thinking of them as meditative, for example, while fishing, listening to quiet music, or becoming absorbed in art.

In centered focus meditation we quietly attend to a simple stimulus, like a sunset (Naranjo & Ornstein, 1971). In open focus meditation we attend to the flow of all stimuli (Shapiro, 1980). This is as much as can be said now. If you complete the entire Relaxation Dynamics program, you will meet meditation again at the end of your journey and have a chance to understand this subtle approach more fully.

We have just sampled some of the approaches in Relaxation Dynamics. How do you feel compared with before we started? Did you notice any differences among exercises? Which seemed easy? Which seemed challenging? Did you notice that some exercises are entirely physical and others entirely mental? You may have found that some exercises are complex and active, and others simple and passive. Whatever you experienced, it is important to emphasize that these instructions are entirely too brief to have a deep effect. Some of the exercises in this program are quite advanced and need much preparation. In fact, do not be concerned if you are not at all relaxed. Once again, the goal of this lesson was not to learn to relax, but to sample a variety of exercises and develop an inner map of the Relaxation Dynamics program.

The Map

Before we end, let's review the path that Relaxation Dynamics takes. We begin with isometric squeeze relaxation. Here we create relaxation by tensing up and letting go. We move to yogaform stretching and then to breathing exercises. These three approaches—squeezing, stretching, and breathing—are mainly physical. They make up the first phase of the Relaxation Dynamics program.

We then move to several mental approaches. The first three approaches are relatively unrestrictive. In your mind you construct restful pictures and phrases. You think of various types of relaxing body sensations and themes.

The final mental approaches are more restrictive. All you do is quietly attend to a simple stimulus. These are the approaches of contemplation and meditation.

Here is the entire Relaxation Dynamics sequence:

Physical Exercises
　　Isometric Squeeze Relaxation
　　Yogaform Stretching
　　Integrative Breathing

Unrestrictive Mental Exercises
   Somatic Focusing (Beginning Exercises)
   Somatic Focusing (Advanced Exercises)
   Thematic Imagery

Restrictive Mental Exercises
   Contemplation
   Centered Focus Meditation
   Open Focus Meditation

If this is a map, where does it lead? In terms of content, we move from exercises that are exclusively physical to those that are more mental in nature. In terms of direction of focus, we move from exercises that are more external to those that are more internal. Each approach requires that you direct your attention from the hectic pressures of everyday life to a more limited focus. In each you are asked to put aside effortful and goal-directed striving. Some exercises may present experiences that are new and unfamiliar, experiences you will need to tolerate and accept to progress in Relaxation Dynamics.

All these exercises will give you an opportunity to explore and hopefully benefit from new sources of pleasure and meaning. They hold the potential for self-mastery, self-expression, and self-discovery. The joys and meanings of relaxation unfold as we learn to attend with an undivided mind, put aside our urgent daily strivings, and accept and value the rewards of quieting the tensions of body and mind.

You are now ready to begin. In the next lesson you will have an opportunity to think about what you want from relaxation training and to set up your own relaxation training program.

Lesson 3

Selecting a Relaxation Training Program

What are your relaxation training goals? Which approaches do you want to explore? How much time are you willing to devote to training? These are some of the basic questions that you need to answer before starting Relaxation Dynamics training. In answering these questions you will be setting up a personal relaxation training program.

What Are Your Relaxation Goals?

Relaxation Dynamics presents nine approaches to relaxation training. Each approach can be useful in and of itself, and some exercises can prepare for others. You may choose to explore a broad array of techniques, or any one technique in depth. Either way can be very rewarding, but before you start, you need to decide upon your relaxation goals. Here are a few of the goals people often have.

Getting acquainted with the worlds of relaxation. You may have no reason for or interest in becoming an expert at relaxation, but want to find out what it's all about. For example, you may have heard of progressive relaxation, autogenic training, or yoga, and just want to know what these terms mean. For you, Section I can serve as a useful introduction. Trying a session or two of each exercise can give you a feel for what the technique is all about.

Brushing up on or improving an approach you already know. You may want to brush up on a technique you already know, or learn some preparatory exercises to make your preferred technique work even better. If these are your goals, you can use Section I as a sort of relaxation encyclopedia. Browse through the lessons, and pick exercises that seem interesting. (However, when you decide to do an exercise, be sure to follow the instructions very carefully.) For example, one of my students had completed the transcendental meditation (TM) training program a few years ago. She had stopped practicing, but wanted to begin again. She also wanted to learn some exercises to improve her TM practice. After reading Section I, she decided that muscle tension was distracting her meditation, so she chose to master yogaform stretching (Lesson 8) and integrative breathing (Lesson 9). She even read the lesson on centered focus meditation to get some ideas on how to meditate better. Today this student does 10 minutes of yoga breathing exercises before meditating and finds her meditation much more rewarding.

Learning one particular technique of special interest. You may have heard of one technique and want to learn it. For example, one artist had read about imagery exercises and wanted to learn this approach to enhance his creativity. He went directly to Lesson 11 (thematic imagery) and tried it out. It should be noted that if one technique doesn't work, it may be that you didn't give it enough time. Or perhaps it wasn't the technique for you. It also might be that the technique is too advanced and should be preceded by some other exercises. Whatever the case, Section I can serve as your guide for exploring and mastering different approaches.

Exploring different approaches and developing your own. You may want to complete the entire Relaxation Dynamics program to learn all approaches and develop your own personalized relaxation sequences, sets of exercises targeted to specific goals. You will need to proceed through Section I lesson by lesson, devoting about a week to each level of training.

Teaching self-relaxation to others. If you are a health professional interested in teaching self-relaxation to patients and clients, this also is an appropriate professional textbook. The lessons present information appropriate for beginners in a down-to-earth style. They provide a model for a manner of instruction most people find understandable and interesting. Section II presents a variety of possible training programs and important technical information about training.

If you are not a health professional, do not attempt to teach Relaxation Dynamics to others without professional supervision. It may seem that students would do better to learn from a person than from a text, even though instruction might not be as good as it would be with a trained professional. However, the Relaxation Dynamics lessons, worksheets, and taped instructions have been carefully developed and tested to maximize success and minimize possible dangers. The program has been designed to work best either when presented by professionals or when used alone for self-study. It is impossible for a nonprofessional to teach this material without introducing something that might jeopardize training. For instance, every time a question is asked, the teacher invariably adds something new. The teacher's tone of voice when giving instructions can significantly affect the results of the exercises. And the relationship between teacher and student can be the most important part of training (psychologists often spend years learning the complexities of the therapeutic relationship). If you wish to learn more about medical and psychological precautions for teaching relaxation training, see the following: Bernstein and Borkovec (1973); Budzynski (1974); Carrington (1978); Iyengar (1981); Jencks (1977); Kapleau (1965); LeShan (1974); Luthe (1977); Masters and Houston (1972); Rama et al. (1976); Rama, Ballentine, and Hymes (1979); Shapiro and Walsh (1984); Smith (1978); Turk et al. (1983); Woolfolk and Lehrer (1984).

Choosing and Following Your Program

Once you have selected a relaxation training goal, you need to decide which approaches to explore and how many weeks to practice. There are two paths you can follow. You may continue reading Section I, lesson by lesson. As each relaxation approach is introduced, you will follow the instructions provided (or use the taped instructions in the Relaxation Dynamics Cassette Series). This is the simplest way to explore Relaxation Dynamics.

A more rigorous way to learn self-relaxation is to follow one of the programs presented in Chapter 1 of Section II. This is one of the most important parts of Relaxation Dynamics. It outlines several training schedules, telling you which exercise sets to practice and which worksheets to complete. The schedules tell you how to learn Relaxation Dynamics and guide you every step of the way. Here are summaries of three training schedules students have found particularly useful.

The Complete 14-Week Training Program

Week 1: Orientation
Week 2: Measuring Stress and Relaxation
Week 3: Setting Time Aside for Rest
Week 4: Isometric Squeeze Relaxation
Week 5: Yogaform Stretching

Week 6: Integrative Breathing
Week 7: Consolidating, Experimenting, and Setting Up a Quieting
Sequence
Week 8: Somatic Focusing (Beginning Exercises)
Week 9: Somatic Focusing (Advanced Exercises)
Week 10: Thematic Imagery
Week 11: Contemplation
Week 12: Centered Focus Meditation
Week 13: Open Focus Meditation
Week 14: Setting Up a Personalized Relaxation Program

The 4-Week Training Program

Week 1: Orientation and Isometric Squeeze Relaxation
Week 2: Yogaform Stretching or Integrative Breathing
Week 3: Mental Relaxation: Thematic Imagery or Centered Focus
Meditation
Week 4: Setting Up a Personalized Relaxation Program

The 2-Week Training Program

Week 1: Orientation, Grand Tour, Review of All Approaches, and
Selection of Approach(es)
Week 2: Review and Fine-Tuning of Selected Approach(es)

As part of your training, you may develop a personalized relaxation program for yourself (as discussed in Lesson 15). This will mean modifying or combining the exercises you have learned to meet your personal goals. To help in identification and listing, each exercise has been given a Relaxation Dynamics (RD) code number. For example, the stretching and breathing exercise we encountered in the Grand Tour of Lesson 2 has the code RD 27. An RD number is presented beside the instructions for each exercise. A complete numbered listing of all Relaxation Dynamics exercises appears at the beginning of Lesson 15.

Guidelines

Relaxation Dynamics is a discipline of personal growth and discovery. As in any personal discipline, there are beginning guidelines, rules, and precautions.

First, try not to approach Relaxation Dynamics with an urgent purpose or goal. Relaxation Dynamics should be done for self-expression, self-mastery, and, most important, for the simple fun of it.

Learning relaxation is like learning any other skill, whether it be swimming, driving a car, or singing: you have to start with the basics and build up; you have to practice; and you have to be patient. To ensure maximum benefit, you should practice your techniques twice daily, 20–30 minutes a session. Moderate benefits can be obtained by practicing once a day. Less frequent practice can be useful for those who are not interested in mastering the skill of self-relaxation, but desire a simple demonstration of specific techniques.

Don't expect immediate results, as few skills are mastered overnight. Often the effects are gradual. And different exercises will work for different people. Some exercises in this program simply may not be the right ones for you.

One important piece of advice applies to every exercise presented in this program. If an exercise makes you uncomfortable in any way, first try shortening it (doing it for 15 minutes instead of 25) and exerting less effort. If it still makes you uncomfortable, drop the exercise unless you are under professional supervision. This advice is so important that it merits repeating: if an exercise hurts, makes you dizzy, anxious, or depressed, or feels unpleasant or uncomfortable in *any* way, ease up and spend less time at it. If the problem continues, stop the exercise, unless you are under professional supervision.

Finally, do not attempt Relaxation Dynamics unless you are in reasonably good health. You should have a physical checkup before beginning. Let your physician know that the program can require a moderate level of exertion, and let him read the precautions listed here.

On rare occasions relaxation exercises can have unwanted physical effects. While for most people self-relaxation is comfortable and safe, seek medical permission before beginning training if you have now or have had in the past any of the following conditions:

Backaches (constant or progressive)
Blackouts
Cerebro-vascular accident
Depression (severe)
Diabetes
Glaucoma
Heart disease
Hypoglycemia
Hypertension
Pregnancy (third trimester)

Thyroid disorder

Transient ischemic attacks

Any recent or serious disorder affecting bones, ligaments, or muscles

If you are learning Relaxation Dynamics in order to reduce physical pain or discomfort, it is important that a physician determine the probable source of your condition and the advisability of learning self-relaxation. If while practicing Relaxation Dynamics you notice the worsening of any symptom, consult your physician at once.

Virtually every relaxation training manual, including this one, warns that relaxation training can alter the required dosage levels for prescription medication, particularly for patients undergoing treatment for hypertension, diabetes, depression, anxiety, and any disorder influenced by changes in general metabolic rate. Although the potential for risk has not been consistently demonstrated, the state of relaxation itself is frequently associated with changes in general metabolic rate. As a result, need for medication may decrease (and in a few paradoxical cases temporarily increase). If you are taking medication, be sure to obtain medical approval to begin Relaxation Dynamics and inform your physician that required dosage level may change during the course of training. Frequent monitoring of dosage level is advised. However, do not assume that Relaxation Dynamics will eliminate the need for any medication you are taking.

Although Relaxation Dynamics can be used as a psychotherapeutic tool, it is not a substitute for psychotherapy. By itself, it is not designed to help solve problems of loneliness, shyness, anger, depression, anxiety, or low self-esteem. These psychological problems can be treated quite effectively by qualified health professionals such as psychologists, psychiatrists, and clinical social workers.

Finally, it is important to say a few words about stress management. Any relaxation technique is in itself usually not enough for effective stress management. Relaxation training should be used in combination with other, often more active, techniques.

Preparing for Practicing

Relaxation Dynamics is designed to be easy to practice. The techniques require no special equipment and can be done just about anytime and anywhere. However, the area you choose to practice in should be quiet, where you will not be interrupted by phone calls, people, or excessive outside noise. You also will need a comfortable chair or sofa, preferably one with a padded back (and without a built-in desk). Although some exercises might work better if you were lying down (isometric squeeze relaxation) and some while standing (yogaform stretching), it is recommended that all exercises be practiced in a seated position. In this way you learn to associate relaxation with sitting by consistently doing every exercise in a chair. Since most stressful situations are encountered while you are seated, rather than lying in bed or standing and moving actively, it makes more sense to practice in a seated position. Also, while reclining, you run the risk of falling asleep. While that might be excellent proof that you are indeed relaxed, you can't practice and experience Relaxation Dynamics while you're asleep. Finally, you will discover that some exercises are refreshing and energizing, others absorbing and interesting, and still others soothing. If you practiced all your exercises in bed, you might begin to associate lying in bed with experiences not conducive to sleep. You might find yourself going to bed and suddenly feeling alive, alert, and refreshed, instead of sleepy.

In order for relaxation training to be successful, you must be careful to select an appropriate time for daily practice. This is so important that a large part of Lesson 6 is devoted to how to set time aside for relaxation. That lesson presents four guidelines, which are worth mentioning here:

1. Do not select a time that is within 1 hour after eating. During that interval blood is directed to the stomach to help digest food. As a result, you may not experience the full benefit of some relaxation exercises.

2. Do not select a time when you are likely to be interrupted or distracted. For instance, if you ordinarily fix lunch at noon, it would not be a good idea to make noon your practice time, since you would probably spend much of your time thinking about what you had to do.

3. Do not select a time when you should be doing something else or when there is pressing unfinished business. All other concerns should be put aside for the duration of the session.

4. Select a time that will be relatively easy for you to stick with.

For some, Section I may be enough to learn self-relaxation. You will find on the following pages detailed explanations and instructions for every technique. However, if you are serious about mastering the Relaxation Dynamics approach, you probably should also get the Relaxation Dynamics Cassette Series. The Cassette Series presents audio-taped instructions for each approach, which make practicing easier for most people. Finally, any relaxation training book (or tape) is even more effective when presented by a personal instructor. No book or tape, no matter how well written, can answer all your questions or meet all your training needs.

The most important prerequisite is one this book cannot provide—motivation and commitment to practice. This must come from you. Those who benefit most from relaxation training are not necessarily those who are the most intelligent, strong, or talented. Instead, it is those who have one important quality in common: a sincere interest in exploring the worlds of rest-related states. They approach relaxation training not as passive recipients, but as active and involved participants. And they value the inner potentials made available by quieting the tensions of body and mind.

You are now ready to begin your adventure into Relaxation Dynamics. If you complete the entire program, you will learn a new approach each week. Some you may like, some you may not; different approaches will probably have quite different effects on you. Your role is somewhat like that of an explorer traveling into a new world. You need to observe carefully what you encounter and note the peaks and the valleys, what you find promising and what you find disappointing. Be creative in your adventure and make careful note of your own discoveries. Then, at the end of this program several weeks from now, you can return to each of the 58 exercises that you have sampled and construct an approach to relaxation that is truly your own. So take careful notes. But above all, have fun!

Part II

Getting Ready

Lesson 4

Stress Management and Beyond

In this lesson we will take a close look at the goals of Relaxation Dynamics, starting with stress management. Most relaxation training programs are sold as ways of managing stress (Woolfolk & Lehrer, 1984), and while Relaxation Dynamics goes far beyond this single objective, it is a useful place to begin.

The Costs of Stress

Stress affects everyone. Even everyday pressures and demands can damage our health, work effectiveness, and well-being. The costs can be serious and pervasive. Experts used to warn us of a handful of "stress illnesses" such as ulcers and heart disease, but it is now known that perhaps the majority of symptoms reported to the family physician are stress related (Pelletier, 1977). Stress contributes significantly to heart disease, cancer, lung ailments, accidental injuries, cirrhosis of the liver, and suicide—all leading causes of death in this country (Wallis, 1983). It is not surprising that three of this country's best-selling drugs are an ulcer medication (Tagamet), a hypertension drug (Inderal), and a tranquilizer (Valium) (Wallis, 1983).

At first these claims may seem a bit overstated. After all, if stress is such a problem, why aren't we inundated with public pronouncements and warnings? The fact is that few health professionals are adequately trained in the problems of stress. Only within the last few years have many of the most serious costs been clearly demonstrated. But now we know that the costs are real.

To understand these costs, we must begin with the human nervous system. A useful if somewhat oversimplified view is that each of us is born with an emergency energy mobilization or "flight or fight" reaction (Cannon, 1932). In an emergency, our bodies awaken and energize for quick, hard work. Outside of awareness, our brain's "stress trigger," the hypothalamus, sends messages to the heart, lungs, circulatory system—virtually all organs—to awaken and energize them for action. Stress mobilization is the pounding of the heart you experience when attacked by a street dog, the shortness of breath you experience when rushing to catch a bus, and the cold sweaty palms you feel before giving a speech. That quick shot of energy can be essential for self-defense and survival.

Unfortunately, even minor threats can trigger stress mobilization. And the effects accumulate. This process can be seen in the average day of a hard-driven, harried executive. Our executive is awakened by his alarm clock and experiences his first shot of stress energy. He rushes to the train and nearly misses it, triggering the emergency system again. He dashes into his office and notices on his desk yesterday's report, still unfinished. By now his heart is pounding, his muscles are getting tense, and his stomach feels queasy. The boss enters and announces that the report is needed by noon. The secretary complains about being over-worked. Our pressured executive begins to worry about whether he can finish the job on time. He wonders if he has what it takes for this line of work. Stress builds, this time from thoughts and worries, not external threats and demands. As the day continues, our executive confronts one minor emergency after another, a series of pressures and uncertainties. He finds himself trying to accomplish as much as possible in a short period of time and against the pressures and demands of others and himself. By the end of the day he is exhausted.

Although our hypothetical example may be a bit extreme, it illustrates quite well that everyday pressures and demands, especially those that are self-imposed, add up. What are the costs of such chronic stress? Research now tells us that continued high levels of stress mobilization subject the body to real and measurable wear and tear. Years are added to the heart, circulatory system, lungs, and digestive system. More ominously, the body's immune system, its built-in defense against virtually all illness, is impaired. Put briefly, stress places the body under poten-tially damaging pressure, and reduces its ability to resist and recover from illness (Pelletier, 1977).

We have just considered the "general arousal response" view of stress. It is a view widely presented in the popular press, simple to understand and useful for waking people up to the seriousness of stress. However, it would be oversimplifying matters to claim that stress is only general physical emergency mobilization. Often our bodies do not react in a wholesale, all-or-none fashion to stress (Smith & Siebert, 1984). We will see in the next lesson that people may respond to stress in different specific ways—some react with muscle tension, some with shallow breathing, some by perspiring, and so on.

More important, a complete view of stress has to encompass how we view ourselves and our world. Arousal need not only be physical; it can be mental and emotional. We can feel worry, fear, and anger. In addition, we are most likely to trigger stress arousal, whether it be physical, mental, or emotional, when we see a threat to our well-being and when we think there is little we can do about it (Ellis, 1975; Lazarus & Folkman, 1984). Arousal, of course, can be desirable when it prompts us to cope more effectively with such threats. However, we have already seen that excessive and chronic physical arousal can have physical costs. In addition, excessive worry and upset can distract us from coping; reduce our ability to think flexibly and creatively; contribute to performance-sapping fatigue; prompt ill-considered, impulsive action; and lead us to give up prematurely (Cohen, 1980; Lazarus & Folkman, 1984). The costs of stress go beyond simple physical wear and tear.

Perhaps the most dangerous cost of stress is that it is possible to get used to it, just as we might get used to poorly fitting shoes. It is easy to become numb to the chronic strain of life's pressures and demands. In fact, some researchers speculate that we can become addicted to our own stress hormones and actually crave chronic stress mobilization. Stress may be a hidden and addicting killer (Selye, 1976).

Our poor harried executive is at high risk for all of these costs. Not only does he complain of back tension and stomach pain, but his physician has warned him that his blood pressure is high. Last month he was out of work 3 days with the flu—right during the busy season. At work, he lacks the creative energy he had when he started 3 years ago. He approaches complex new problems with mechanical old solutions. Put briefly, our executive is a victim of stress. And more unfortunately, he is a victim of his own ignorance. He attributes his stomach pain to poor diet, his blood pressure to excessive salt, and his propensity to catch the flu to just plain bad luck. He's not even aware that his performance is not what it used to be. Yet all of these symptoms can be related to stress, and excessive stress can be prevented and managed.

The Successful Coper

The Relaxation Dynamics system is based on observations of individuals who are particularly successful at coping with life's demands. Coping has been defined in a variety of ways, for example, in terms of attempting to change threatening aspects of the environment. "Emotion-focused" coping involves in part reducing excessive, potentially damaging or disruptive stress arousal (Lazarus & Folkman, 1984). Good copers indeed experience stress, often at considerable levels. However, a moment-by-moment analysis of their day's activities reveals that they are quite adept at relaxing. Indeed, periods of relaxation and recuperation appear to follow periods of activity and tension. This pattern can be referred to as the *activity/rest cycle* (Stoyva & Anderson, 1982).

In addition successful copers value their rest activities as rewarding and interesting in their own right. Rest activities help them prepare for stress, recover from stress, prepare for sleep, and awaken at the beginning of the day. Rest activities are experienced as integrated and interrelated rather than fragmented and episodic. Finally, rest often lends meaning and structure to the rest of the day's activity.

The importance of the activity/rest cycle can be seen in the log of the day's activities of a successful coper in Figure 1. Note that rest, whether it be physical, mental, or emotional, follows activity.

It is clear that this individual experiences a balance of tension and relaxation in her life. Mundane activities like daydreaming or appreciating a flower have a deeper significance. They are accompanied by genuine decreases in stress mobilization. If we were to continue with this log and look at logs of other days, we would see an even greater variety of restful activities: aesthetically appreciating the surrounding beauty; thinking pleasant tunes; self-praising after resolving conflict; taking a deep stretch after a long period of reading; and deeply sighing. The activities are not random and trivial; they are experienced as self-affirming and life-affirming. Underlying most is an implicit or even explicit recognition that "I am OK" or "Life is good," or even thoughts of a more spiritual or existential nature. During each of these activities, physiological, mental, and emotional tension decrease. The coper is better prepared for effective action, and quite likely less at risk for stress-related illness as well.

In a more technical sense our successful coper has a variety of skills. She can detect tension in its early stages. She can differentiate tension from relaxation. She can direct her mind from the hectic outer world and attend to inner sources of simple restfulness. And she can put aside active and effortful striving and let herself experience the pleasures of letting go. Most important, she accepts and values the rewards she gets from self-relaxation.

Figure 1
Day's Log of a Successful Coper

Time	Activity	Source of Rest
7:00 a.m.	Awakens	
7:30 a.m.	Showers	Enjoyable source of physical relaxation
8:00 a.m.	Drives to work	
8:30 a.m.	Arrives at work; takes time to appreciate arrangement of plants in window	Mind diverted from hectic drive; physiological tension declines
8:35 a.m.	Calls boss; starts work on annual report	
10:00 a.m.	Finishes report; praises self for good job; engages in pleasant fantasy over best parts of report	Enjoyable source of physical and mental relaxation; attention focuses on internal and relaxing activity
10:01 a.m.	Discusses project with secretary	
11:15 a.m.	Finishes work; takes deep breath and stretches back and neck	Relaxation of muscles
11:20 a.m.	Dictates letters	
12:00 p.m.	Goes to lunch with friend, does not discuss work	Diversion from pressures of day
1:00 p.m.	Meets with potential clients	
3:00 p.m.	Finishes meeting; leans back in chair, reads newspaper	Cognitive relaxation
3:06 p.m.	Resumes work	

Self-Relaxation and Stress Management

Let's return once again to our harried executive. His excessive level of stress arousal can be seen as the result of many factors—a lack of skill at managing and scheduling his time (resulting in stressful backlogs of work); unassertiveness (shown by his unwillingness to talk to his boss about possibly excessive responsibilities); and low self-esteem (reflected in his tendency to take minor setbacks as personal threats). Any or all of these factors may be present. However, at the end of the day the simplest observation to be made is that he experiences an unhealthy level of tension for an unhealthy period of time. Eventually he may do well to consider learning to manage time more effectively, or deal with others more directly and assertively. He might even consider psychotherapy to deal with issues that contribute to his low self-esteem. But at the end of the day his most pressing need is to somehow reduce the excessive level of stress energy that has been mobilized throughout the day. Put simply, he needs to relax.

On the surface this might seem like an easy task. After all, what could be more simple than sitting in front of the television, or drinking a few beers, or even falling asleep? But most likely these attempts to escape the pressures of the day would not be enough to reduce the stress. What our executive needs is deep relaxation.

The deep relaxation referred to is often unfamiliar to us in the West. We learn very well how to create stress and tension in ourselves; we are stress mobilization experts. But few of us are experts at *demobilizing* stress, at generating states of inner rest sufficiently profound to counteract stress.

Self-relaxation is indeed a skill. But what kind of skill is it? Remember our discussion of physical stress mobilization? When triggered, all organs of the body are automatically awakened and energized for emergency activity. The body also has the capacity for the opposite response, one in which it quickly enters a state of deep and recuperative rest. This relaxation response has been given many technical names, including *hypometabolic state, trophotropic state,* and *quieting response.* Whatever this state is called, it appears to be the mirror opposite of stress mobilization.

But self-relaxation is much more than the simple skill of producing a hypometabolic state. There is another level at which relaxation training can be understood.

Beyond Simple Stress Management: Basic Relaxation Skills

The goal of Relaxation Dynamics is self-exploration and self-development. It is a discipline that involves learning to appreciate, master, and enjoy the inner rewards that come from quieting the tensions of body and mind. Such rewards come from mastering three skills: (1) focusing, the ability to identify, differentiate, maintain attention on, and return to simple stimuli for an extended period; (2) passivity, the ability to stop unnecessary goal-directed and analytic activity; and (3) receptivity, the ability to tolerate and accept uncertain, unfamiliar, and paradoxical experiences. Let's examine each of these skills and then consider certain "meta-skills" at the very heart of self-relaxation.

Focusing

Imagine you are resting by the seashore with a friend. You are gazing quietly at the vast sky overhead. Suddenly your friend calls out, "Look, what a beautiful seagull!" You look everywhere but see nothing. The seagull is simply too small and the sky too big. She cries out again, "Look, there it is!" You look very carefully. You think you've found it, but it turns out to be a cloud floating by. Then you notice something moving, but it is only a leaf floating away. Finally you see it, but only for a brief second. Something else catches your attention, and before you know it you have lost sight of the gull.

This example illustrates the notion of focusing. In order to watch the seagull, you first have to detect and identify it. This may be difficult given its small size. You must also discriminate between other stimuli and the seagull. You must not get caught up in looking at clouds and leaves. You must be able to deploy your attention for more than a brief second, and when you are distracted, you must be able to return to the object of your attention. The skill of focusing involves identifying a stimulus, differentiating it from other stimuli, maintaining attention on the stimulus for a period of time, and returning attention after distraction. It is a skill central to all relaxation, even reading for pleasure, as is shown next.

Imagine you have returned home from a hectic day of work. You decide to relax by reading a pleasant book. You browse through your books and have trouble even finding one you want to read. Clearly, before you can relax with a book, you must find one, or in terms of focusing, identify what you want to read. Imagine you find a few books: a simple mystery novel, a biography of a famous composer, and a textbook for a course you are taking. You aren't sure which to read, so you pick the textbook. You start studying, not quite recognizing you have selected a homework chore rather than a restful activity. You have failed to *discriminate* between books that are potentially relaxing and those that are not. Finally, imagine you quickly discover your text is not at all relaxing and turn to the mystery novel. You begin reading. It is indeed an enjoyable and relaxing story. However, after a few minutes you feel you must put the book aside to check the mail. You do so and return to the novel. A few minutes later you realize you haven't fed the cat. You interrupt your reading again to feed the cat. After a few more interruptions it becomes clear that your reading task is not particularly relaxing simply because you do not stay with it. You do not attend for a sufficient period of time to enjoy what you are doing and you are not particularly diligent at returning your attention once you notice you have been distracted.

Focusing, and its component skills of identifying, discriminating, attending, and returning, are essential to all levels of relaxation.

Passivity

In our culture the term *passivity* has some undesirable connotations. It can suggest weakness or giving up. However, there is a different meaning. Passivity is a special and very powerful skill. It is the ability to put aside unnecessary and unproductive goal-directed striving and thought. Often active and effortful activity wastes energy and prevents us from noticing what is important. A football player may be so involved with the game that he is unaware of a serious injury. A college student may be so preoccupied with worry that she does poorly on an exam. And have you ever been so caught up in trying to win or gain something that you were unable to enjoy yourself? An additional skill basic to relaxation is the ability to calm the noise of effortful and deliberate activity.

Goal-directed striving can take four forms. Instead of quietly enjoying something, you could strive to analyze, evaluate, direct, or avoid it. Imagine you are listening to restful music. All you need to do is sit back and enjoy. The experience would be interrupted if you became preoccupied with analyzing when it was written, who the composer was, the instruments involved, and so on. You might also be distracted if you spent your time judging whether or not the piece should win an award. You would surely be missing something if you became preoccupied with deciding where the piece should be going or what its lyrics should be. And if you kept turning off the music because you felt guilty about wasting your time relaxing, your attempts at avoidance would prevent you from enjoying anything. The ability to put aside all types of goal-directed striving, whether it be effortful analysis, evaluation, direction, or avoidance, is central to all self-relaxation.

Receptivity

Often the effects of self-relaxation are not immediate. Skill at relaxation can take time to develop. You may not know when a technique will take hold, what its effects will be, or even if it will eventually be right for you. To master relaxation you must be willing to tolerate and accept such uncertainties.

Most of us spend our days responding to outside demands and pressures. In many ways the experience of relaxation is just the opposite—internal, simple, and passive. For this reason, many find rest-related experiences new. Unless you can tolerate and accept what might be unfamiliar, skills at maintaining focus and passivity are of little value.

And learning self-relaxation can be an adventure filled with paradox. You might be told to try to relax while maintaining a stance of "not trying." You might be advised not to seek the result you desire, or even desire the result that may be your initial justification for doing a technique. Paradoxes such as these cannot be explained away. You must be willing to at least give the approach a try.

Receptivity is the ability to tolerate and accept what is uncertain, unfamiliar, and paradoxical. This is the most important of relaxation skills. It is a skill required at all levels. At the very beginning you must be willing to trust that simply taking a break from life's hectic routine may have value. In advanced approaches receptivity becomes more and more a part of the very definition of self-relaxation. With this brief (and possibly cryptic) discussion, let's consider the "meta-skills" of self-relaxation—and keep an open mind to their promise.

The "Meta-Skills" of Relaxation

More important than the skills of focusing, passivity, and receptivity are the "meta-skills" of relaxation. These are the skills of experimenting with and using relaxation principles. In traditional relaxation training you might be taught one or two techniques—muscle relaxation, for example, or possibly meditation. You might be told to mechanically practice this technique every day because it is supposed to be good for you. Once you have mastered the technique, you might be taught how to shorten it and use it in special situations. If you are successful, you have learned a health chore, a task analogous to taking vitamins or tranquilizers.

The key to relaxation is *not* complying with some set of externally imposed instructions. It is learning to (1) evaluate and compare the effects of different techniques in different situations and (2) select, tailor, and construct exercises for specific ends. The goal of Relaxation Dynamics is to help you discover what is best for you.

The Rewards of Mastering Self-Relaxation

What are the rewards of learning the skills of self-relaxation? Many relaxation manuals promise too much and offer too little. Claims are made that meditation, yoga, progressive relaxation, and the like can improve memory, lengthen life, improve sexual performance, and solve an impressive array of life's problems. Then relatively little information is given as to how to actually do the promised techniques.

My strategy is somewhat different. Here I present as much actual instruction as a book can. It is then up to you to test the techniques out and find what works for your needs. Rather than promise an impressive array of benefits, I challenge you to experiment and to keep an open mind. It is in this spirit that the benefits others claim to have obtained from mastering relaxation are discussed.

Stress recovery. As noted earlier, the simplest benefit of knowing the skill of self-relaxation is that it can provide a tool for recovering from the pressures and tensions of the day, or from specific stressful events. Many describe self-relaxation as a way of taking a "refreshing vacation" after work, or even during a work break. It is a way of putting past pressures aside to go on.

Adjunct to therapy. As a therapeutic tool, self-relaxation is at least partly a mode of cognitive distraction or diversion (Ellis, 1984). As Ellis has put it, the human mind usually focuses on one major thing at a time; consequently, when you concentrate on self-relaxation "you cannot simultaneously concentrate on how badly you are performing at something or what a worm you are for performing this badly. You focus, instead, on *what* you are doing rather than *how* you are doing; at least temporarily, you find it almost impossible to worry" (p. 671). More important, as you practice self-relaxation, "you often (consciously or unconsciously) make a philosophic change as well. You tell yourself for example, 'I now have a technique of controlling or changing my disturbed feelings; and I therefore *can* function more effectively' " (p. 671). However, it should be emphasized that self-relaxation is not a form of psychotherapy in itself. Rather, it can be a useful *part* of psychotherapy. For more information on the therapeutic use of self-relaxation, see Section II, Chapter 2.

Stress preparation. At times excessive stress can interfere with our ability to do our best. Often affected are communication and listening skills, creativity, memory, thinking, perception, and so on. Self-relaxation can be a useful way of minimizing the costs of excessive stress before an important task. Self-relaxation can be energizing, refreshing, and invigorating.

Preparation for sleep. Insomnia is one of the most common side effects of excessive and prolonged stress mobilization. Some self-relaxation exercises can help alleviate the day's cares and worries and serve as preparation for sleep.

Preparation for the day's activities. Some self-relaxation exercises are ideal for preparing for the day's activities. They offer a refreshing and stimulating way of starting the day off.

Pain management. All pain is real. However, pain is aggravated by worry, physical tension, feelings of helplessness, and a tendency to become preoccupied with pain itself. The skills targeted in Relaxation Dynamics can provide the pain sufferer with tools for reducing worry and physical tension, developing a feeling of control, and diverting attention from painful stimuli.

Creativity and problem solving. Have you ever had a good idea or insight while taking it easy, perhaps while on vacation, listening to music, or even resting? Deep relaxation can help us break out of mental ruts and logjams that sometimes can interfere with creativity and effective problem solving.

Balance to life's activities. As noted earlier, in a balanced and healthy life, rest follows activity, and activity follows rest. Individuals who are especially adept at coping have made this pattern a part of their daily routine. Although a successful coper may appear to be involved deeply in the rush of the day's events, she will also interrupt activity with periods of rest and recuperation. What is interesting is that both periods of rest and periods of activity are valued. Both are enjoyable, rewarding, and interesting in their own right. However, the activity/rest cycle is often forgotten when we are under pressure—at the very time it is needed most. Learning the skill and discipline of self-relaxation can help restore this fundamental life cycle.

Self-exploration. Self-relaxation was just discussed as an approach to stress management. It is important to remember that this is just the beginning. The world of rest-related states is at least as rich and varied as the world of stress and tension. Self-relaxation is more than a tranquilizer; it can be an avenue of personal discovery and meaning.

Lesson 5

Taking Stock of Stress and Relaxation

In the previous lesson some ideas basic to Relaxation Dynamics were examined. In this lesson it will be your personal experience that is considered, that is, how you feel stress and relaxation. What are your stress early warning signs? How do you know when you are deeply and completely relaxed? Learning your inner signs of stress and relaxation is one of the first steps in self-relaxation training. These signs can serve as cues or reminders to relax (cues often ignored by the stress-prone individual). They also can help you discover the impact of different exercises. An awareness and appreciation of the signs of stress and relaxation can sensitize you to and remind you of the potentials of relaxation training.

General Stress Symptoms

General stress symptoms can be seen as early warning signs that stress is present. After researching over 3,000 general stress symptoms over the last 8 years, I have found 32 symptoms that I consider to be the most important ones (for details, see Section II, Chapter 2). These 32 fall into six categories. Let's begin with physical symptoms.

Basic Physical Stress Symptoms

Your body's stress mobilization mechanism supplies you with quick energy for what your mind perceives to be an emergency. Your body gets ready for "fight or flight." Muscles tighten up and become more active in

41

preparation for action. Heart rate and breathing rate increase and become more vigorous to supply muscles with needed blood and oxygen. As we have seen, this basic stress reaction can be triggered too often and by events that realistically are not serious emergencies. When this happens, stress becomes a problem. We may feel like saying:

My heart beats fast, hard, or irregularly.

My breathing feels hurried, shallow, or uneven.

My muscles feel tight, tense, or clenched up.

I feel restless and fidgety.

Secondary Physical Stress Symptoms

Excessive or prolonged stress can trigger a group of related secondary "fight or flight" symptoms. These too can be signs of increased stress mobilization. However, unlike quickened heart rate and breathing or tightening of the muscles, such symptoms are not directly important for accomplishing an emergency action. We may be experiencing excessive secondary stress symptoms when we feel like saying:

I feel tense or self-conscious when I say or do something.

I perspire too much or feel too warm.

I feel the need to go to the rest room even when I don't have to.

I feel uncoordinated.

My mouth feels dry.

Physical Stress Aftereffects

Third, prolonged stress mobilization can contribute to chronic or delayed symptoms of "wear and tear." Such symptoms typically persist after a stress emergency is over. Often it is difficult to trace the stress trigger for such aftereffects. We may be experiencing stress aftereffects when we feel like saying:

I feel tired, fatigued, worn out, or exhausted.

I have a headache.

I feel unfit or heavy.

My back aches.

My shoulders, neck, or back feels tense.

The condition of my skin seems worse (too oily, blemishes).

My eyes are watering or teary.

Digestive Tract Symptoms

Symptoms involving the digestive tract are so prevalent and noticeable that they form a category of their own. When we have these symptoms, we may feel:

My stomach is nervous and uncomfortable.

I have lost my appetite.

Cognitive Stress Symptoms

Just as the body reacts to stress, so does the mind. Mental, or cognitive, symptoms of stress include all forms of worry. And worrying itself can do much to aggravate stress. For example, having a flat tire while driving to work can be a moderate nuisance. However, if you start worrying that this unfortunate event is "the end of the world, a complete catastrophe," you experience much more stress. Similarly, if you are taking an exam and come across a question you can't answer, you can probably go right on to the next question and hope for the best. However, if you dwell upon and ponder over the question, and start worrying, "I'm so stupid, I can't do anything right; I'm going to be a complete failure," you are taking things a bit too seriously. And your worry makes the stress worse.

There are eight types of cognitive stress symptoms, or unproductive and unrealistic worry.

Excessive self-blame. In order to cope it is important to take responsibility for your actions. However, passively dwelling upon and exaggerating your deficiencies and mistakes simply makes things worse. If you were a self-blaming individual, you might think:

I worry too much about not having what it takes to handle things.

Excessive blaming of work or the tasks at hand. Sometimes it is useful to constructively identify the sources of stress at work. However, constructive criticism is different from nonstop complaining that has no purpose other than to aggravate problems that might be present. In such a situation you might think:

I worry too much about how difficult or punishing my tasks are.

Excessive blaming of outside factors. Once again, constructive criticism or problem analysis can be a good way to deal with stress. It is not so useful to chronically worry about how "Society," "Fate," "God," "The Job," or "Certain Others" are always making things bad for you. If you felt this way, you might think:

I worry too much about the outside demands and pressures in my way.

Excessive worry about how complex things are. If, instead of trying to solve a problem, you idly worry about how complicated and difficult it is, you are simply multiplying your problem. You might feel like saying:

I worry too much about how complicated things are.

Excessive worry about how uncertain things are. Another way to waste your time with a problem is to preoccupy yourself with all the things you don't know, all the facts that are unclear, and all the ambiguities and uncertainties that confront you. A successful coper tries to answer the questions that need to be answered and tolerate the uncertainties that remain. However, the stress-prone worrier is more likely to think:

I worry too much about not knowing where I stand.

Excessive worry about unmet needs and wishes. It is important to identify your needs and wishes and attempt to meet them in a realistic, satisfying, and appropriate way. However, if you passively do nothing about your needs except worry about how serious they are, you are just creating stress. In this case, your thought might be:

I worry too much about my frustrations.

Exaggeration. All of the previous types of worry involve taking something too seriously, blowing a problem out of proportion, and making mountains out of molehills. Excessive generalization, exaggeration, personalization, and "awfulization" are so important as sources of stress that they are worth mentioning in their own right. Such an exaggeration-prone person is likely to think:

I take things too seriously and do not see things in perspective.

Idle worry. Similarly, all of the types of worry we've discussed involve replacing direct and active coping with idle thought. It is true that a certain degree of thoughtful preparation, and even painful recollection and anticipation, are often essential precursors to effective coping. However, stress is aggravated when thought replaces action and you become stuck in a "worry rut" and start worrying about worry itself. When this happens, you are more likely to think:

I am burdened by my thoughts and worries.

Negative Emotions

We have seen that stress symptoms can be physical or cognitive. They can also be emotional. Stress can evoke a variety of unpleasant emotions we might wish to avoid. However, it can be healthy to fully experience and share with others the emotions generated by stress. It is often an important part of coping. In addition, the presence of negative emotions indicates that some action needs to be taken. There are six basic emotions often associated with stress:

I feel too distressed (discouraged, downhearted, or sad).

I feel too irritated or angry (annoyed, provoked, mad, or defiant).

I feel too much contempt.

I feel too much distaste or disgust.

I feel too shy or sheepish.

I feel too fearful.

What about emotions like depression and anxiety? Depression and anxiety are complex experiences that usually involve a combination of basic emotions, as well as physical and cognitive symptoms. For example, one person may experience anxiety as a combination of a pounding heart (a physical symptom), excessive self-blame (a cognitive symptom), and the basic emotions of distress, anger, and fear. Another person might experience anxiety quite differently. However it is manifested, a person experiencing negative emotions might think:

I feel too depressed.

I feel too anxious.

Summary of Stress Symptoms

Thus, research suggests there are six general categories of stress symptoms:

1. *Basic Physical Stress Symptoms*
   Rapid, pounding, uneven heartbeat
   Rapid, shallow, uneven breathing
   Muscle clenching
   Restlessness

2. *Secondary Physical Stress Symptoms*
   Tense, self-conscious activity
   Perspiration and warmth

Frequent urge to urinate
Lack of coordination
Dry mouth, thirst

3. *Physical Stress Aftereffects*
Fatigue and lack of energy
Headaches
Feelings of unfitness or heaviness
Backaches
Shoulder, neck, and back tension
Skin problems
Watery eyes

4. *Digestive Tract Symptoms*
Stomach trouble
Lack of appetite

5. *Cognitive Stress Symptoms*
Self-blame
Blame of work or the tasks at hand
Blame of outside factors
Worry about how complex things are
Worry about how uncertain things are
Worry about unmet needs and wishes
Exaggeration
Idle worry

6. *Negative Emotions*
Distress
Irritation or anger
Contempt
Distaste or disgust
Shyness or sheepishness
Fear
Depression
Anxiety

General Signs of Relaxation

Just as there are general symptoms that indicate stress, there are also general signs that indicate restful, "anti-stress" states. Although we may not realize it, there are as many ways to experience restfulness as to feel stress. This is an idea that may seem strange at first. Indeed, most psychologists (who ironically are quite comfortable talking about hundreds of types of stress) think of relaxation as a single, unified state. Our Western emphasis on hard work and achievement has fostered a bias or prejudice against rest-related states. We tend to see rest as "laziness," a "waste of time," or at best a way of preparing for more hard work. This bias is unfortunate. It leads us to discount the potential meaning and satisfaction that can be discovered in rest-related states.

Table 1 is a list of some of the world's relaxation-based disciplines. The pervasiveness of such traditions suggests the diversity of relaxation-related states. In a recent study I attempted to catalog the variety of rest-related states associated with such relaxation disciplines by going through 200 books from all these traditions. Each one was searched for relaxation terms. When the study was done, there were 400 terms

Table 1
Relaxation Traditions

Aikido
Alexander Technique
Autogenic Training
Brahma Yoga
Clinically Standardized Meditation
Concentrative Meditation
Hatha Yoga
Judeo-Christian Contemplation and Prayer
Kung Fu
Kriya Yoga
Kundalini Yoga
Mazdaznan
Mindfulness Meditation
Prana Yoga
Progressive Relaxation
Psychosynthesis
Quieting Response Training
Raja Yoga
Sufi Contemplation
Tantra Yoga
T'ai Chi
Taoist Meditation
Transcendental Meditation
Zen Meditation

(Smith, 1984). Of these, 287 referred to states most frequently reported by those who learn Relaxation Dynamics (Smith, 1984). These terms are listed in the Checklist of Rest-Related States (Appendix, Worksheet 1).

Clearly there are many ways of experiencing rest. But what is a rest-related state? At the very least rest is the absence of tension, whether it be physical, cognitive, or emotional. It is a state of being physically, mentally, or emotionally at ease. But rest is more than this. It can be a state of comfortable drowsiness before a good sleep, or refreshing alertness at the beginning of a good day. And even more than this, rest can be a way to activate a variety of strengths and potentials. It can be possible to be both relaxed and alert, perceptive, and creative when distracting tensions and preoccupations have been put to rest. When conflict and indecision are eliminated, we can be both at ease and forceful, vigorous, and effective. We can be deeply loving and caring when we trust enough to relax defensive barriers. And deeper states of rest can have their own meaning, whether it be aesthetic, existential, or spiritual. The worlds of rest are at least as rich and varied as the worlds of stress and tension. And self-relaxation can be much more than stress management. With this idea in mind we begin our adventure into Relaxation Dynamics.

Appraising Your Progress

Often the effects of an approach to relaxation are subtle and easy to miss. If you wish to master self-relaxation, it is important to take notes on your progress. This book provides you with worksheets to facilitate your note taking. These notes can help you notice changes that may be taking place and enable you to compare and contrast approaches to relaxation. In a broader sense, they can serve as a guide, helping you identify relaxation goals and develop personalized relaxation sequences.

In the Appendix you will find four sets of worksheets to be used while you are mastering self-relaxation. They are:

First Session
Daily Logs
Final Assessments
Personal Thoughts

These worksheets are integrated into the programs outlined in Section II. However, if you are not following a specific program, it might be useful to take a glance at these exercises in order to become acquainted with what they measure. Here is a description of those exercises.

First Session

The First Session worksheet is to be done only the very first time you practice each technique. If you look carefully you will note that this exercise is actually two identical pairs of questionnaires, one to be completed immediately before and one immediately after you practice the technique for the first time. This before-after format is useful for noting any changes produced by the technique. Often the first exposure to an approach to relaxation is special and can yield insights into its overall potential.

Daily Log

The Daily Log is a recording sheet with a column for each day of the week. On this sheet you note the effects of your technique each day you practice. Many people find that an approach to relaxation has different effects on different days. When the effects of several days are recorded, patterns can emerge. Note that there are different Daily Logs for different approaches to relaxation.

Final Assessment

When you have finished with a technique, you are ready to complete the Final Assessment worksheet. This exercise is a highly structured questionnaire that asks you to evaluate in general terms the strengths and weaknesses of what you have learned and record any special observations or insights you may have. Questions are provided for every facet of training. Once again, there are different Final Assessment exercises for different approaches to relaxation.

Personal Thoughts

The Personal Thoughts worksheet is also to be done when you have finished learning a technique. It is simply a blank page provided for you to express in any way you wish your overall impression of the approach you have learned. You may choose to write an essay, a poem, or a letter to yourself (as in a diary). You may even draw a picture. In Personal Thoughts you describe the approach in whatever way is best for you.

You may want to complete all four sets of worksheets, which are designed to complement each other. Or, you might want to do only one or two, for example the Final Assessment or Personal Thoughts worksheets. Some people seem to express their reactions better with a Daily Log format, and others appear to prefer less-structured formats.

Lesson 6

Learning to Set Time Aside for Rest

The most difficult problem beginners have with relaxation training is learning to set aside a specific daily time for relaxation. This might seem like an easy thing to do, but it is important not to underestimate the difficulties. There are many hidden forces that can get in the way. First, our society has a deep and often hidden prejudice against inactivity and rest. Relaxation is associated with laziness and wasting time. Society tells us it is OK to take it easy *after* we have completed our work; Relaxation Dynamics views rest as being just as important and meaningful as work. Second, we often have the mistaken belief that success must always be preceded by strain and toil. It can take time to see that rest-related skills are equally important.

There is a third, more insidious resistance as well. People with a high-stress pattern of living may actually become accustomed to and perhaps even crave a chronic, high level of stress arousal. Just as the alcoholic craves alcohol when sober, the "stressoholic" craves stressful activity, even when at rest.

When you begin practicing Relaxation Dynamics you will probably experience the combined effects of society's pressures and your own addiction to stress. You may feel impatient, bored, and restless. You may want things to happen immediately. You may worry that your exercises are not working. In fact, in other relaxation programs over 50% of those who start simply quit after the first few weeks (Shapiro, 1980; Smith, 1978).

Relaxation Dynamics is specially designed to counter this resistance. It incorporates an approach called *shaping*. Here's how it works. A very powerful way of learning a difficult skill is to take it in easy and rewarding steps. If we wanted to help a small child overcome her fear of the water and learn to swim, a very effective approach would be to break the task into manageable and pleasant steps. We might first have her wade into the water and play with a beachball. We then would have her wade in farther and play with the beachball some more. Later we might have her try floating and playing with a toy boat. Eventually we would have her attempt to swim. Notice that not only are we having her approach the task of swimming (and overcoming fear of water) in small steps, or *successive approximations,* but each step is rewarding and pleasurable in and of itself. This is exactly the procedure we will be using in Relaxation Dynamics.

Other relaxation programs begin with advanced techniques like deep muscle relaxation, yoga, or meditation (Woolfolk & Lehrer, 1984). I believe this is a mistake. You don't teach someone to swim by starting in deep water. Relaxation Dynamics begins with a technique absolutely everyone can do and find enjoyable. In fact, all the early exercises incorporate activities familiar to most people.

This week you are going to select an easy, restful activity you already know how to do and enjoy. Then you will choose a *time-off period and place,* a time and setting when you will practice Relaxation Dynamics. By making your Relaxation Dynamics breaks easy and pleasurable, you will help counter your addictions and prejudices against relaxation. You will condition your body and mind to accept taking time off for relaxation. Once you have learned this healthy habit, you probably will begin to treat your time-off periods as special and guard them jealously for yourself. At this time you will have mastered the first and most difficult skill of Relaxation Dynamics—setting time aside on a daily basis.

Selecting a Time-Off Relaxation Activity

This week try to practice a rewarding and restful activity for 20 to 30 minutes every day. You need to first select your activity, then decide when to practice. When selecting this week's time-off activity it is important to keep in mind that it should be easy for you and pleasant to do. Remember that you will be using time-off relaxation to condition your body and mind to accept the discipline of setting time aside on a daily basis.

Guidelines for Selecting an Activity

When considering which activity to select, try to follow these guidelines:

1. Select an activity that involves a minimum of physical movement and effort. Thus, avoid jogging, sports, dancing, and similar pastimes.

2. Choose an activity that can be done alone without outside distraction. Avoid talking over the phone, chatting with friends, playing games, engaging in sexual activity, and the like.

3. Make sure your activity is not especially goal-directed or analytic. Avoid activities that have a serious purpose, such as doing homework, practicing a musical instrument (for a class or professional purposes), solving highly complex puzzles, doing difficult reading, planning the day's activities, or working on personal problems.

4. Pick an activity that is different than what you usually do. Try to think of something you find restful and enjoyable that you just haven't had time to do recently. Avoid activities you already do. For example, if you already spend time each day listening to pleasant music, do not choose this as your time-off activity.

5. Choose something that is indeed fun and easy. Don't make it a chore or burden. You should like doing it.

6. Take care to select an activity that will last no less than 20 minutes and no more than 30 minutes. It is important that you stick to this time period very carefully. If you are restless after 10 minutes, continue until you have finished 20 minutes (don't let your stress addiction get to you). If after 30 minutes you aren't finished and want to continue, stop anyway. It is important that you condition your mind and body to understand that a certain period of time is for time off and nothing else. Consistency and discipline are very important when teaching small children, and a stress-addicted mind and body often acts like a cantankerous child. Be firm.

7. Finally, avoid the following: eating; drinking; smoking; taking drugs; sleeping.

Here are some time-off activities people have chosen in the past:

Reading
Listening to quiet music
Sewing or knitting
Solving easy puzzles
Drawing
Playing a simple musical instrument just for fun
Daydreaming
Looking at pictures

Activity Brainstorming

What restful and rewarding activities would be easy for you to do? Before making your choice, it might be helpful to brainstorm a bit. Think of as many potential relaxation activities as possible, then write them in the following spaces. At this time it is not important that the activities be desirable or possible. Just put your critical and evaluative mind aside. Let yourself be creative, and think of all the relaxation activities you are capable of doing:

Potential Time-Off Relaxation Activities

1. _____
2. _____
3. _____
4. _____
5. _____
6. _____
7. _____
8. _____
9. _____
10. _____
11. _____
12. _____

Now, look back over this list. Think about the guidelines you read. Which of the activities you wrote down would be best for you? Which would you be most likely to stick with for 7 days? Which would do the best job of conditioning your mind and body to accept taking time off on a daily basis? Make your selection, and describe it in the following space:

Description of This Week's Time-Off Relaxation Activity

Effectiveness of Your
Time-Off Relaxation Activity

Now that you have selected the first activity you will do in Relaxation Dynamics, you might be interested in what science says about its potential effectiveness. There are a number of scientific studies that have compared the effectiveness of regular, informal self-relaxation activities (like reading, listening to music, or just sitting and daydreaming) with well-known approaches such as transcendental meditation and progressive relaxation (Beiman, Israel, & Johnson, 1978; Boswell & Murray, 1979; Fenwick et al., 1977; Marlatt, Pagano, Rose, & Marques, 1984; Michaels, Huber, & McCann, 1976; Puente & Beiman, 1980; Smith, 1976; Travis, Kondo, & Knott, 1976). These studies have found that for many (and possibly most) people, regular informal relaxation is just as effective in reducing stress and tension. So your very first "exercise" in Relaxation Dynamics may be just as powerful as exercises popular in stress programs across the country. But keep in mind, this is just the beginning. This week's training is an important stepping stone for things to come.

Selecting a Time-Off Period

Your next task is picking a time to practice. As mentioned earlier, you need to practice your Relaxation Dynamics techniques at least once a day, preferably twice a day, for 20 to 30 minutes. The time you choose to practice will have considerable impact on how successful training is for you. You need to consider carefully what the best practice times are.

Here are a few guidelines:

1. Do not select a time that is within 1 hour after eating. During that interval blood is directed to the stomach to help digest food. As a result, you may not experience the full benefit of some relaxation exercises.

2. Do not select a time when you are likely to be interrupted or distracted. For example, if your friends usually call in the early evening, it would not be a good idea to make this your practice time.

3. Do not select a time when you should be doing something else or when there is pressing unfinished business. Remember, your relaxation time is yours and yours alone. All other concerns should be put aside for the duration of the session.

4. Select a time that will be relatively easy for you to stick with.

On the next page is a calendar for 1 week with a space for each day. Spend a few minutes thinking about what your week is typically like, and then, on your calendar, reserve one or two 30-minute practice periods each day. On the same calendar, indicate what you would ordinarily be doing the hour before and the hour after each practice period.

What is your overall assessment of your proposed schedule? Think about any problems that might arise. Now is the time to be very critical.

TENTATIVE PRACTICE CALENDAR

	Mon	Tues	Wed	Thurs	Fri	Sat	Sun
8:00							
8:30							
9:00							
9:30							
10:00							
10:30							
11:00							
11:30							
12:00							
12:30							
1:00							
1:30							
2:00							
2:30							
3:00							
3:30							
4:00							
4:30							
5:00							
5:30							
6:00							
6:30							
7:00							
7:30							
8:00							
8:30							
9:00							
9:30							
10:00							
10:30							
11:00							
11:30							

Lesson 6

It is very easy to write a schedule, but it can be very difficult to stay with it. Here are some questions to help you evaluate your schedule.

What interruptions might come up during your time-off period?

How do you plan to deal with these interruptions?

Can you think of a time when there would be fewer interruptions?

If other people are going to be around (family, roommates), what are you going to tell them so they won't interrupt you?

What mechanical interruptors can you remove (disconnect phone, turn off TV, close window)?

Selecting a Time-Off Place

Where you practice your relaxation can have a considerable impact on how well your relaxation works. It is important to pick a setting conducive to physical and mental calm. The place should be dimly lit, and your relaxation chair should be comfortable. You also should try to minimize possible sources of distraction, such as radio, TV, noisy neighbors, ringing phones, and playing children. Distracting sources of discomfort (heat, noise, odors) should be eliminated as well.

You may wish to adjust your surroundings to further enhance relaxation. If you are devoting a room or a corner of a room to your relaxation exercises, you might want to select a painting, sculpture, rug, or plant that is suggestive of relaxation to you. Some people find the burning of incense during relaxation particularly helpful.

Checking the Start Off Checklist

Before going on a trip, have you ever made a checklist of things not to forget? Your list might have included such things as "Turn off the lights"; "Put gas in the car"; "Lock the doors." The following is a "Start Off Checklist" for relaxation. Be sure to read it carefully before beginning your exercise.

Start Off Checklist

___ Have you selected practice times during which you are relatively unlikely to be distracted? Remember: it is often not a good idea to practice when you have some other duty that has to be performed.

___ Do you have a comfortable relaxation chair?

___ Do you have a quiet place in which to practice? If you are going to practice in a place where there are other people, try to make sure you won't be interrupted. Close the door to your room. Ask friends or family members not to interrupt while you are "resting." And it's OK to take the phone off the hook.

___ You should not take a nonprescription drug (marijuana, amphetamines, barbituates, psychedelic drugs) or alcohol for at least a day before practicing. Such drugs can make it more difficult to relax or focus attention on what you are doing. At the very least, they can limit the extent to which the effects of relaxation will generalize outside the session.

___ You should not have a drink containing caffeine (coffee, tea, cola) for at least 2 hours before practicing. Caffeine can make it more difficult to relax and focus attention on what you are doing.

___ You should not smoke tobacco for at least an hour before practicing.

___ You should not eat any food for at least an hour before practicing. If you are absolutely starving, eat a carrot.

___ When you are finished, come out of relaxation very slowly and gently. Arising too abruptly can be jarring and even make you feel dizzy. Take about 60 seconds to easily open your eyes all the way. Then stretch your arms to your sides and take a deep breath.

Part III

Physical Exercises

Lesson 7

Isometric Squeeze Relaxation

Most people have some difficulty continuing with a relaxation program. As mentioned earlier, this may be due partly to addiction to stress as well as society's prejudice against inactivity. However, there may be another reason. Informal relaxation often has its own limitations. For example, if your form of relaxation is listening to music on the radio, you must have a radio present, and the music must be to your liking. If sketching is your form of relaxation, you can't very well do it while driving. And if your favorite way of taking it easy is to lie on a fur rug in front of the fireplace, you must do something else while at the office (or in the summer). It is clear that one serious problem with informal relaxation is that it is often dependent on outside circumstances. Another problem is that informal relaxation can become very monotonous. It often lacks diversity and direction. It can be simple, boring, and aimless.

Relaxation Dynamics is based on self-relaxation techniques. Exercises have been selected that are minimally dependent on the constraints of outside circumstances. Self-relaxation is something you can do by yourself, on your own, virtually anytime and anywhere. Relaxation Dynamics is also varied and directed. Each week you learn a different technique, and in many cases, techniques build upon each other. It is an adventure into new worlds of rest-related states.

It is appropriate that we begin Relaxation Dynamics with isometric squeeze relaxation. Not only is this approach the most popular in stress clinics, but it is the only completely American technique in our program. In addition, it is an approach that can teach us much about the nature of muscle tension and relaxation. It can refine our sensitivity to subtle, often missed sources of tension. And finally, it is relatively easy to learn.

However, it is important to remember that isometric squeeze relaxation is only one of many approaches we will explore. While some people will find that it is the approach of choice for them, it can also be used to prepare for or complement other approaches. It has its own unique effects, different from those of other muscle relaxation techniques. This point is often overlooked in stress management programs, where isometric squeeze may be the sole technique taught.

An important part of the idea underlying isometric squeeze relaxation was first suggested by Edmund Jacobson nearly 50 years ago (1938). Jacobson observed that anxiety and tension are often accompanied by a measurable tightening of muscle fibers. He developed a set of "progressive relaxation" exercises that involve reducing muscle tension by systematically tensing and letting go of various muscle groups while discriminating and attending to resulting sensations of tension and relaxation. Although Jacobson's approach was time-consuming (requiring 50 or more sessions over several months or even years) and not particularly scientific, it has been frequently revised and improved. In the 1950s Joseph Wolpe (1958) introduced a condensed version of progressive relaxation requiring only six 20-minute training sessions. Today many health professionals use the progressive relaxation training manual of Bernstein and Borkovec (1973). This work set new standards for scholarship and practicality and influenced the isometric squeeze system described here.

There are two ways to generate and use muscle tension. You can use your muscles to complete an overt action or movement. This is called *isotonic* activity. Or, you can tense up your muscles while keeping them relatively motionless. This second approach is *isometric.* You may have heard of isometric muscle building exercises. Isometric squeeze relaxation is different. The goal is to relax, not develop muscles. This is illustrated by this exercise:

> First, rest both arms in your lap. Now, gently shrug your shoulders. Pull them up or back, whatever feels better. Squeeze the muscles more and more until the squeeze feels most complete and pleasurable. Now, release the tension. Let your shoulders hang. Let the tension begin to flow out. Notice how you can create both feelings of tension and relaxation in your shoulders. For about 30 seconds let your shoulders relax more and more and attend to the pleasant sensations. If you had some difficulty discovering how to generate pleasurable tension, you might try asking someone to gently squeeze and massage the muscles of your shoulders. Have the person

easily squeeze and press into the muscles, gradually increasing the pressure until it feels most complete and pleasurable. Then ask the person to relax. Let go. Let the tension begin to dissolve. It is this kind of pleasurable tension and tension-release many people experience with isometric squeeze relaxation.

Why initially create tension in order to relax? Why not simply sit back and let go of the tension in each muscle group? One of Jacobson's most useful ideas was that initially squeezing a muscle group actually helps it relax. To illustrate, imagine you are sledding down a snow-covered hill with a slight incline, barely enough for good sliding. You might push your sled uphill a bit to get a running start. When you let go and start sliding, the extra momentum created by starting uphill helps you go farther. Similarly, by first tensing up a muscle group you give it a "running start." When you let go of the tension, the momentum generated helps the muscle relax more than if you simply sat back and tried to relax. A second reason for squeezing before letting go is that the isometric tension associated with squeezing demonstrates what muscle tension feels like, and how it differs from muscle relaxation. As a result, you gradually develop the skill of differentiating subtle states of tension and relaxation.

The Pleasures of Isometric Squeeze Relaxation

When exploring isometric squeeze relaxation, try to identify its unique sources of pleasure and satisfaction. Relaxation can, of course, be rewarding in and of itself. However, the isometric approach can be enjoyable in other ways. First, some find the act of squeezing muscles a special source of pleasure, something like a massage. You might want to see if this is true for you. Try actively shrugging your shoulder muscles to a point where it simply feels good. Squeeze farther until you reach a point of maximum pleasurable tension, as if you were giving yourself a very thorough and deeply satisfying shoulder massage. Then release the tension. When you practice isometric squeeze relaxation, you might want to see if other muscles can be squeezed to a point of maximum pleasurable tension.

Some people do not find the idea of squeezing muscles to a point of maximum pleasurable tension particularly useful. For them, a somewhat different source of pleasure comes from the process of building up and releasing tension. Many of life's pleasures involve a temporary increase in tension and excitement followed by a release. Imagine, for example, the buildup of excitement when climbing to the top of a diving board and the release of tension when diving into the water. Or try picturing the buildup of suspense and anticipation while watching a mystery thriller followed by a sigh of release at the conclusion. You might even want to think of the buildup in tension when aiming a bow and arrow and the release of tension when the arrow is sent sailing. In each of these examples, tension builds and is released. Feelings of excitement and anticipation are followed by feelings of release and relief. What is pleasurable is not so much either the tensing or the letting go, but both, the buildup and the release. This too can be an important source of pleasure in isometric squeeze relaxation.

There is a third potential source of pleasure in isometric squeeze relaxation—the skill of controlling isolated groups of muscles. When you practice, try to tense up only one isolated muscle group. Let the other muscles remain relaxed. This is a skill that takes time to acquire. As you practice you will likely find yourself getting better and better at it. In fact, skill at "turning on" and "turning off" tension in whatever muscle group you desire can be one of the more rewarding challenges of isometric squeeze relaxation. It is a type of self-control that is often fun to master.

The Isometric Squeeze Exercises

The entire isometric squeeze sequence involves tensing and letting go of 11 major muscle groups. You will squeeze and relax each muscle group twice before moving on to the next. Each time you relax a muscle group on one side of the body, you will relax the corresponding muscle group on the other side. And when you have completed the entire sequence, you will quietly check each muscle group to see if any tension remains. If a muscle is still tight, first squeeze and release the squeeze a few more times. If that doesn't work, try isolating specific muscles in the group and squeezing and relaxing them separately. For example, you will be squeezing your entire face all at once. If your face muscles remain tense after a few squeezes, try tensing up and relaxing just the forehead. When it is relaxed, move to the nose and cheeks, then to the lips, and go on to the jaws. Finally, experiment with different types of squeezes. See what works best. Here are three squeeze strategies to get you started. (Try each out on the same muscle group—the hand or arm, for example.)

The Quick Squeeze Strategy. Quickly tense the muscle group, keeping the rest of the body relaxed. Create as much tension as you can (without pain). Hold the tension for about 6 seconds. Now let go. Let your muscles drop, as if you were a floppy rag doll. Let them hang for about 30 seconds.

The Slow Squeeze Strategy. Slowly and gently tense the muscle group. Go easy. Gradually increase the tension. Keep the rest of the body relaxed. Now slowly decrease the tension. Easily and gently let go until your muscles are completely relaxed. For about 30 seconds attend to the muscles as they become more and more relaxed.

The Minimal Squeeze Strategy. Gently tense the muscle group—just enough so you feel a slight and noticeable increase in tension. The idea is to squeeze as little as you can and still notice it. Keep the rest of the body relaxed. Now hold the tension for about 5 seconds. Then let go of the tension and let your muscles relax for about 30 seconds.

Here are the 11 isometric squeeze exercises you will do:

1. Hand Squeeze (right hand twice, then left)
2. Arm Squeeze (right arm twice, then left)
3. Arm and Side Squeeze (right side twice, then left)
4. Back Squeeze (twice, or bend right and then left)
5. Shoulder Squeeze (twice)
6. Back of Neck Squeeze (twice)
7. Face Squeeze (twice)
8. Front of Neck Squeeze (twice)
9. Stomach and Chest Squeeze (twice)
10. Leg Squeeze (right leg twice, then left)
11. Foot Squeeze (right foot twice, then left)

Check muscle groups for remaining tension.

Repeat exercises for muscles still tense, or divide muscle group into components, squeezing each part.

Verbatim instructions for each of these exercises are presented at the end of the chapter in a script. Within the script, each exercise (hand squeeze, arm squeeze, etc.) has a different code number (RD 1, RD 2, etc.). For directions on making a relaxation tape from the script or reading the instructions to someone else, see "Reading a Script" in Lesson 15.

Now that you know the basic idea underlying the isometric squeeze relaxation approach, you are better prepared to understand why it is first in the program. Of all the approaches in Relaxation Dynamics, isometric squeeze relaxation is typically the most familiar to the beginner. It incorporates a type of activity most people already know how to do—tensing up or squeezing various muscle groups. Think of all the activities that involve exerting considerable muscle tension while accomplishing relatively little movement: making a fist, trying to push a car out of a pothole, attempting to remove a stuck jar lid. You already know the idea underlying isometric squeeze relaxation. The only alteration you make is letting go after the squeeze and attending to the "momentum" or process of relaxation. In line with the principle of shaping discussed earlier (i.e., learning a task in small, easy steps), we begin with the isometric squeeze approach.

It might also be useful at this point to conclude by reviewing how isometric squeeze exercises help develop the basic relaxation skills mentioned in Lesson 4, particularly the skill of focusing. Isometric squeeze relaxation teaches us to divert attention from external pressures and demands, as well as from worry and deliberate analytic thought. Instead, we focus inwardly on sensations associated with tension and relaxation. While we are involved with squeezing various muscle groups it is relatively difficult to also attend to and worry about our problems. Thus, in a very basic sense, isometric relaxation teaches the skill of focusing.

There are other, somewhat more subtle ways in which isometric relaxation trains us to focus. As already noted, by attending to the sensations associated with squeezing and letting go you learn to distinguish the subtle sensations associated with muscle tension and relaxation. If you wish to let go of muscle tension, you first need to know that it is there. You will be using this ability to discriminate throughout the program. Also, muscle tension, particularly "clenching up," generates stimuli that mask subtler sources of stimuli from within. Such tension is a type of static that prevents us from noticing relatively quiet internal phenomena. Have you ever unknowingly hurt yourself while doing something that takes considerable physical effort? You might not have noticed the pain until you were finished with your work. This is partly because the muscle tension created by working masked the pain from the injury. The isometric squeeze relaxation approach is designed to quiet some of this internal noise.

Starting and Ending Exercises

For each of the physical exercises we will begin and end each practice session with a brief special exercise sequence. We will start with a few breathing exercises designed to help us settle down and become more aware of tension and relaxation. We later will end with a few minutes of silence so we can observe the feelings of relaxation produced by the exercise. Both special exercises are designed to increase your sensitivity to the effects of each week's approach. The instructions for the special starting and ending exercises are included in the following script for isometric squeeze relaxation.

Start Off Checklist

(Do before starting this week's exercises)

— Have you selected practice times during which you are relatively unlikely to be distracted? Remember: it is often not a good idea to practice when you have some other duty that has to be performed.

— Do you have a comfortable relaxation chair?

— Do you have a quiet place in which to practice? If you are going to practice in a place where there are other people, try to make sure you won't be interrupted. Close the door to your room. Ask friends or family members not to interrupt while you are "resting." And it's OK to take the phone off the hook.

— You should not take a nonprescription drug (marijuana, amphetamines, barbituates, psychedelic drugs) or alcohol for at least a day before practicing. Such drugs can make it more difficult to relax or focus attention on what you are doing. At the very least, they can limit the extent to which the effects of relaxation will generalize outside the session.

— You should not have a drink containing caffeine (coffee, tea, cola) for at least 2 hours before practicing. Caffeine can make it more difficult to relax and focus attention on what you are doing.

— You should not smoke tobacco for at least an hour before practicing.

— You should not eat any food for at least an hour before practicing. If you are absolutely starving, eat a carrot.

— When you are finished, come out of relaxation very slowly and gently. Arising too abruptly can be jarring and even make you feel dizzy. Take about 60 seconds to easily open your eyes all the way. Then stretch your arms to your sides and take a deep breath.

Isometric Squeeze Relaxation

In this exercise sequence we are going to relax by squeezing and letting go of various muscle groups. While doing this we will be attending to and comparing the pleasurable sensations that go with muscle relaxation.

Before you begin, make sure you are seated upright and are comfortable. Rest your hands in your lap and your feet flat on the floor.

PAUSE

Now gently close your eyes and let yourself settle into a position that is comfortable. We will begin with a preparatory breathing sequence.

PAUSE

Preparatory Breathing

Now quietly direct your attention to your breath.

PAUSE

Without forcing yourself to breathe in any particular way, simply relax. Take a deep breath.

PAUSE

And let go. Let the tensions dissolve and flow away.

PAUSE

Let yourself breathe in a way that feels easy and comfortable.

PAUSE 5 SECONDS

Let your breathing be even and complete. Take your time. There is no need to hurry.

PAUSE 5 SECONDS

We are now going to reach up while breathing in, and bow over while breathing out. Slowly, as you breathe in, raise your arms in front of you, higher and higher, until they eventually reach straight over your head, pointing to the sky. Stretch and reach as high as you can.

And when you are ready, let out the air while slowly lowering your arms and bowing over. Let your arms and head hang limp. Do not exert any effort.

PAUSE

When you are ready, once again gently and easily sit up and reach toward the sky, taking in a deep breath. And then bow over and breathe out.

PAUSE

Continue breathing this way... reaching and breathing in, bowing and breathing out ... for the next minute or so.

PAUSE

Move easily and gently.
Do not force yourself to breathe in any particular way.

PAUSE

Take your time.

PAUSE

Move in a way that feels natural and unforced.

PAUSE 1 MINUTE

Now, when you are ready, place your hands in your lap and relax.

PAUSE 5 SECONDS

Let yourself breathe easily and comfortably. Attend to the easy flow of breath ...in and out.

PAUSE 5 SECONDS

Now, as you breathe out, gently open your lips. Quietly breathe out through your lips, making the flow of air as gentle and smooth as possible ...as if you were blowing at a candle flame so that it barely flickered. When you are ready, breathe in through your nose.

PAUSE 5 SECONDS

Continue breathing this way... in through your nose, and gently and quietly out through your lips ... very smoothly and gently.

PAUSE

Let your breathing be full, comfortable, and unforced.

PAUSE

Notice the easy rhythm of your breath.

PAUSE

Gently in ... and gently out. Breathe at your own pace.

PAUSE 5 SECONDS

We are now ready to begin the isometric squeeze sequence.

Hand Squeeze (RD 1)

We'll begin by focusing attention on the right hand. While keeping the rest of your body relaxed, squeeze the fingers together by making a fist. Do this **now.**

Squeeze the fingers together, making them tighter and tighter.
Let the tension build completely.
Notice the tension . . . and **let go.**

PAUSE

Let yourself relax.
Let the tension go. You might want to think of a tight ball of string slowly unwinding.
Focus on your hand as it begins to relax more and more.
Attend to the good feelings as the momentum of relaxation begins to carry the tension away.

PAUSE

Once again, squeeze the fingers together **now.**
Hold the tension as if you were wringing it out.
Hold it tight . . . and **let go.**

PAUSE

Let the muscles of your right hand begin to sink into a deeper and deeper state of comfort.
Let the tension go.
Notice how the muscles of the right and left hand compare.
Let your tension start to melt away into relaxation.
Let tightness float away.

PAUSE

We are now ready to move to the other hand.
Make a tight fist **now.**
Hold the tension.
Make your fist tighter and tighter . . . and **let go.**

PAUSE

Let any tightness slowly dissolve and flow away.
Just let your muscles go and think about nothing but the very pleasant feelings of relaxation.
Notice how your hand feels when the process of relaxation begins.
Notice the changes you can bring about.
Compare the sensations in your left hand with your right hand.

PAUSE

Once again, make a tight fist with your left hand **now.**
Can you feel the tension?
And once again, **let go.**

PAUSE

Let the muscles of your hand become more and more deeply relaxed.

Let the momentum of relaxation begin to carry away feelings of tightness.

Let your tension start to unwind.

Just experience the pleasant sensations and the feelings of relaxation you can create.

Arm Squeeze (RD 2)

This time move to your right arm. While keeping the rest of your body relaxed, squeeze your lower and upper right arm together, bending at the elbow. You might want to imagine you are trying to touch your shoulder with your hand.

Do this **now.**

Let the tension build until the squeeze feels most satisfying and complete.

Squeeze them together more and more.

And **let go.**

PAUSE

Let your arms go limp like a floppy rag doll.

Enjoy the feelings of relaxation you create as your muscles smooth out.

Compare how your right arm feels with your left arm.

Just notice what it feels like as the muscles start to become more and more deeply relaxed.

PAUSE

Once again, squeeze the parts of your arm together **now.**

Can you feel the tension?

Notice the feelings as the muscles squeeze.

And **let go.**

PAUSE

Let the momentum of relaxation carry the tension away.

Let the muscles go on relaxing more and more deeply.

There's nothing for you to do but focus your attention on the very pleasant feelings of relaxation flowing into your arm.

Let yourself enjoy these sensations.

PAUSE

This time move to the other arm and squeeze the lower and upper parts together **now.**

Let the squeeze be satisfying and complete.

Notice the control you have over your muscles.

Tighten only the muscles of the left arm.
And **let go.**

PAUSE

Let the tension go.
Focus your mind on the feelings associated with relaxation.
Let the tension melt away into relaxation.
If you notice any little bit of tension, just let go and become more and more relaxed.

PAUSE

Once again, squeeze the parts of your arm together **now.**
Let the tension grow to where it feels good and complete.
Hold the muscles tight, as if you were squeezing out the tension.
And **let go.**

PAUSE

Notice how you can create and release tension.
Let the muscles begin to sink into a deeper and deeper state of peaceful comfort.
Let yourself become more and more calm.
Just let your muscles go, and think about nothing but the feelings of relaxation.
Notice how the sensations from your left and right arms compare.

Arm and Side Squeeze (RD 3)

Now, rest your right hand in your lap. Focus your attention on your right arm and side and press them together, as if you were squeezing a sponge in the pit of your arm. Keep the rest of your body relaxed. Do this **now.**
Create a good, complete squeeze.
Can you feel the tension?
Now **let go.**

PAUSE

Let the tension unwind like a tight ball of string slowly unwinding.
Let the muscles of your arm and side become more and more deeply relaxed.
Let the tension unwind, like a tight ball of string slowly becoming more and more loose.
Focus on your right arm and side as they start to relax more and more.

PAUSE

Once again, tighten the arm and side **now.**
Make the muscles tense.

Let the muscles get more and more hard.
And **let go.**

PAUSE

Let yourself relax more and more.
Enjoy the sensations of relaxation as your muscles smooth out.
Compare the muscles of your right and left arm and side.
Focus completely on your muscles as the momentum of relaxation creates more and more relaxation.

PAUSE

This time move your attention to your left side.
While keeping the rest of your body relaxed, squeeze the arm and side together **now.**
Can you feel the buildup in tension?
And **let go.**

PAUSE

Let the momentum of letting go relax you more and more thoroughly.
Enjoy the pleasant feelings of relaxation.
Let the muscles go on relaxing more and more.
Pay attention only to the sensations of relaxation as the relaxation process takes place.

PAUSE

Once again, tighten your left arm and side **now.**
Can you notice the difference when you squeeze the muscles harder and harder?
Only tighten the muscles on your left side.
And **let go.**

PAUSE

Let the momentum of relaxation begin to carry your tension away.
Let any tightness float away.
If you notice any little bit of tension, just let go and become more and more relaxed.
See if you can tell any difference in how your right and left side feel now.

PAUSE

Back Squeeze (RD 4)

Focus your attention on the back muscles that are below the shoulders.
Tighten up these muscles in whatever way feels best. You might arch your back (and extend your stomach and chest out) . . . or squeeze your

Isometric Squeeze Relaxation   73 back muscles together... or bend to one side and then the other... or even press and rub your back against the back of the chair as if you were rubbing an itch. In whatever way feels best, tighten up your back muscles **now.**

Gently hold the tension.

Let it build to where it feels good and complete.

And **let go.**

PAUSE

Let the tension flow out as your back starts to become more and more relaxed.

Let the momentum of relaxation carry the tension away.

It's OK to shift your back around to help it relax.

Enjoy the pleasant feelings as your back relaxes more and more.

PAUSE

And once again, tighten up your back muscles **now.**

Notice any good sensations as you squeeze and tighten the muscles.

Hold the tension.

And **let go.**

PAUSE

Let your back muscles sink into a state of deeper and deeper relaxation.

Notice the changes you can bring about as you squeeze and let go.

Give the muscles plenty of time to relax.

Let the muscles unwind like a tightly coiled ball of string.

PAUSE

Shoulder Squeeze (RD 5)

This time move your attention to your shoulders. Keep the rest of your body relaxed.

Squeeze them in whatever way feels best ... by shrugging them up ... by pulling them behind you ... or by making a slow circling motion. Squeeze them **now.**

Feel the good tension as it grows to a point where it is most satisfying and complete.

Squeeze every muscle fiber.

Notice how you can generate a complete squeeze.

And **let go.**

PAUSE

Let the momentum of relaxation begin to melt away the tension.

Let your muscles go and think about the pleasant feelings of relaxation in your shoulders.

Give your shoulder muscles time to relax.

Let relaxation flow into every muscle.

PAUSE

And again, squeeze your shoulder muscles **now.**

Let the tension build to a point that feels satisfying and complete.

Tense only the shoulder muscles.

And **let go.**

PAUSE

Let yourself become more and more calm.

Let the muscles sink into a deeper and deeper state of peaceful comfort.

Let any tightness slowly begin to dissolve and flow away.

Can you notice how your muscles feel compared with before?

Can you notice the changes you can bring about?

PAUSE

Back of Neck Squeeze (RD 6)

This time move your attention up to your neck and gently tilt your head back. While keeping the rest of your body relaxed, gently press the back of your head against your neck **now.**

Let the tension grow, this time not too tightly.

Create a good, complete squeeze.

And **let go.**

PAUSE

Let the muscles of your neck relax like a floppy rag doll.

Let the tension unwind.

Enjoy the feelings of relaxation.

Let the momentum of relaxation carry the tension away.

PAUSE

Once again, gently tilt your head back.

Squeeze the muscles at the back of your neck **now.**

Hold the tension.

Can you feel the muscles get nice and hard?

And **let go.**

PAUSE

Let tightness begin to float away.
Let the momentum of relaxation dissolve your tension.
Keep your mind on the sensations of relaxation.
Can you feel any difference in how the muscles of your neck and shoulders feel?

PAUSE

Face Squeeze (RD 7)

This time move to the muscles of your face.
While keeping the rest of your body relaxed, squeeze your jaws, tongue, lips, nose, eyes, eyebrows, and forehead . . . all together **now.**
Squeeze your entire face together very tightly.
Feel tension build and spread over your entire face.
And **let go.**

PAUSE

Let the muscles of your face become more and more deeply relaxed.
Let tightness slowly dissolve and flow away.
Enjoy the feelings in the muscles as they smooth out and become more relaxed.
Attend to the sensations of relaxation.

PAUSE

Squeeze your jaws, tongue, lips, nose, eyes, eyebrows, and forehead . . . all together **now.**
Make it a good, complete squeeze.
Squeeze every muscle.
And **let go.**

PAUSE

Let the tension unwind.
Enjoy the pleasant feelings of relaxation.
Let the muscles smooth out and become more and more relaxed.
Notice how your face feels now compared with before.

PAUSE

Front of Neck Squeeze (RD 8)

This time move to the front of your neck. Bow your head and gently press your chin down to your chest. Do this **now.**
Feel the nice squeeze you can create in the muscles of your neck.
Make the muscles tight.
And **let go.**

Let the momentum of relaxation carry away the tension.

Let yourself feel more and more calm.

Just let your muscles go and think about nothing but the very pleasant feelings of relaxation.

Just experience the sensations of deep relaxation flowing into your neck muscles.

PAUSE

Once again, tighten your neck **now.**

Don't squeeze too hard, just enough to feel the tension.

Notice the sensations.

And **let go.**

PAUSE

Let the tension melt away into relaxation.

Enjoy the pleasant sensations of relaxation.

If you notice any bit of tension, just let go and become more and more relaxed.

How does your neck feel now compared with before?

PAUSE

Stomach and Chest Squeeze (RD 9)

This time tense your stomach and chest in whatever way feels best . . . by pulling your stomach in . . . pushing it out . . . or tightening it up. Do this **now.**

Notice the feelings of tension build.

And **let go.**

PAUSE

Let yourself relax more and more completely.

Enjoy the sensations of relaxation as your muscles smooth out.

Just notice what it is like as the muscles become more and more deeply relaxed.

How do your chest and stomach feel?

PAUSE

Once again, tense your chest and stomach **now.**

Hold the tension.

Notice how the muscles feel when tightened up.

And **let go.**

PAUSE

Let your tension melt away into relaxation.

If you notice any little bit of tension, just let go and become more and more relaxed.

Let yourself relax more and more completely.

Notice what it feels like as the muscles become more and more relaxed.

PAUSE

Leg Squeeze (RD 10)

This time move to your right leg.

While keeping the rest of your body relaxed, tense the muscles in whatever way feels best . . . by pushing your foot against the leg or back of your chair . . . or by pressing your right leg tightly against your left. Tense your right leg **now.**

Notice the tension build.

Notice how you can make your right leg more and more tight.

Keep the rest of your body relaxed.

And **let go.**

PAUSE

Let your tension melt away into relaxation.

Just let your muscles go and think about nothing but the pleasant feelings of relaxation.

Let yourself become more and more calm.

How do your right and left legs compare?

PAUSE

Once again, tighten your right leg **now.**

Hold the muscles very tightly.

Notice the tension build.

And **let go.**

PAUSE

Let yourself become more and more calm.

Let the momentum of letting go relax you more and more thoroughly.

Let the muscles sink into a deeper and deeper state of comfort.

Notice the sensations you have created by squeezing and letting go.

PAUSE

This time move to your left leg, and make it tense **now.**

Notice the muscles become tighter.

Tighten only the muscles of the left leg.

And **let go.**

Enjoy the pleasant feelings of relaxation.
Let the tension unwind.
Enjoy the feelings as the muscles loosen up.
There's nothing for you to do but focus your attention on the very pleasant feelings of relaxation flowing into your leg.

PAUSE

And again, tighten the left leg **now.**
Let the tension grow so you can feel it build.
Can you feel the muscles get hard?
And **let go.**

PAUSE

Let any tightness slowly dissolve and flow away.
Let the muscles of your leg become more and more deeply relaxed.
Let the muscles go on relaxing more and more deeply.
How does your left leg compare with your right?
Just attend to the pleasant sensations of relaxation.

PAUSE

Foot Squeeze (RD 11)

This time focus your attention on your right foot.
Curl your toes into the floor while pushing down. Do this **now.**
Feel the tension build as you squeeze the muscles.
Notice the tightness in your foot and leg.
And **let go.**

PAUSE

Let the momentum of relaxation carry the tension away.
Let the tightness float away.
Let all your tension go.
Focus all your attention on the feelings associated with relaxation flowing into your right foot and leg.

PAUSE

And again, tighten your right foot and leg **now.**
Gently make them tighter and tighter.
Notice the sensations of tension.
And **let go.**

PAUSE

Just let yourself become more and more calm.

Let your muscles go and think about nothing but the very pleasant feelings of relaxation.

Compare the sensations from the right and left feet.

Notice how the muscles feel as they relax.

PAUSE

This time focus your attention on your left foot.

Curl the toes and push down **now.**

Notice the tension build.

Attend to the sensations of tension.

Tense only the left leg and foot.

And **let go.**

PAUSE

Enjoy the sensations of relaxation as your muscles smooth out.

Relax more and more completely.

Let all the tension go as you sink into a deeper and deeper state of relaxation.

Compare your left and right leg and foot.

PAUSE

Once again, tighten your left leg and foot **now.**

Gently hold the tension.

Notice the sensations as the muscles squeeze more and more.

And **let go.**

PAUSE

Let the momentum of relaxation carry your tension away.

Let the muscles go on relaxing more and more deeply.

Let the muscles of your foot and leg become more and more relaxed.

Let any tightness slowly dissolve and flow away.

PAUSE

Review

And how does your entire body feel? If you notice any areas of leftover tension, simply let go, this time without first squeezing and creating tension.

PAUSE 5 SECONDS

Attend to your hands and arms. If you feel any tension here, simply let go.

PAUSE 5 SECONDS

Notice the feelings of relaxation you have created.
Let any tightness in your arms and sides dissolve.

PAUSE 5 SECONDS

Move your attention to your back muscles. If you feel any tension remaining here, release the tension. Let your back muscles become more and more relaxed.

PAUSE 5 SECONDS

Now focus on your neck and shoulder muscles. Is there any tightness remaining? If so, simply let go as before. Let your shoulders and neck become more and more relaxed.

PAUSE 5 SECONDS

How do the muscles in your face feel?
Let any tightness in your face dissolve and flow away.

PAUSE 5 SECONDS

Move your attention to your stomach and chest. If you still feel any tension here, let go and relax. Let the tension unwind.

PAUSE 5 SECONDS

How do the muscles of your legs feel? Let go of any tension you may feel. Let your legs sink into a deeper and deeper state of relaxation.

PAUSE 5 SECONDS

Let your toes, feet, and legs become more and more peacefully relaxed.

PAUSE 5 SECONDS

If you notice any area of tension in your body, let the tension flow away.
Or squeeze and relax that part of the body a few more times.
If you need to, focus on one specific part and squeeze and relax it a few times.
For the next 2 minutes let yourself enjoy the pleasant feelings of relaxation.

PAUSE 2 MINUTES

Now slowly open your eyes.

PAUSE 5 SECONDS

Take a deep breath.

PAUSE 5 SECONDS

And stretch.

PAUSE 5 SECONDS

This completes the isometric squeeze exercise sequence.

Lesson 8

Yogaform Stretching

In this lesson we will explore yogaform stretching, an approach that, like isometric squeeze relaxation, focuses on muscle relaxation. Taken together, isometric and stretching exercises are probably the most widely used approaches to relaxation. However, there are several important differences. Isometric relaxation is a fairly new Western technique; yoga originated in India nearly 3,000 years ago (Eliade, 1969). Isometric relaxation is a purely secular technique; yoga has deep ties to religion and philosophy. Different isometric relaxation systems incorporate from 10 to 20 exercises, while yoga exercises number in the hundreds. And finally, isometric relaxation is little more than an approach to muscle relaxation; yoga traditions often incorporate a wide range of activities including restrictions on diet and sexual activity (Iyengar, 1965).

The word *yoga* comes from a root that has a variety of meanings: to bind, join, attach and yoke; to direct and concentrate one's attention; and to use and apply. It can also mean union or communion with God (Eliade, 1969). These meanings reflect the many goals of yoga. There are yoga exercises claimed to cleanse the body, activate the nervous system, increase one's intelligence, improve one's sexual life, develop presumed paranormal powers, and heal virtually every organ system. Indeed, there is no such thing as a single yoga discipline; there are many yogas. In such an ancient and varied tradition there is much of value. There is also much superstition and pseudoscience (Iyengar, 1965; Rama et al., 1976).

The approach you will learn this week is derived from yogic tradition. However, some important changes have been made. Spiritual, religious, and metaphysical references have been avoided. Potentially dangerous and superfluous exercises have not been included. Generally, this approach incorporates only those exercises that are mentioned most frequently in introductory yoga texts and that have proven to be easy, effective, and enjoyable. This approach is called yogaform stretching to indicate that, although these exercises borrow from yogic tradition, they avoid much that is advanced or is of questionable value.

The key activity underlying the yogaform exercises is the focused stretch. You will slowly, smoothly, and gently stretch and unstretch the same 11 muscle groups you squeeze-relaxed last week. Because you will direct your attention to these same muscle groups, you will have an opportunity to compare and contrast the relaxing effects of squeeze (isometric) and stretch (isotonic) relaxation.

A tense muscle can be likened to a tightly coiled spring. If we wanted to loosen the spring we could easily stretch it out and then release the stretch. Similarly, in the yogaform exercises we slowly, smoothly, and gently stretch each muscle, and then easily release the stretch. The process is quite different from that involved in isometric squeeze relaxation. The most obvious difference is that the squeeze exercises involve relatively rapid constriction followed by 20 to 30 seconds of inactivity, whereas the yogaform exercises involve continuous smooth movement—stretching and unstretching.

However, there are other differences that are a bit more subtle. A smooth and continuous stretch requires us to focus our attention for the duration of the stretch; squeezing requires relatively less sustained attention. This point can be easily illustrated. Quickly make a fist and then let go. That action required little focused attention. Indeed, we often "clench up" automatically when threatened. Now, slowly open your fingers. Do this very slowly, smoothly, and gently, as if there were feathers resting on each finger. Notice how you had to attend more carefully to your fingers. By focusing your attention in a sustained manner you will be developing a skill that is important for the more advanced Relaxation Dynamics exercises.

There are other equally important differences. Isometric exercises are all active, whereas many yogaform stretches are slightly more passive. This can be illustrated by the following example.

> First tense up the muscles at the back of your neck as in iso-
> metric squeeze relaxation. Tilt your head back and squeeze
> the muscles tightly. Then let go. Now, as in the yogaform
> sequence, stretch the same muscles at the back of the neck.
> Let your head fall gently forward. You don't have to exert any
> effort whatsoever. Simply let gravity do all the work for you.

Let the heavy weight of your head pull it slowly, smoothly, and gently toward your chest, easily stretching the muscles at the back of your neck. Take a few seconds to do this. Now lift your head up.

Did you notice a difference in the feelings associated with squeezing and stretching the muscles at the back of the neck? Squeezing was active, effortful, and deliberate. Stretching was passive and effortless. The neck muscles stretched automatically as gravity pulled your head forward. Most of the yogaform exercises are equally passive and effortless. In each exercise, the major muscle to be stretched remains at rest while a smaller muscle (or gravity) does the work. Passive and effortless relaxation is another skill that will be very important in exercises later in this program.

Of course, there are some important similarities between the approaches of isometric squeeze relaxation and yogaform stretching. The stretching exercises continue to train us to divert our attention from external, goal-directed activity and thought. They continue to teach us to detect subtle tension. And they continue to soothe or quiet internal sources of noise. However, somewhat more than the isometric approach, yogaform exercises are designed to develop a capacity to passively sustain attention on an internal focus and discover sources of quiet inner fulfillment.

The Yogaform Stretching Exercises

We will slowly, smoothly, and gently stretch and unstretch the same muscle groups we squeezed last week. As noted earlier, this way you can compare the pleasures and effects of stretching and squeezing on the very same parts of the body. Also, if you learned the isometric squeeze sequence, you already know what parts of the body to focus on in yogaform stretching.

For each yogaform exercise, take about 20 seconds to stretch the indicated muscle group. When a muscle is stretched, hold the stretch and attend to the pleasant sensations for a few seconds. Then take about 20 seconds to unstretch. Take your time. Try to move as slowly, smoothly, and gently as possible. Keep your mind focused on what you are doing. As before, do each exercise twice. For each exercise done on the right side of the body, repeat on the left side. When you are finished, scan your body for any sources of residual tension. Repeat stretches for areas that are still tense. If an area is still tense, try breaking an exercise into parts; for example, stretch the lips, mouth, and forehead separately rather than stretching the whole face together. Experiment with new or combined stretches if those presented here are not satisfactory. Here are the muscle groups again:

1. Hand Stretch (right hand twice, then left)
2. Arm Stretch (right arm twice, then left)
3. Arm and Side Stretch (right side twice, then left)
4. Back Stretch (twice)
5. Shoulder Stretch (twice)
6. Back of Neck Stretch (twice)
7. Face Stretch (twice)
8. Front of Neck Stretch (twice)
9. Stomach and Chest Stretch (twice)
10. Leg Stretch (right leg twice, then left)
11. Foot Stretch (right foot twice, then left)

Repeat for muscle groups still tense.

Stretch component muscles if necessary.

Experiment with new or combined stretches.

As with the isometric exercises presented earlier, yogaform exercises initially should be done in a comfortable chair. This way you learn to relax in a position most often associated with tension—sitting. However, many find that some yogaform exercises can be even more rewarding when done while standing. You might want to try this and see what you think.

Start Off Checklist

(Do before starting this week's exercises)

— Have you selected practice times during which you are relatively unlikely to be distracted? Remember: it is often not a good idea to practice when you have some other duty that has to be performed.

— Do you have a comfortable relaxation chair?

— Do you have a quiet place in which to practice? If you are going to practice in a place where there are other people, try to make sure you won't be interrupted. Close the door to your room. Ask friends or family members not to interrupt while you are "resting." And it's OK to take the phone off the hook.

— You should not take a nonprescription drug (marijuana, amphetamines, barbituates, psychedelic drugs) or alcohol for at least a day before practicing. Such drugs can make it more difficult to relax or focus attention on what you are doing. At the very least, they can limit the extent to which the effects of relaxation will generalize outside the session.

— You should not have a drink containing caffeine (coffee, tea, cola) for at least 2 hours before practicing. Caffeine can make it more difficult to relax and focus attention on what you are doing.

— You should not smoke tobacco for at least an hour before practicing.

— You should not eat any food for at least an hour before practicing. If you are absolutely starving, eat a carrot.

— When you are finished, come out of relaxation very slowly and gently. Arising too abruptly can be jarring and even make you feel dizzy. Take about 60 seconds to easily open your eyes all the way. Then stretch your arms to your sides and take a deep breath.

Yogaform Stretching

In this exercise sequence we are going to relax by slowly, smoothly, and gently stretching and unstretching various muscle groups.

Before you begin, make sure you are seated upright in a comfortable position with your hands in your lap. Are your feet flat on the floor?

PAUSE

Now gently close your eyes and let yourself settle into a position that is comfortable.

PAUSE

We will begin with a preparatory breathing sequence.

Preparatory Breathing

Now quietly direct your attention to your breath.

PAUSE

Without forcing yourself to breathe in any particular way, simply relax. Take a deep breath.

PAUSE

And let go. Let the tensions dissolve and flow away.

PAUSE

Let yourself breathe in a way that feels easy and comfortable.

PAUSE 5 SECONDS

Let your breathing be even and complete. Take your time. There is no need to hurry.

PAUSE 5 SECONDS

We are now going to reach up while breathing in, and bow over while breathing out. Slowly, as you breathe in, raise your arms in front of you, higher and higher, until they eventually reach straight over your head, pointing to the sky. Stretch and reach as high as you can.

And when you are ready, let out the air while slowly lowering your arms and bowing over. Let your arms and head hang limp. Do not exert any effort.

PAUSE

When you are ready, once again gently and easily sit up and reach toward the sky, taking in a deep breath. And then bow over and breathe out.

PAUSE

Continue breathing this way. . . reaching and breathing in, bowing and breathing out . . . for the next minute or so.

PAUSE

Move easily and gently. Do not force yourself to breathe in any particular way.

PAUSE

Take your time.

PAUSE

Move in a way that feels natural and unforced.

PAUSE 1 MINUTE

Now, when you are ready, place your hands in your lap and relax.

PAUSE 5 SECONDS

Let yourself breathe easily and comfortably. Attend to the easy flow of breath . . . in and out.

PAUSE 5 SECONDS

Now, as you breathe out, gently open your lips. Quietly breathe out through your lips, making the flow of air as gentle and smooth as possible . . . as if you were blowing at a candle flame so that it barely flickered. When you are ready, breathe in through your nose.

PAUSE 5 SECONDS

Continue breathing this way. . . in through your nose, and gently and quietly out through your lips . . . very smoothly and gently.

PAUSE

Let your breathing be full, comfortable, and unforced.

PAUSE

Notice the easy rhythm of your breath.

PAUSE

Gently in . . . and gently out. Breathe at your own pace.

PAUSE 5 SECONDS

We are now ready to begin the yogaform stretching sequence.

Hand Stretch (RD 12)

We'll begin with the right hand.

Slowly, smoothly, and gently open your fingers and easily stretch them back and apart.

Try not to stretch so it hurts.

PAUSE

Just enough to feel a good stretch.

PAUSE

Take your time.

PAUSE

Stretch every muscle completely.

PAUSE

Then hold the stretch.

PAUSE

And slowly, smoothly, and gently release the stretch.

PAUSE

Let your fingers very slowly return to their original relaxed position.

PAUSE

Notice the sensations as the muscles unstretch.

PAUSE

Take your time, there is no need to hurry.

PAUSE

Now let's try that again.
Without hurrying, very easily and gently open the fingers of your right hand.

PAUSE

Open them wide apart so you can feel a good complete stretch.

PAUSE

Let each finger open more and more.

PAUSE

Notice the sensations of stretching.

PAUSE

Then hold the stretch.

PAUSE

Then slowly, smoothly, and gently release the stretch.

PAUSE

Let your movement be smooth.

PAUSE

Take your time.

PAUSE

Easily return your fingers to their original position.

PAUSE

We are now ready to move to the other hand.

PAUSE

Slowly, smoothly, and gently open the fingers.

PAUSE

Move them farther and farther apart.

PAUSE

Make sure your right hand remains relaxed.

PAUSE

Open them more and more so you feel a good complete stretch.

PAUSE

Then hold the stretch.

PAUSE

And gently and easily release your fingers.

PAUSE

Let your fingers gently and smoothly return to their resting position.

PAUSE

There is no need to hurry.

PAUSE

Move at a pace that feels comfortable for you.

PAUSE

And let's try that once again.

PAUSE

Very easily and gently open the fingers.

PAUSE

Notice how it feels as your fingers stretch farther apart.

PAUSE

Let the movement be smooth and graceful.

PAUSE

Each finger farther and farther apart.

PAUSE

And hold the stretch.

PAUSE

And gently and easily release the stretch.

PAUSE

Let the fingers gently return.

PAUSE

Try not to hurry or rush.

PAUSE

Notice the pleasant feelings of relaxation.

Arm Stretch (RD 13)

Now move to your right arm.

PAUSE

Slowly, smoothly, and gently slide your hand down your leg.

PAUSE

Extend your arm farther and farther.

PAUSE

Reach out and extend your arm in front of you.

PAUSE

Very gracefully, like you are balancing a feather on each hand.

PAUSE

And hold the stretch.

PAUSE

Then slowly, smoothly, and gently release the stretch.

PAUSE

Gently rest your hand on your leg and slide your arm back to its resting position.

PAUSE

Take your time.

PAUSE

Slowly and gently unstretch your arm.

PAUSE

And once again, slowly, smoothly, and gently reach and stretch.

PAUSE

Open your arm more and more.

PAUSE

Reach out in front of you.

PAUSE

Feel a good complete stretch.

PAUSE

And hold the stretch.

PAUSE

Then gently and easily return your arm.

PAUSE

Do not hurry or rush.

PAUSE

Let your arm relax and return.

PAUSE

Notice the pleasant sensations of stretching and relaxing.

PAUSE

Now move to your other arm.

PAUSE

Once again, quietly and easily reach and stretch.

PAUSE

Let your hand and arm slide down your leg.

PAUSE

Stretch more and more so you feel a good complete stretch.

PAUSE

Make sure your right arm remains relaxed.

PAUSE

Then hold the stretch.

PAUSE

And slowly and easily let your arm return.

PAUSE

Take your time.

PAUSE

Let the hand and arm gently and gracefully unstretch.

PAUSE

Notice the sensations of stretching and unstretching.

PAUSE

Now, once again, reach and stretch.

PAUSE

Slowly, smoothly, and gently.

PAUSE

Make a good complete stretch.

PAUSE

Notice the sensations of stretching.

PAUSE

And hold the stretch.

PAUSE

Then easily return your arm.

PAUSE

Let it slide back to its resting position.

PAUSE

Very smoothly and easily.

PAUSE

Let it relax.

PAUSE

Arm and Side Stretch (RD 14)

Now let both your arms fall limply to your sides.

PAUSE

Lesson 8

Slowly, smoothly, and gently circle your right arm and hand up and away from your body, like the hand of a clock or the wing of a bird.

PAUSE

Let your arm extend straight, and circle higher and higher.

PAUSE

Let it circle to the sky.

PAUSE

And then circle your arm over your head so your hand points to the other side . . . stretch and arch your body as you reach and point farther and farther, like a tree arching in the wind.

PAUSE

Now gently and easily.

PAUSE

Like the hand of a clock or the wing of a bird.

PAUSE

Circle your arm back over your head . . . to your side.

PAUSE

Finally to the resting position.

PAUSE

And let your arm hang.

PAUSE

Let's do that once again.

PAUSE

Circle your arm.

PAUSE

Very easily and gently, up to the side.

PAUSE

Higher and higher, over your head.

PAUSE

Pointing to the other side.

PAUSE

Reaching and stretching farther and farther. Feel a good complete stretch in your entire body as it arches.

PAUSE

Then slowly circle your arm back.

PAUSE

Evenly and gently without rushing.

PAUSE

Like the hand of a clock or the wing of a bird.

PAUSE

Take your time.

PAUSE

Easily return your arm to your side and let it hang again.

PAUSE

Now the other side.

PAUSE

Smoothly and gently circle your arm and hand up to your side.

PAUSE

Like the hand of a clock or the wing of a bird.

PAUSE

Let it reach higher and higher.

PAUSE

Until it is pointing to the sky.

PAUSE

And reach and stretch to the other side.

PAUSE

Feel a good complete stretch all along your body.

PAUSE

Hold the stretch.

PAUSE

Then slowly and easily.

PAUSE

Like the hand of a clock or the wing of a bird.

PAUSE

Circle your arm back to the side.

PAUSE

Gracefully and gently let it circle down.

PAUSE

Try not to hurry.

PAUSE

And return your arm to your side.

PAUSE

Once again.

PAUSE

Very easily and gently.

PAUSE

Circle your arm up, higher and higher.

PAUSE

Up to your side.

PAUSE

Gradually over your head, pointing up.

PAUSE

Reach to the other side, and feel a good complete stretch.

PAUSE

Then gently release the stretch.

PAUSE

Gently return your arm.

PAUSE

Like the hand of a clock or the wing of a bird.

PAUSE

Slowly and gently to the side.

PAUSE

Lower and lower.

PAUSE

Until your arm is again hanging comfortably by your side.

Back Stretch (RD 15)

Now focus your attention on your back, below your shoulders. Slowly, smoothly, and gently relax and bow over.

PAUSE

Let your arms hang limply.

PAUSE

Let your head fall forward, as you bow forward farther and farther in your chair.

PAUSE

Do not force yourself to bow over... let gravity pull your body toward your knees . . . farther and farther. It's OK to take a short breath if you need to.

PAUSE

Feel the stretch along the back.

PAUSE

Let gravity pull your body forward, as far as it will go.

PAUSE

Then gently and easily sit up.

PAUSE

Take your time.

PAUSE

Inch by inch, straighten up your body.

PAUSE

Until you are seated comfortably in an upright position.

PAUSE

Now again.

PAUSE

Let gravity pull your body down toward your knees.

PAUSE

Farther and farther.

PAUSE

Feel the stretch along your back.

PAUSE

Let your entire torso bend forward, farther and farther.

PAUSE

Let your head hang limply.

PAUSE

Now gradually sit up.

PAUSE

Move at a pace that feels comfortable.

PAUSE

Gently straighten your back.

PAUSE

Return to your original erect position.

PAUSE

And make sure you are seated comfortably.

Shoulder Stretch (RD 16)

Now lift both arms straight ahead in front of you and let your fingers touch.

PAUSE

Slowly, smoothly, and gently circle them around together, as if you were squeezing a big pillow.

PAUSE

Let your hands cross, pointing in opposite directions.

PAUSE

Squeeze farther and farther, so you can feel a stretch in your shoulders and back.

PAUSE

Hold the stretch.

PAUSE

And gently release the stretch.

PAUSE

Gradually return your arms to your side.

PAUSE

Take your time, there is no need to hurry.

PAUSE

Let your arms relax.

PAUSE

Now again.

PAUSE

Lift both arms, and slowly, smoothly, and gently cross them in front of you.

PAUSE

Imagine you are squeezing a big pillow.

PAUSE

Stretch the shoulders and back.

PAUSE

Hold the stretch.

PAUSE

Then gently release your arms.

PAUSE

Gradually return your arms to their original position.

PAUSE

Let your arms relax.

PAUSE

Move at a pace that feels comfortable.

PAUSE

And when you are done, rest your hands comfortably in your lap.

Back of Neck Stretch (RD 17)

Now, while sitting erect, let your head tilt easily toward your chest.

PAUSE

Try not to force it down.

PAUSE

Simply let gravity pull your head down.

PAUSE

Farther and farther.

PAUSE

Feel the stretch in the back of your neck.

PAUSE

As the force of gravity easily and slowly pulls your head down.

PAUSE

When you are ready.

PAUSE

Gently and easily lift your head.

PAUSE

Lift it until it is again comfortably upright.

PAUSE

Now, again, let gravity pull your head down.

PAUSE

Let your head fall farther and farther toward your chest.

PAUSE

Feel the muscles in the back of your neck stretch.

PAUSE

Do not force your head down, let your neck relax.

PAUSE

And let gravity do the work for you.

PAUSE

And when you are ready.

PAUSE

Gently and easily lift your head.

PAUSE

Gradually move your head to an upright position.

PAUSE

Until your head is comfortably erect.

PAUSE

Face Stretch (RD 18)

Now attend to the muscles of your face.

PAUSE

Slowly, smoothly, and gently open your jaws, mouth, and eyes while lifting your eyebrows.

PAUSE

Open wide.

PAUSE

Feel every muscle of your face stretch more and more.

PAUSE

Hold the stretch.

PAUSE

Then gently and easily release the stretch.

PAUSE

Let the muscles smooth out as they relax.

PAUSE

Let your face settle into a comfortable position.

PAUSE

Once again, gently and easily open your jaws, mouth, and eyes.

PAUSE

Open them more and more so you can feel a good complete stretch in your entire face.

PAUSE

When you are stretching as far as you can, gently hold the stretch.

PAUSE

Attend to the sensations of stretching.

PAUSE

Then gently and easily release the stretch.

PAUSE

Let the muscles of the face smooth out.

PAUSE

Let your face muscles relax more and more.

PAUSE

Until they are in a relaxed and comfortable position.

Front of Neck Stretch (RD 19)

Now, like before, let your head tilt, this time backward.

PAUSE

Let gravity pull your head back, but not too far, just enough to feel the stretch.

PAUSE

Do not force it back.

PAUSE

Let gravity do the work for you as it pulls the heavy weight of your head back farther and farther.

PAUSE

Gently and slightly open your mouth, and let your head relax and fall back.

PAUSE

Notice the muscles in the front of the neck stretch.

PAUSE

Gently hold the stretch.

PAUSE

Then gently and easily lift your head.

PAUSE

Gradually return it to its upright position.

PAUSE

Take your time, there is no need to hurry.

PAUSE

Now again.

PAUSE

Let gravity pull your head back.

PAUSE

Just enough to feel the stretch.

PAUSE

Easily and gently, so you can feel the stretch in your neck.

PAUSE

Try not to exert any effort.

PAUSE

Just let go, and let your head gently tilt back.

PAUSE

Then easily and gently.

PAUSE

Let your head return to an upright position.

PAUSE

And let your head rest comfortably.

Stomach and Chest Stretch (RD 20)

Now lean back comfortably in your chair.

PAUSE

Slowly, smoothly, and gently, arch your stomach and chest out.

PAUSE

Do this slowly and gently.

PAUSE

Feel a stretch along your torso.

PAUSE

Arch and stretch.

PAUSE

Then gently and easily release the stretch.

PAUSE

Slowly and easily return to an upright position.

PAUSE

Take your time. There is no reason to hurry.

PAUSE

And again.

PAUSE

Slowly and easily arch your stomach and chest out.

PAUSE

Arch your back more and more.

PAUSE

Feel a complete stretch all along your torso.

PAUSE

Then gently and easily release the stretch.

PAUSE

Gradually return your back to its original position.

PAUSE

And sit comfortably in an upright position.

Leg Stretch (RD 21)

Now focus your attention on your right leg.

PAUSE

Slowly and easily stretch the leg out in front of you.

PAUSE

Stretch and twist, so you can feel the muscles pulling.

PAUSE

Do this easily and gently.

PAUSE

Feel a good complete stretch all along your leg.

PAUSE

Then gently release the stretch.

PAUSE

Slowly let your leg return to its original resting position.

PAUSE

Take your time.

PAUSE

Gently unstretch your leg.

PAUSE

And let it rest.

PAUSE

Now once again, easily and gently stretch your leg out.

PAUSE

Easily and gently, stretch farther and farther.

PAUSE

Notice the sensation of stretching.

PAUSE

Then hold the stretch.

PAUSE

Now slowly and easily unstretch.

PAUSE

Let the leg easily return.

PAUSE

Take your time. There is no need to hurry.

PAUSE

Notice the sensations of unstretching.

PAUSE

Now focus on your left leg.

PAUSE

Slowly and evenly stretch the leg out.

PAUSE

Feel every muscle pulling and stretching.

PAUSE

Notice the pleasant sensations associated with stretching.

PAUSE

Stretch all the way.

PAUSE

And hold the stretch.

PAUSE

Now easily and gently release the stretch.

PAUSE

Take your time.

PAUSE

Release the stretch very gently.

PAUSE

Return your leg to its original resting position.

PAUSE

Now, once again, gently and easily stretch.

PAUSE

Stretch the leg out farther and farther.

PAUSE

Feel the sensations of stretching.

PAUSE

Take your time stretching.

PAUSE

And hold the stretch.

PAUSE

Now gently release the stretch.

PAUSE

Inch by inch, move your leg back to its resting position.

PAUSE

Move your leg as smoothly as possible.

PAUSE

Notice the sensations associated with unstretching.

PAUSE

Foot Stretch (RD 22)

Now focus your attention on your right foot.

PAUSE

While resting your heel on the floor, gently pull your toes and foot up, as if they were being pulled by strings.

PAUSE

Let the foot and leg stretch more and more.

PAUSE

Feel the complete stretch in every muscle fiber.

PAUSE

Stretch all the way.

PAUSE

And hold the stretch.

PAUSE

Now easily and gently release the stretch.

PAUSE

Let the foot slowly and smoothly relax.

PAUSE

Inch by inch, let the foot return.

PAUSE

Unstretch the foot until it is resting again on the floor.

PAUSE

Once again, slowly lift the foot and toes, resting your heel on the floor.

PAUSE

Feel the stretch all along your foot and leg.

PAUSE

Feel a good complete stretch.

PAUSE

Slowly and gently.

PAUSE

And hold the stretch.

PAUSE

Now gently lower the foot.

PAUSE

Easily return the foot.

PAUSE

Take your time, return your foot gently.

PAUSE

And let your foot relax.

PAUSE

Now focus your attention on your left foot.

PAUSE

Imagine strings are pulling your left toes and foot up.

PAUSE

Stretch the foot, toes, and leg more and more.

PAUSE

Feel the stretch all along your foot and leg.

PAUSE

Feel a good complete stretch.

PAUSE

And hold the stretch.

PAUSE

Then slowly release the stretch.

PAUSE

Gently relax the toes and foot.

PAUSE

Slowly lower them to the floor.

PAUSE

Take your time. Go easily and gently.

PAUSE

Once again, stretch the left foot and toes up.

PAUSE

Stretch more and more.

PAUSE

Feel every muscle stretching.

PAUSE

Notice the sensations of stretching.

PAUSE

And hold the stretch.

PAUSE

Then slowly and gently release the stretch.

PAUSE

Without hurrying, lower the foot.

PAUSE

Inch by inch, let the foot return to the floor.

PAUSE

And let the foot and leg relax in a resting position.

Review

And how does your entire body feel? If you notice any areas of leftover tension, simply let go, this time without first stretching and unstretching.

PAUSE 5 SECONDS

Attend to your hands and arms. If you feel any tension here, simply let it flow away.

PAUSE 5 SECONDS

Notice the feelings of relaxation you have created.
Let any tightness in your arms and sides dissolve.

PAUSE 5 SECONDS

Move your attention to your back muscles. If you feel any tension remaining here, let the tension flow away. Let your back muscles become more and more relaxed.

PAUSE 5 SECONDS

Now focus on your neck and shoulder muscles. Is there any tightness remaining? If so, simply let the tension dissolve. Let your shoulders and neck become more and more relaxed.

PAUSE 5 SECONDS

How do the muscles in your face feel?
Let any tightness in your face dissolve and flow away.

PAUSE 5 SECONDS

Move your attention to your stomach and chest. If you still feel any tension here, let it flow away. Let the tension unwind.

PAUSE 5 SECONDS

How do the muscles of your legs feel? Let your legs sink into a deeper and deeper state of relaxation.

PAUSE 5 SECONDS

Let your toes, feet, and legs become more and more peacefully relaxed.

PAUSE 5 SECONDS

If you notice any area of tension in your body, let the tension flow away.

Or stretch and unstretch that part of the body a few more times.

If you need to, focus on one specific part and stretch and unstretch it a few times.

For the next 2 minutes let yourself enjoy the pleasant feelings of relaxation.

PAUSE 2 MINUTES

Now slowly open your eyes.

PAUSE 5 SECONDS

Take a deep breath.

PAUSE 5 SECONDS

And stretch.

PAUSE 5 SECONDS

This completes the yogaform stretching exercise sequence.

Lesson 9

Integrative Breathing and Scanning

Breathing exercises have a special place in the Relaxation Dynamics system. Their importance reflects the significance of breathing to life itself. We can live days without food and water, but only minutes without air. We maintain continuous and intimate contact with the outside world through breathing. Breathing is the only basic physiological process that is both voluntary and involuntary; ordinarily we breathe automatically, but if we wish we can deliberately alter our breathing. Even physiologically our lungs hold a central position, next to and closely connected with the heart itself.

The way we breathe accurately reflects our tension and relaxation. We breathe quickly and choppily when angry, momentarily hold our breath when afraid, gasp when shocked, and choke when in despair. In contrast, we sigh deeply when relieved. When we are deeply relaxed our breathing is full, even, and unhurried.

To understand the importance of breathing to the process of relaxation, you need to know something about how we breathe. We breathe, of course, through our lungs. However, the lungs do not do the work of drawing in and expelling air. This is accomplished by the surrounding ribcage and collarbone, and by the diaphragm, an important drum-like muscle under the lungs that separates the chest cavity from the stomach.

Relaxed breathing begins with the diaphragm. Like a piston, it pulls down (pushing against the stomach) and draws air into the lower portion of the lungs. The ribcage expands outward and the collarbone moves up, drawing air into the middle and upper regions of the lungs.

113

Thus, when we inhale, muscles pull down (diaphragm) and out (ribcage and collarbone), and the lungs expand. When we exhale, these muscles relax inward. The diaphragm, in piston-like fashion, swings up. The ribcage closes and the collarbone moves down. Air is forced out (Guyton, 1976).

Diaphragmatic breathing is efficient and associated with relaxation; chest breathing is inefficient and associated with tension. This can be demonstrated easily.

> First sit up comfortably with your feet flat on the floor. Place a clock or watch with a second hand in front of you. When the second hand reaches 12, hold your ribcage and collarbone as still as possible and breathe in through your stomach as slowly as you can. Imagine you are filling your stomach with air. See how long you can draw out the inhalation and exhalation. How slowly did you breathe? Now place your hands over your stomach and hold your stomach as still as you can. Try not to let it move at all. Breathe by moving only your ribcage. See how slow you can make this breath.

Most people find they can breathe more slowly and with less strain "through the stomach" than "through the chest." This is because stomach breathing involves primarily the diaphragm and is more efficient.

Why is diaphragmatic breathing more efficient? First, there are more blood vessels in the lower part of your lungs, near the diaphragm. Your diaphragm pulls air to where it will do the most good. Also, because of our upright position, gravity tends to pull blood to the lower part of the lungs, toward the diaphragm. In contrast, chest or ribcage breathing is less efficient. Since less blood travels in the midportion of the lungs, the ribcage must work harder to enrich blood with oxygen. As a result breathing becomes more rapid.

Not only is diaphragmatic breathing more efficient, it is more relaxed. The diaphragm uses the least amount of energy to accomplish the work of breathing. If you observe an infant sleeping, you may notice the stomach expanding and contracting, a good illustration of relaxed diaphragmatic breathing. When tense, we are more likely to breathe using the ribcage, just as a tense runner heaves his chest while breathing. In fact, stress mobilization automatically tightens the chest muscles and prepares us for vigorous defensive action. If you ever have the opportunity to observe a boxing match, notice how the boxers' chest muscles tighten as they raise their fists. Although a tightened chest may serve as body armor to cushion the blows of others, it does little to foster efficient and relaxed breathing.

In addition to being diaphragmatic, relaxed breathing has a special rhythm. Exhalation is slow, even, and relatively passive. Muscle tension generated through inhalation is "let go" or "given up." The chest muscles and diaphragm relax automatically while air is quietly expelled. Although air is flowing up through the lungs and out, there is a sinking movement associated with the automatic relaxation of the breathing muscles. When air has been exhaled, there is a pause until the need for oxygen prompts an automatic and relaxed inhalation. The inhalation phase occurs quietly and easily (Jencks, 1977).

In contrast, the rhythm of tense breathing is more active and forced. Inhalation is more effortful and pronounced. The breath is retained too long until tension or discomfort forces a rapid exhalation.

The Integrative Breathing Exercises

The breathing exercises we will try are designed to encourage relaxed, full, and rhythmical breathing as well as increase the ability to detect and differentiate relaxed and tense breathing. They are meant to help us breathe deeply and diaphragmatically, evenly, and slowly—the opposite of how we breathe under stress. These exercises were selected from hundreds suggested by practitioners of yoga and related disciplines. Only those that are easy, effective, and safe have been retained.

Some of the exercises involve simply attending to the breath. This tends to foster more relaxed breathing and increase awareness of the breathing process. Some involve extensive arm and torso stretches designed to open the diaphragm and chest fully. Some involve breathing carefully through the nose or lips in order to facilitate an even rhythm, particularly the passive exhalation phase. The exercises include:

1. Deep Breathing
2. Arm Swing Breathing
3. Body Arch Breathing
4. Breathing and Bowing
5. Bowing and Stretching
6. Stomach Squeeze Breathing
7. Active Diaphragmatic Breathing
8. Inhaling Through Nose
9. Exhaling Through Lips
10. Focused Breathing
11. Thinking the Word *One*
12. Thinking a Relaxing Word

As with all other exercises in this program, practice in a comfortable chair. Since some breathing exercises incorporate stretching, you might want to try practicing in a standing position. Once again, experiment and find out what works best for you.

Scanning (RD 35)

To do our best in most activities we must have a certain amount of tension. For example, it would be impossible to drive a car if every muscle were completely limp with relaxation. However, often we carry unnecessary tension. There is no need to tense our face muscles while driving, and yet we may routinely do it. Unnecessary tension can waste our energy and keep us from doing our best.

Scanning involves checking for and letting go of unnecessary tension. It is done in pace with breathing, like this:

BREATHE IN—SCAN FOR TENSION

BREATHE OUT—RELEASE TENSION

To scan, first settle into a position that is relatively relaxing. If you are at a desk, simply stop what you are doing and close your eyes. If you are driving, pull to the side of the road and remain in the driver's seat. Let yourself settle into a position that is comfortable. Attend to your breath for a few seconds, letting it be as full, even, and unhurried as possible. Then, direct your attention to each major muscle group (see Lesson 7), one at a time. As you breathe in, focus on one muscle group and ask yourself "Am I tense here?" For example, focus on your hands and arms to see if they are tense. As you breathe out, let go of any tension you may have found in your hands and arms. You may need to squeeze or stretch a few times. It might be helpful to take a few deep breaths. With every inhalation move your attention to another muscle group and check for tension; with every exhalation let go of any tension you may find. Scanning is like looking at an inner "tension mirror" or taking an instant photo or X-ray of your tension "hot spots."*

As you can see, scanning involves checking for tension. Checking is something most of us already do on a regular basis. For instance, if you are driving a long distance, when are you most likely to check your gas? Probably when you pass a service station. Similarly, when do you find yourself checking your appearance during the day? Most of us more or less automatically do this at specific times—in the rest room, while waiting for a bus, or perhaps when passing by a mirror. Checking is something we do in response to specific checking cues, such as gas stations

---

*For a similar exercise that does not involve checking for tension in pace with breathing, see mental isometric relaxation (RD 37, Lesson 10).

or mirrors. Part of the skill of scanning involves establishing certain checking cues, outside stimuli that become automatic reminders to scan for tension.

Scanning should be incorporated into your daily activities. It is during the day that you are most likely to experience unnecessary and wasteful tension. For example, when writing a report there is no need for you to tighten your back or leg muscles. These muscles are not needed for writing, and any tension there represents wasted energy.

In order for scanning to work you need to establish a set of daily checking cues or reminders. Whenever these cues occur, scan for tension. You can choose any regularly occurring stimulus as a checking cue: the hourly chime of a bell, a ringing phone, times when you are combing your hair or getting on the bus—anything. Before you begin this week's exercises, list the stimuli that might work as checking cues for you:

Potential Scanning Cues

1. _____
2. _____
3. _____
4. _____
5. _____
6. _____
7. _____

Now, place a check by the cues you plan to use this week.

The Integrative Nature of Breathing Exercises

The breathing exercises presented here hold a special place in the Relaxation Dynamics program: they are integrative. As mentioned earlier, breathing ties the inside world with the outside, and voluntary activity with involuntary. In research I have found that the experience of breathing is unique: tense breathing is associated with both heart symptoms and overt muscle tension, and relaxed breathing with relaxed heart activity and decreased muscle tension. Changes in breathing are associated with both visceral (or autonomic) and muscular manifestations of tension. Indeed, tense breathing is close to a universal symptom of stress.

Integrative breathing ties those exercises you learned earlier to those you will learn later in the program. Many of the breathing exercises incorporate the type of stretching movement you practiced last week. In fact, many students discover their breathing changes spontaneously while doing yogaform stretching or isometric squeeze exercises. In the future you may find that some breathing exercises help integrate relaxation exercises or provide a useful underlying rhythm or pace. Finally, integrative breathing defines a significant transition in the Relaxation Dynamics sequence. It is at this point we proceed from exercises that are primarily physical to exercises that are primarily mental.

Focus, Passivity, and Receptivity in Breathing Exercises

This week's approach continues our movement into worlds of rest involving greater degrees of internal focus, passivity, and receptivity. Both isometric squeeze relaxation and yogaform stretching incorporate motions that are often externally directed. We tighten up and extend our limbs when interacting with the outside world. Breathing involves actions and processes that are more internal, and more difficult to identify and discriminate. Rarely do we inhale and exhale to modify our environment. And, of course, the lungs are more internal than the muscles, bones, and ligaments. Sensations associated with relaxed breathing also require a greater degree of focus. It is often difficult to identify, discriminate, and attend to the easy flow of breath along its path of inhalation and exhalation.

Isometric relaxation is a relatively active approach. Yogaform stretching can be a bit more passive. Although some breathing exercises are as active as yoga stretches, their objective is alteration of a process that is essentially passive, the flow of breath. Indeed, relaxed breathing can often be facilitated by doing little more than attending to the breathing process itself or to a breathing-related fantasy. And truly relaxed breathing is utterly effortless and passive.

Finally, breathing exercises often confront us with new and unfamiliar experiences. The activity of attending to breathing may in itself be somewhat foreign. Also, as a result of increased oxygen in the blood, we might be distracted by a variety of novel sensations, such as feelings of increased mental clarity or alertness. In the face of such experiences, our task is to maintain a stance of receptivity, to accept such experiences, and to return to the exercise.

Start Off Checklist

(Do before starting this week's exercises)

__ Have you selected practice times during which you are relatively unlikely to be distracted? Remember: it is often not a good idea to practice when you have some other duty that has to be performed.

__ Do you have a comfortable relaxation chair?

__ Do you have a quiet place in which to practice? If you are going to practice in a place where there are other people, try to make sure you won't be interrupted. Close the door to your room. Ask friends or family members not to interrupt while you are "resting." And it's OK to take the phone off the hook.

__ You should not take a nonprescription drug (marijuana, amphetamines, barbituates, psychedelic drugs) or alcohol for at least a day before practicing. Such drugs can make it more difficult to relax or focus attention on what you are doing. At the very least, they can limit the extent to which the effects of relaxation will generalize outside the session.

__ You should not have a drink containing caffeine (coffee, tea, cola) for at least 2 hours before practicing. Caffeine can make it more difficult to relax and focus attention on what you are doing.

__ You should not smoke tobacco for at least an hour before practicing.

__ You should not eat any food for at least an hour before practicing. If you are absolutely starving, eat a carrot.

__ When you are finished, come out of relaxation very slowly and gently. Arising too abruptly can be jarring and even make you feel dizzy. Take about 60 seconds to easily open your eyes all the way. Then stretch your arms to your sides and take a deep breath.

Integrative Breathing

In this exercise sequence we are going to relax by breathing in a way that is full and even and unhurried.

Before we begin, make sure you are seated upright in a comfortable position.

PAUSE

Rest your hands comfortably in your lap.

PAUSE

Make sure your feet are placed flat on the floor.

PAUSE

Now gently close your eyes and let yourself settle into a position that is comfortable.

PAUSE

For the next few minutes let your body become more and more quiet.

PAUSE

Let yourself begin to settle down and relax as you remain still.

PAUSE 30 SECONDS

What is your breathing like?

PAUSE

Is it shallow or full?

PAUSE

Even or jerky?

PAUSE

Rushed or unhurried?

PAUSE

Deep Breathing(RD 23)

Now take a deep breath. And when you are ready, slowly and evenly exhale.

PAUSE 5 SECONDS

Let yourself breathe in a way that is comfortable.

PAUSE

Slow, easy, and rhythmical.

PAUSE

Take your time. Try not to force yourself to breathe in any particular way.

PAUSE

Let your stomach and chest slowly fill and empty with air.

PAUSE

Keep breathing this way.

PAUSE

Slowly in and slowly out.

PAUSE 15 SECONDS

Arm Swing Breathing (RD 24)

Now let your arms hang by your sides.

PAUSE 5 SECONDS

This time, as you breathe in, circle your arms behind you in whatever way feels best. And when you are ready to breathe out, gently and easily circle your arms around to your front and let them cross your chest as if you were hugging a big pillow. Try breathing this way for a while.

PAUSE 5 SECONDS

Continue breathing this way... breathing in while gently circling your arms to your back ... and pausing ... and breathing out while circling your arms to your front.

PAUSE 5 SECONDS

Breathe gently and easily at an unhurried pace. Take your time.

PAUSE 5 SECONDS

Go easily.

PAUSE 5 SECONDS

Let each breath be full and complete.

PAUSE 5 SECONDS

And let yourself breathe without strain and without effort.

PAUSE 5 SECONDS

Without hurrying and without rushing.

PAUSE 5 SECONDS

Now let your arms hang by your sides.

PAUSE 5 SECONDS

Body Arch Breathing (RD 25)

This time, as you inhale, gently arch and stretch your back and let your head tilt back slightly. Let your lungs fill completely with air. And when you are ready, exhale and relax and return to a comfortable upright position. Gently tilt your head forward.

PAUSE 5 SECONDS

For a few seconds, continue breathing this way, gently and easily. Arch your back as you gently breathe in. And sit up as you breathe out. Do this gently and easily.

PAUSE 15 SECONDS

Breathing and Bowing (RD 26)

Now, with your arms still hanging by your sides, sit up again.

PAUSE 5 SECONDS

Now, again, arch and stretch your back, taking in a deep breath. But this time when you are ready to exhale, gently and slowly bow over in your chair, letting your chest and head move toward your knees. Let your arms hang limply. Let gravity pull you down, squeezing all the air out. If you need to take a short breath from time to time, that's OK. And when you are ready, slowly and gently inhale while sitting up.

PAUSE 5 SECONDS

Continue breathing this way for about a minute, in an easy and unhurried way. Breathe at your own pace, easily in and out.

PAUSE 5 SECONDS

Let each breath be full and complete.

PAUSE 5 SECONDS

Breathe at a pace that feels comfortable and unhurried.

PAUSE 5 SECONDS

Do not force yourself to move; let gravity do the work.

PAUSE 5 SECONDS

Notice the relaxed and easy flow of breath.

PAUSE 5 SECONDS

Take your time.

PAUSE 5 SECONDS

Breathe fully and evenly.

PAUSE 5 SECONDS

Breathe in a rhythm that feels comfortable to you.

PAUSE 5 SECONDS

Let your breathing be easy and relaxed.

PAUSE 5 SECONDS

Now, as you sit up, stay in that position for a few minutes, and breathe deeply and easily in your own way.

PAUSE 5 SECONDS

Let your stomach and chest fill and empty completely of air.

PAUSE 5 SECONDS

Take your time.

PAUSE

Breathe at a pace that feels comfortable for you.

PAUSE 5 SECONDS

Let each breath carry out the tensions of your body.

PAUSE

Let the air that fills your lungs dissolve any tension you might feel.

PAUSE 15 SECONDS

Bowing and Stretching (RD 27)

Now, as you inhale, reach and stretch. Arch your back and gently circle both arms up toward the sky like the hands of a clock or the wings of a great bird. When you are ready to exhale, slowly circle your arms down so they are hanging heavily, and gently bow over, as before, squeezing out all the air. Let gravity pull your body down farther and farther. There is nothing for you to do. Continue breathing this way for a while. Breathe at whatever pace feels most comfortable. If you need to take a short breath from time to time, that's OK.

PAUSE

Continue breathing this way at your own pace. Reach up and breathe in; pause; and let go and bow over while breathing out. Do this very slowly and evenly, without hurrying and without rushing.

PAUSE 5 SECONDS

Make your movements very smooth and even.

PAUSE 10 SECONDS

Let yourself breathe deeply and fully, at your own pace.

PAUSE 10 SECONDS

Notice the easy flow of air as it moves in and out of your lungs.

PAUSE 5 SECONDS

Take your time, do not force yourself. Breathe comfortably and fully.

PAUSE 5 SECONDS

Now, as you sit up, place your hands in your lap. Stay in this position for a little while.

PAUSE

Let yourself breathe in a natural and easy way.

PAUSE 15 SECONDS

Attend to your stomach and chest.

PAUSE

How does it feel to breathe in a deep and relaxed manner?

PAUSE

You might want to think of a large, soft balloon that slowly fills, pauses, and empties of air.

PAUSE 5 SECONDS

Let each breath soothe your body, and make it more and more relaxed.

PAUSE 5 SECONDS

Stomach Squeeze Breathing (RD 28)

Now sit up in your chair and open your hands and fingers and place them over your stomach.

PAUSE

Spread your fingers comfortably apart so they cover your entire stomach, with your thumbs touching the bottom part of your chest.

PAUSE 5 SECONDS

Now, very easily, take a full breath, filling your stomach and chest completely. And when you are ready to exhale, firmly press in with your hands and fingers, squeezing in.

And when you are ready to inhale, gradually release your fingers, and let your stomach relax and breathe in as if your stomach were filling with air.

PAUSE

Breathe easily and completely.

PAUSE 5 SECONDS

Now continue breathing this way, squeezing your stomach as you are breathing out, and relaxing your fingers as you are breathing in.

PAUSE

Do not force yourself to breathe at a hurried pace.

PAUSE

Take your time.
Breathe very gently and very easily.

PAUSE 5 SECONDS

Notice what it feels like to breathe completely and fully.

PAUSE 5 SECONDS

At your own pace, continue breathing evenly in and evenly out. Do not hurry. Take your time.

PAUSE 5 SECONDS

Notice the even flow of air as it rushes in and out of your lungs.

PAUSE 10 SECONDS

Now, when you are ready, exhale completely, and relax your fingers.

PAUSE

Active Diaphragmatic Breathing (RD 29)

This time, let your fingers remain relaxed over your stomach. As you breathe in, let the air come in on its own, as if it were filling your stomach.

Feel the stomach filling, like a large, soft balloon filling completely.

And when you are ready to exhale, this time do not press in with your fingers. Relax, and let the air flow out on its own, gently and slowly. When you have breathed out, pull your stomach in toward your backbone, not using your fingers. Squeeze out any remaining air.

PAUSE

Continue breathing this way for a little while, breathing completely and deeply.

PAUSE 5 SECONDS

Fill and empty your stomach and chest.

Integrative Breathing

PAUSE 5 SECONDS

Take it easy, do not force yourself to breathe in a way that feels uncomfortable.

PAUSE 5 SECONDS

Breathe without strain.

PAUSE 5 SECONDS

Easily and completely.

PAUSE 5 SECONDS

Notice how it feels as breathing helps you become more and more relaxed.

PAUSE 15 SECONDS

And now, when you are ready, rest your hands in your lap. Let yourself breathe deeply and easily, without strain and without effort.

PAUSE

Now attend to the flow of air in and out of your nose.

PAUSE

How does it feel as the air rushes in and out?

PAUSE 5 SECONDS

Inhaling Through Nose (RD 30)

This time, as you breathe in, imagine you are sniffing a very delicate flower. Let the flow of breath into your nose be as smooth and gentle as possible, so you barely rustle a petal. Take a full breath.

PAUSE

And relax, letting yourself breathe out naturally, without effort.

PAUSE 5 SECONDS

Continue breathing this way, breathing in and out quietly and evenly at your own pace.

PAUSE 5 SECONDS

Notice the inner calm that comes with breathing in a way that is slow, full, and even.

PAUSE 5 SECONDS

Notice the relaxing and refreshing rush of air as it quietly moves in and out of your lungs.

PAUSE 5 SECONDS

See how far you can follow the inward flow of air.

PAUSE 5 SECONDS

Can you feel it move past your nostrils?

PAUSE 5 SECONDS

Can you feel the air in the passages of your nose?

PAUSE 5 SECONDS

Can you feel the air flowing into your body?

PAUSE 10 SECONDS

Take your time. Breathe easily and fully.

PAUSE 10 SECONDS

Let yourself become more and more quiet, more and more relaxed.

PAUSE 10 SECONDS

Exhaling Through Lips (RD 31)

Now take a slow deep breath and pause.

And breathe out slowly through your lips, as if you were blowing at a candle flame just enough to make it flicker, but not go out. Continue breathing out, emptying all the air from your stomach and chest.

PAUSE

Then breathe in through your nose.

PAUSE

Continue breathing this way, making the stream of air that passes through your lips as you exhale as smooth and gentle as possible.

PAUSE 5 SECONDS

Let the tension flow out with every breath.

PAUSE 5 SECONDS

Let the gentle movement of air dissolve any feelings of tension you might have.

PAUSE 10 SECONDS

Notice the easy flow of air as it relaxes and refreshes you.

PAUSE 10 SECONDS

Let each breath fill you with feelings of peaceful relaxation.

PAUSE 10 SECONDS

Notice the inner calm that comes with breathing in a way that is slow and full and even.

Focused Breathing (RD 32)

Now continue breathing in a relaxed manner, in and out through your nose.

PAUSE 5 SECONDS

Try not to force your breathing.

PAUSE 5 SECONDS

Notice the air as it rushes in and out, flowing into and out of your lungs, filling your body with refreshing and relaxing air.

PAUSE 5 SECONDS

Notice the unhurried rhythm of your breathing. Let yourself breathe effortlessly, without strain.

PAUSE 10 SECONDS

Notice the even flow of air as it moves in and out of your lungs through your nose.

PAUSE 10 SECONDS

Notice how the easy flow of air relaxes and refreshes you.

PAUSE 10 SECONDS

And attend to the feelings of inner calm that come from breathing in a way that is slow and full and even.

PAUSE 15 SECONDS

Thinking the Word *One* (RD 33)

This time, as you breathe out, gently let the word *one* repeat itself in your mind. Let it repeat effortlessly, like an echo.

PAUSE

There is nothing for you to do but attend to the word *one* every time you relax and exhale.

PAUSE 5 SECONDS

If your mind wanders, that's OK.
Gently and easily let the word *one* begin repeating itself in your mind. Let it repeat in any way it wishes.

PAUSE 5 SECONDS

Continue breathing this way for the next minute or so.

PAUSE 1 MINUTE

Now gradually let go of the word *one.*

PAUSE 5 SECONDS

Let yourself breathe effortlessly and without strain.

PAUSE

Thinking a Relaxing Word (RD 34)

This time, every time you relax and breathe out, let a relaxing word of your own choosing repeat itself in your mind.

PAUSE 5 SECONDS

Let your word repeat effortlessly, like an echo, following the easy pace of your breathing.   ,

PAUSE

Let yourself breathe this way for about a minute or so.

PAUSE 1 MINUTE

Now, very gently and easily, let go of the word.

PAUSE 5 SECONDS

Let it quietly float away, like a cloud.

PAUSE 5 SECONDS

Now, for the next few minutes, simply sit quietly and gently.

PAUSE

Attend to how you feel.

PAUSE

Let yourself enjoy the pleasant feelings of relaxation.

PAUSE 3 MINUTES

Now slowly and easily open your eyes.

PAUSE 5 SECONDS

Take a deep breath.

PAUSE 5 SECONDS

And stretch.

PAUSE 5 SECONDS

This completes the integrative breathing exercise sequence.

Part IV

Unrestrictive Mental Exercises

Lesson 10
Somatic Focusing
(Beginning and Advanced Exercises)

Lesson 11
Thematic Imagery

Lesson 10

Somatic Focusing

We have just completed a series of physical relaxation exercises. In this lesson we are going to begin our exploration of an entirely new approach, mental relaxation. We will first explore somatic focusing and thematic imagery, mental approaches that are relatively unrestrictive in that they give you considerable leeway in what you can do. We will then consider the relatively restrictive approaches of contemplation and meditation.

Let's begin with somatic focusing. Somatic focusing works because of the strong link between the body and mind. It is a link demonstrated nearly every day. You think of a delicious meal—your mouth waters. You imagine an upcoming exam—your muscles tighten up. You fantasize a relaxing vacation spot—you sigh in relief. In somatic focusing we are going to create and enhance relaxation by doing nothing more than thinking certain kinds of thoughts that go with physical relaxation. Let's see what this means.

How does your body feel after a hot bath or thorough massage? What kinds of thoughts and images go through your mind? How did you feel after trying the squeezing, stretching, and breathing exercises described in previous lessons? You might have felt warm or heavy, or your breathing might have seemed cool and refreshing. You even might have pictured a warm beach or a refreshing breeze. Such experiences are normal and usually reflect that physical, or *somatic*, relaxation is taking place. When you are tense, the blood vessels in your fingers constrict. This results in the cold, clammy hands many experience under stress. However, when you relax, these same blood vessels dilate or expand. Blood flow to the extremities increases, and you feel warm. Similarly, when your muscles relax, you are more likely to feel their weight (have you ever been so relaxed that you felt that you simply couldn't get up?). There are many physical sensations that signify that relaxation is taking place. It is possible to create and enhance relaxation by doing nothing more than thinking thoughts related to such somatic relaxation processes. This is a strategy frequently used in hypnosis (Bower, 1976), autogenic training (Luthe, 1963, 1965, 1977), kundalini yoga (Rama et al., 1976), and some forms of Zen meditation (Kapleau, 1965). It is the idea underlying somatic focusing.

Somatic focusing makes use of a special type of mental activity called *passive thinking.* This way of using the mind can be demonstrated easily.

> First, let's demonstrate its opposite, active thinking. Let your right hand drop to your side. Now, actively and effortfully try to make your hand feel warm and heavy. Work at it. Exert as much effort as you can trying to actively and deliberately will your hands to feel warm and heavy.
>
> Now, simply relax. Let your hand fall limply by your side. Without trying to accomplish anything, simply let the phrase "My hand is warm and heavy" repeat in your mind. Let the words repeat on their own, like an echo. All you have to do is quietly observe the repeating words. Don't try to achieve warmth and heaviness. Just quietly let the words go over and over in your mind. While thinking the words *warm and heavy,* you might want to imagine your hand in warm sand, or in the sun, or in a warm bath. Pick an image that feels comfortable, and simply dwell upon it.

The first exercise illustrates active thinking, the second passive thinking. Most people find that passive thinking is more effective at fostering relaxation processes. The idea behind passive thinking is to quietly let certain phrases or images pass through the mind, as if they were echoes. There is no attempt to deliberately accomplish anything. However, not just any phrase or image will do. In order to work, the phrases or images must somehow be associated with or symbolize the somatic processes that go with relaxation; they must be *supporting phrases* or *supporting images.* The words *warm and heavy* or the image of the warm sun on the hand are excellent examples.

Unlike previous exercises in the Relaxation Dynamics system, somatic exercises are not to be done alone (although this can be attempted, with interesting effects). Instead, it is preferable to use somatic images and phrases to enhance and modify the effects of other exercises. That is, you might want to take specific phrases and pictures presented in this and the next lesson and weave them into your favorite sequence. For example, when you tense and let go of your hand muscles in isometric relaxation, you might want to think the phrase "My hands are warm and heavy."

Beginning Somatic Exercises

In this lesson we will first learn to relax by passively thinking phrases and images associated with four kinds of relaxation: relaxed breathing; the letting go of tension in isometric relaxation (and scanning); a relaxing massage; and the feelings of warmth and heaviness. We start with these because they are relatively simple and are closely related to the exercises we have already performed. We will then explore some somatic exercises that are a bit more advanced.

In integrative breathing you learned to inhale and exhale in a way that is slow, deep, and even. At the end of this exercise, your breathing might have felt cool and relaxed. The first somatic focusing exercise involves passively thinking thoughts related to relaxed and effortless breathing. You will simply repeat phrases such as "My breathing is slow, deep, and even" or "My breath is cool and relaxed."

In isometric squeezing you first tensed up and then let go of various muscle groups. Our next somatic focusing exercise involves a mental version of this approach. Here you direct attention to each muscle group and simply think thoughts related to the release of muscle tension; for example, you might think "Tightness is dissolving and flowing out of my muscles."

Both isometric squeezing and yogaform stretching result in a deliberate releasing, pulling, pushing, and kneading of muscles. This produces a tingling massage-like effect for many. In addition, blood flow increases to the extremities, bringing on a feeling of being warm and heavy. In the final beginning somatic focusing exercises you think phrases and images related to a massage-like tingling as well as warmth and heaviness.

Advanced Somatic Exercises

In the exercises just described we focused on sensations, phrases, and images associated with deliberate muscle relaxation as well as relaxed breathing. These are physical processes that are to some extent under direct voluntary control; we can deliberately tense, stretch, and relax our muscles and alter our breathing. In addition, these processes are relatively easy to attend to; most people can quickly direct their attention to a tightened fist or the process of breathing. We will now focus on physical processes and organs that are usually not under voluntary control and are generally outside of awareness.

We will begin by attending to nerves deep in the pit of the stomach close to the backbone. This area is called the solar plexis. When relaxed, people at times feel a warm glow in this area, similar to what might be felt after swallowing a warm, soothing liquid. We will then briefly guide our attention to the spine. Next, we will attend to the heart and sensations associated with a slow, even heartbeat. We then will direct our attention up the spine to the base of the throat. For reasons that are not entirely understood, feelings of relaxation sometimes center here. Finally, we will direct our attention farther up the spine, into the head, and end by focusing at the space between and slightly above the eyes. We will attend to visual phenomena associated with spontaneous neurological activity in the retina (phosphene activity) and possibly other parts of the visual system. Seen as brief spots or flashes of light, or possibly vague forms of light, such activity is at times associated with relaxation.

Throughout the entire exercise we will take care to keep our backs erect and relaxed. There is a good reason for this. When the spine is erect, it is in a position that facilitates both alertness and relaxation. When we begin a task that requires full awareness (typing, playing a video game, etc.), we typically sit up straight. This position also encourages relaxation. Imagine the backbone as a stack of bricks. If bricks are stacked at a tilt, like the Tower of Pisa, you have to brace them with your hands to keep them from falling over. If they are stacked straight, they rest quietly on top of each other, requiring no further effort. Similarly, an erect spine requires little effort to stay erect. The muscles of the body can remain relaxed.

Somatic Deepening Suggestions (RD 45)

The images described previously (such as "My hands are warm and heavy") simply depict physical states and changes that go with relaxation. It is possible to enhance relaxation by repeating phrases and images that suggest deeper states of relaxation. Somatic deepening suggestions involve thinking of a conceivable consequence of the somatic thoughts and phrases being repeated. That is, thinking the thought "My hands and arms are warm and heavy" is one somatic exercise. What would be a conceivable consequence if your hands and arms were actually warm and heavy? They might feel so heavy that they almost seemed hard to lift. This consequence could be incorporated into your somatic relaxation sequence as a deepening suggestion. For instance, in addition to slowly repeating the phrase "My hands and arms are warm and heavy," you could occasionally think, "My hands and arms are getting so heavy I can barely lift them . . . it feels as if bricks are holding them down." Some other somatic deepening suggestions include:

> My eyelids are so comfortably warm and heavy they feel glued shut.

> My feet and legs are so pleasantly heavy it feels as if I could barely lift them off the ground.

> The muscles in my fingers are so relaxed it feels as if I would be unable to open them even if I tried.

> My entire body is so pleasantly heavy and relaxed it feels as if I would be unable to get up and walk away.

Whatever somatic deepening suggestions you discover, remember to make them *pleasurable*. If you don't like the idea of bricks holding your hands down, think of something else, a heavy blanket perhaps. If you don't like thinking about your eyelids being glued shut, imagine you have been given eyedrops to make them heavy. You choose the suggestions that feel best.

Quieting Sequences

For all mental exercises, from somatic focusing to contemplation and meditation, it is often best to devote a little time to physical relaxation before starting. Physical relaxation can be useful for "quieting" some of the tension that can interfere with cognitive techniques. However, of the three approaches to physical relaxation (isometric squeeze relaxation, yogaform stretching, and integrative breathing), different approaches or combinations of approaches may work better for different people. One way to find out which works best for you is to try several, testing out a different one each session before you do a mental exercise. Worksheet 18 in the Appendix will help you to develop your own quieting sequence.

Start Off Checklist

(Do before starting this week's exercises)

___ Have you selected practice times during which you are relatively unlikely to be distracted? Remember: it is often not a good idea to practice when you have some other duty that has to be performed.

___ Do you have a comfortable relaxation chair?

___ Do you have a quiet place in which to practice? If you are going to practice in a place where there are other people, try to make sure you won't be interrupted. Close the door to your room. Ask friends or family members not to interrupt while you are "resting." And it's OK to take the phone off the hook.

___ You should not take a nonprescription drug (marijuana, amphetamines, barbituates, psychedelic drugs) or alcohol for at least a day before practicing. Such drugs can make it more difficult to relax or focus attention on what you are doing. At the very least, they can limit the extent to which the effects of relaxation will generalize outside the session.

___ You should not have a drink containing caffeine (coffee, tea, cola) for at least 2 hours before practicing. Caffeine can make it more difficult to relax and focus attention on what you are doing.

___ You should not smoke tobacco for at least an hour before practicing.

___ You should not eat any food for at least an hour before practicing. If you are absolutely starving, eat a carrot.

___ Be sure to precede your practice with a physical quieting sequence.

___ When you are finished, come out of relaxation very slowly and gently. Arising too abruptly can be jarring and even make you feel dizzy. Take about 60 seconds to easily open your eyes all the way. Then stretch your arms to your sides and take a deep breath.

Somatic Focusing: Beginning Exercises

In this exercise sequence we are going to relax by attending to phrases and images that are associated with the process of physical relaxation.

PAUSE

First, make sure you are seated in an upright position.

PAUSE

Are your feet flat on the floor?

PAUSE

Rest your hands comfortably in your lap.

PAUSE

Now gently close your eyes and let yourself settle into a position that is comfortable.

PAUSE

For the next few minutes let your body become more and more quiet. Let yourself begin to settle down and relax as you remain still.

PAUSE 1 MINUTE

Breathing (RD 36)

Let your breathing be slow, rhythmical, and full.

PAUSE 5 SECONDS

Take your time, do not force yourself to breathe in any particular way.

PAUSE 5 SECONDS

Simply observe the breath as it easily flows in . . . and out.

PAUSE 5 SECONDS

Breathe in, and relax and let go as you breathe out. In . . . and out as you relax and let go.

PAUSE 5 SECONDS

Imagine ocean waves, flowing in . . . and out . . . as your breathing flows in and out.

PAUSE

Feel what is set into motion with the rising wave of inhalation . . . allow the wave of breath to decline and fade, as if into a great distance.

PAUSE 10 SECONDS

Let your breath flow easily... smoothly and rhythmically...like waves on the ocean.

PAUSE 10 SECONDS

Quietly observe the easy pace of your breathing.

PAUSE 10 SECONDS

There is nothing for you to do but passively observe the breath as you breathe in, and relax and let go as you breathe out.

PAUSE 15 SECONDS

You might want to imagine yourself breathing in through your fingertips. Your breath flows in, very smoothly and calmly, through your fingertips.

PAUSE

Up the arms into the shoulders.

PAUSE

And then as you exhale, relax and let go as the breath flows down the trunk and stomach and legs and leisurely out at the toes.

PAUSE 10 SECONDS

Let the breath flow in, easily and gently, and out as you relax and let go.

PAUSE 15 SECONDS

What images or words best describe the quiet and rhythmic flow of breath?

PAUSE 5 SECONDS

What images or words best describe the relaxation and letting go you feel at the end of every breath?

PAUSE

Is your breathing refreshing, cool, gentle, sinking, light?

PAUSE

Let whatever images or words that describe the smooth and gentle flow of breath come to mind . . . let these words or pictures repeat in your mind with every breath . . . like an echo or like clouds floating by in the sky. Do this for the next minute or so.

PAUSE 1 MINUTE

Mental Isometric Relaxation (RD 37)

Now quietly attend to your hands and fingers.

PAUSE

With every breath, let go of any tension you might feel.

PAUSE

Let your hands and fingers become more and more relaxed.

PAUSE

Let tension flow from your arms with every breath.

PAUSE

Simply let go, and let the tension release, like a tightly rolled ball of string slowly unwinding.

PAUSE

Let any feelings of tightness you might have in the muscles of your back flow away.
Let the tension go with every outgoing breath.

PAUSE

As you breathe out, let go of any tension you might feel in your shoulders.
Let yourself become more and more limp, like a floppy rag doll.

PAUSE

Let your shoulder muscles become more and more relaxed.

PAUSE

Let your mind dwell on any words or pictures that might go with letting go of tension.
Let your shoulder muscles sink into a pleasant state of comfortable relaxation.

PAUSE

Let any feelings of tension in your neck muscles dissolve and flow away.
Let your neck become more and more comfortably relaxed.

PAUSE

With every outgoing breath, let tension gently flow from the muscles of your face.

PAUSE

Let your jaws, mouth, tongue, and lips become more and more relaxed.

PAUSE

If you feel tightness around your eyes, let the tension flow away with every outgoing breath.

PAUSE

Let any tension you might feel in your chest and abdomen flow away with every outgoing breath.

PAUSE

Let yourself become more and more comfortably relaxed with every outgoing breath.

There is nothing for you to do but experience the pleasant feelings of relaxation as you let go of areas of tension.

PAUSE

Attend to the muscles of your legs and thighs and, with every outgoing breath, let go of any tension you might feel.

Let the tension pleasantly flow away.

Let your leg muscles sink into a deeper and deeper state of pleasant comfort.

PAUSE

And let your feet and toes become more comfortably relaxed.

Let the tension flow away.

Let your feet become more and more completely relaxed with every outgoing breath.

PAUSE

Now, for the next minute or so, let your entire body become more and more relaxed. Let go of any tension you may feel. It is OK to let pictures or words come to mind that go with relaxation.

PAUSE 1 MINUTE

Mental Massage (RD 38)

Now once again attend to your hands and fingers.

PAUSE 5 SECONDS

Imagine a gentle relaxing massage of your hands.

PAUSE 5 SECONDS

You might imagine fingers gently massaging your hands, soothing away the tensions.

PAUSE

Or a soft flow of air or water, or a warm furry kitten brushing against your hand.

PAUSE

Imagine the soothing, tingling, gentle movement against your hands.

PAUSE 15 SECONDS

With every breath you exhale, let go and let the massaging relaxation flow up your arms, dissolving any tension.

PAUSE

It is not important that you actually feel massaging sensations; simply let words and images dwell in your mind. There is nothing else for you to do or experience.

PAUSE 10 SECONDS

Let a relaxing massage flow into your shoulders, back, and neck.

PAUSE 10 SECONDS

Let the gentle relaxation sink deep into the muscles like gently massaging fingers, or a massaging flow of water or air.

PAUSE 10 SECONDS

Let the massaging action dissolve feelings of tension with every outward breath.

PAUSE 10 SECONDS

Let it sink into the very deepest muscles.

PAUSE 10 SECONDS

Let the massaging relaxation continue to flow into your face and smooth away any tightness you may feel in your jaws and lips, any tension you may feel around your eyes and forehead.

PAUSE 10 SECONDS

Imagine the gentle movement of fingers, or air or water, against your face, smoothing away the tension with every outward breath.

PAUSE 10 SECONDS

Let the relaxing massage move to your trunk and stomach and let the tension sink and flow away as you breathe. Let the gentle massage move to your legs and toes, sinking deeply into every muscle, dissolving any tension that may be there.

PAUSE 10 SECONDS

Now, for the next minute or so, let your entire body become more completely relaxed as you feel a gentle massage flowing over every muscle. Let the massage dissolve any tightness you may feel. Let your mind dwell on whatever words or pictures go with relaxation. Attend to and enjoy the feelings associated with massaging relaxation.

PAUSE 1 MINUTE

Warmth and Heaviness (RD 39)

Now attend again to your hands and fingers.

PAUSE 5 SECONDS

With every flow of breath, let yourself think words and images related to warmth and heaviness.

PAUSE

It is not important that you actually feel sensations of warmth and heaviness. Simply let thoughts related to warmth and heaviness float through your mind, like echoes.

PAUSE 10 SECONDS

Think the phrase "My hands and arms are heavy and warm . . . warmth is flowing into my hands and arms."

PAUSE

What pictures or images come to mind that go with warmth and heaviness? You might want to imagine your hands and arms in warm, soothing water, or in the sand. You might want to imagine a warm, relaxing breeze caressing your skin. Let pictures and images come to mind that suggest warmth and heaviness.

PAUSE 10 SECONDS

"My hands and arms are heavy and warm . . . so heavy it begins to feel as if I could barely lift them . . . as if heavy bricks were resting on my hands, pulling them down."

PAUSE 10 SECONDS

"Warmth flows into the spaces between my fingers, into my hands and arms."

PAUSE

Imagine these words quietly and passively, like an echo.

PAUSE

"Warm and heavy, hands and arms are warm and heavy, as blood carries warmth to every muscle."

PAUSE

"My arms and hands are so heavy it feels as if it might be hard to lift them."

PAUSE

"As if heavy bricks were attached to each arm."

PAUSE 10 SECONDS

You might imagine the warm sun shining on your hands and arms.

PAUSE

Or warm water or air, or a soft warm blanket.

PAUSE 10 SECONDS

Let the warmth and heaviness flow up your arms with every breath into your shoulders, back, and neck. You might want to imagine the warm sun, or warm water or air, bringing relaxation to your shoulders, back, and neck.

PAUSE 10 SECONDS

Think "My back is warm and heavy."

PAUSE 10 SECONDS

"My shoulders are warm and heavy."

PAUSE 10 SECONDS

"My neck is warm and heavy."

PAUSE 10 SECONDS

"It feels pleasant as my muscles relax and become warm and heavy, as if the sun were shining down on them, or they were covered by warm water or air."

PAUSE 10 SECONDS

If your mind is distracted, that's OK . . . easily and gently return to thinking "warm and heavy," passively and quietly, as if you were listening to words echo in your mind.

PAUSE 10 SECONDS

Let warmth and heaviness flow into the muscles of your face, dissolving any tension that may be there.

PAUSE 10 SECONDS

Let the flow of blood bring feelings of warmth and heaviness to your face, smoothing out the tension, bringing deeper and deeper relaxation.

PAUSE 10 SECONDS

Let yourself think "warm and heavy" as your face becomes more relaxed.

PAUSE

"My eyelids are comfortably warm and heavy... almost as if they were glued shut."

PAUSE

"I can feel the heavy weight of my eyelids beginning to build as they become so relaxed."

PAUSE

"It would take some effort to open my eyelids ... it feels so good just to let them stay shut ... warm and heavy."

PAUSE 10 SECONDS

Let the warmth and heaviness flow into your trunk and stomach, flowing deeply inside. Let go of any tension with every breath as you think, "I am warm and heavy, warm and heavy."

PAUSE 10 SECONDS

Let warmth and heaviness flow into your legs and feet. Focus on your legs and feet. Notice the pleasant sensations as warmth and heaviness flow with every breath.

PAUSE

Think silently to yourself "My legs and feet are becoming heavy and warm ... warmth is flowing into my feet ... my legs are warm and heavy... my feet are warm and heavy... warmth and heaviness is sinking into my legs and feet as they become more and more relaxed."

PAUSE

Your legs and feet feel more and more warm and heavy... so heavy that you can feel gravity pulling them down ... so heavy that it feels as if it would take some effort to lift them ... warm and heavy... as if heavy weights were resting on each leg ... heavy bricks pulling down.

PAUSE 10 SECONDS

Now, for the next minute or so, let your entire body feel pleasantly warm and heavy. Let waves of pleasant relaxation dissolve any tension you may have. Let every muscle sink and become more completely relaxed . . . warm and heavy.

PAUSE 1 MINUTE

Now, gently let go of what you are attending to.

PAUSE 5 SECONDS

Gently open your eyes.

PAUSE 5 SECONDS

Take a deep breath.

PAUSE 5 SECONDS

And stretch.

PAUSE 5 SECONDS

And this completes your beginning somatic focusing exercise sequence.

Somatic Focusing: Advanced Exercises

In this exercise sequence we are going to relax by quietly attending to parts of our body deep within that are usually silent.

PAUSE 5 SECONDS

Make sure you are seated upright in a comfortable position.

PAUSE 5 SECONDS

Are your feet flat on the floor?

PAUSE 5 SECONDS

Are your hands resting comfortably in your lap?

PAUSE 5 SECONDS

Now gently close your eyes.

PAUSE 5 SECONDS

Make sure your head is erect.

PAUSE 5 SECONDS

Your spine should be poised in an upright and relaxed position.

PAUSE 5 SECONDS

Now take a deep breath, and as you let go, relax.

PAUSE 5 SECONDS

For the next few minutes let your body become more and more quiet.

PAUSE 5 SECONDS

Let yourself begin to settle down and relax as you remain still.

PAUSE 30 SECONDS

Now attend to your breathing.

PAUSE 5 SECONDS

Let your breathing be slow, even, and full.

PAUSE 5 SECONDS

Try not to force yourself to breathe in any particular way.

PAUSE 10 SECONDS

With each outward breath, let go and relax.

PAUSE 10 SECONDS

Let your tensions flow out with every breath.

PAUSE 10 SECONDS

Quietly observe the easy pace of your breathing.

PAUSE 10 SECONDS

There is nothing for you to do but passively observe your breathing, in and out.

PAUSE 15 SECONDS

Thematic Deepening Suggestions (RD 53)

Let yourself sink deeper and deeper with each outgoing breath.

PAUSE 15 SECONDS

With each outgoing breath, count down, one number with each breath, starting with the number 10. Let yourself become more and more relaxed.

PAUSE

Let yourself think 9, sinking deeper and deeper into a pleasant state of relaxation.

PAUSE

8—let yourself become warm and heavy, sinking into a deeper and deeper state of relaxation. You might imagine you are sinking into a soft deep pillow.

PAUSE

7—sinking farther and farther into pleasant relaxation.

PAUSE

6—with every outward breath, let go of your tension, sinking deeper and deeper.

PAUSE

5—let your entire body become more and more relaxed. If you notice any area of tension, let go of the tension, and sink deeper and deeper.

PAUSE

4—let your mind sink deeper into the center of your body.

PAUSE

3—become more centered and relaxed.

PAUSE

2—let relaxation sink deep into the pit of your stomach, deep behind your navel.

PAUSE

Somatic Focusing

1—let your body become completely limp and relaxed as you attend to your center, deep within your abdomen.

PAUSE 10 SECONDS

Solar Plexis (RD 40)

With every breath you exhale, let warmth flow into your abdomen, filling you with a nice relaxed feeling.

PAUSE 10 SECONDS

Let the warm outgoing breath warm you inside.

PAUSE 10 SECONDS

You might imagine drinking something that warms you nicely inside with every outgoing breath ... or that a warm glowing ball is rolling around inside you, or a warm sun gently warming and relaxing you inside with its rays.

PAUSE 10 SECONDS

Let every outgoing breath bring warmth within you.

PAUSE 10 SECONDS

What pictures or words best fit the feelings of relaxation deep within you?

PAUSE 10 SECONDS

Let these images or words come to you in whatever way they want, and let them repeat like echoes in your mind.

PAUSE 10 SECONDS

If any pictures or images come to mind, simply attend to them quietly. Continue relaxing this way for the next minute or so.

PAUSE 1 MINUTE

Erect Spine (RD 41)

Now attend to your backbone.

PAUSE 5 SECONDS

Let it be relaxed and erect, like a chain hanging loosely.

PAUSE

You might imagine you are quietly and gracefully balancing something on the top of your head, or that your back is resting comfortably against a flat surface.

PAUSE 10 SECONDS

Heart (RD 42)

Now let warm and pleasant relaxation flow up to your chest, around your heart.

PAUSE 10 SECONDS

Let warmth flow, like a calm river, or the moving rays of the sun, up to the area of your heart, deep within.

PAUSE 10 SECONDS

And let your breathing be deep and even.

PAUSE 10 SECONDS

Let every incoming breath bring life and energy, and every outgoing breath carry out the tension.

PAUSE 10 SECONDS

And let your heart beat slowly and evenly, slowly and evenly.

PAUSE 10 SECONDS

What words or pictures come to mind as you attend to your calm and even heartbeat?

PAUSE 10 SECONDS

For the next minute or so let these words or pictures run through your mind, like echoes in your mind.

PAUSE 1 MINUTE

Base of Throat (RD 43)

Now let your attention float with every breath farther up your spine, like the flow of water, or the warm rays of the sun, to the base of your throat.

PAUSE 10 SECONDS

Let your throat relax and open fully.

PAUSE 10 SECONDS

Let every breath bring refreshing relaxation to the area around your throat.

PAUSE 10 SECONDS

Let your throat open and relax, as if you were going to say the word "Ahhh" or sing in a way that is free and joyful.

PAUSE 10 SECONDS

What words or images come to mind as you attend to the peaceful energy centered here?

PAUSE 10 SECONDS

For the next minute or so, let these words or pictures run through your mind, like echoes, as you attend to the refreshing sensations of relaxation.

PAUSE 1 MINUTE

Visual Phenomena (RD 44)

Now let your attention move slowly with every breath into your head, into the space between and slightly above your eyes.

PAUSE 10 SECONDS

Attend to this space very quietly.

PAUSE 10 SECONDS

What do you see with your eyes closed?

PAUSE

Darkness, like the night sky?

PAUSE

Flashes or star-like points of light?

PAUSE

Vague forms or colors?

PAUSE

Attend to whatever you see.

PAUSE 10 SECONDS

If restful words or images or even sounds or music come to mind, let them repeat easily and effortlessly, without trying to keep them or push them away.

PAUSE 15 SECONDS

Simply attend to what happens as your attention centers in your mind.

PAUSE 15 SECONDS

If you become caught up in a train of thought or distraction, easily return to attending to the cool space between and slightly above your eyes. Continue doing this for the next minute or so.

PAUSE 1 MINUTE

Now, gently let go of what you are attending to.

PAUSE 5 SECONDS

Slowly and gently open your eyes.

PAUSE 5 SECONDS

Take a deep breath.

PAUSE 5 SECONDS

And stretch.

PAUSE 5 SECONDS

This completes the advanced somatic focusing exercise sequence.

Lesson 11

Thematic Imagery

The approaches introduced in preceding lessons involved physical activity or thoughts about physical relaxation. Thematic imagery is entirely mental. Imagery involves creating in the mind happenings both real and fanciful. Just as the writer and artist use words or pictures to describe their worlds, we can evoke worlds in our minds either verbally or visually. Our mental creations can be as brief or extensive as we desire. We can repeat in our minds relaxing words and sentences, or even tell ourselves restful stories. Or we can visualize relaxing pictures or create a type of inner motion picture (Kroger & Fezler, 1976; Luthe, 1963, 1965, 1977; Masters & Houston, 1972; McCaffery, 1979; Meichenbaum, 1977; Samuels & Samuels, 1975).

The physical relaxation exercises described in previous lessons made some use of imagery. For example, one isometric squeeze exercise had instructions to think of squeezing a sponge while pressing the arm against the side. Part of a breathing exercise was to picture blowing gently on a candle flame while exhaling through the lips. Such pictures and phrases assisted the process of relaxation. This week such thoughts become the primary focus of our attention.

Imagery can be active or passive. You can actively take the role of a director guiding and changing a movie. You can decide where a fantasy goes and every turn it takes. You can even decide to stop a fantasy or change themes. Or you can sit back and passively let thoughts and pictures change and unfold on their own. In that case you are no longer the director but the observer. Processes outside of your immediate awareness are in charge. To put it differently, in active imagery you are in the driver's seat; in passive imagery you are the passenger.

155

The Themes of Imagery

Any of life's relaxing situations can be pictured or described in the mind. We can think thoughts that are simply pleasurable or escapist, as in daydreaming. We can imagine the feelings of self-affirmation and relief that come from successfully mastering a challenge. We can be artists or musicians in our mind's eye. Or we can become immersed in the world of the senses, or commune with the mysteries of the universe. These are the themes of imagery. They are summarized here:

1. Pleasure
2. Escape
3. Reminiscence
4. Mastery
5. Expression
6. Intuition
7. Sensation

Let's begin with three themes familiar to most people: pleasure, escape, and reminiscence.

Pleasure (RD 46)

Most people find it easy to engage in pleasure imagery. All of us have indulged at times in an innocent sexual fantasy or thought about an approaching meal. And for such themes we are typically active participants, although this does not have to be the case. When constructing pleasure imagery, feel free to include anything you wish. Remember, in your mind you have complete freedom to do absolutely anything. Indeed, at times it can be healthy to enjoy an innocent fantasy of something you ordinarily wouldn't do in everyday life.

Escape (RD 47)

Have you ever pictured yourself in a distant land or even on a different world? Have you ever imagined yourself in a time or place far removed from the present moment? These are the fantasies and images of escape. As with pleasure imagery, you have complete freedom to do anything and go anywhere. Escape imagery can be a particularly useful form of self-relaxation, a way of experiencing a quick mental vacation from life's pressures and demands.

You might want to experiment with constructing your own private "escape place." In your mind, picture a setting that is particularly relaxing. Whenever you need a quick break, simply close your eyes and return to this place. Many people find that with practice the private escape place becomes more satisfying and relaxing. Every time they return it becomes more real.

Reminiscence (RD 48)

Have you ever found yourself thinking about something pleasurable that has happened to you in the past? This is reminiscence. It is a form of imagery that, in addition to being pleasurable and relaxing, can help us integrate important experiences into our lives. For example, our memories of loved ones who have passed away remind us of the part they played and still play in our lives.

The next themes, mastery, expression, and intuition, all involve accomplishing a desired end.

Mastery (RD 49)

Through mental pictures or words we can imagine meeting and mastering a challenge. The experience of mastery is also a part of the universe of self-relaxation. From mastery can come feelings of relief and self-affirmation, experiences that allow us to put aside unnecessary physical and mental tensions. Thoughts of mastery can at times actually prepare us for meeting a challenge. For example, one student of Relaxation Dynamics found meeting new people so anxiety-arousing that he often preferred to be alone rather than take part in social events. One night, before going to a party where he was sure to meet a number of strangers, he created for himself a relaxing mastery fantasy.

> I see myself at the party. Anxiety is building. My heart is pounding. I am beginning to think about how awkward I must appear. I decide to stop this uptight, crazy line of thought. I start repeating the phrase "All I have to do is walk up to one person and start talking about all the people at the party... that's all I have to do." I'll take a deep, relaxing breath, and simply do it. I may not come across as a social whiz, but I'll keep at it. OK, let's imagine what this will be like. I'm walking up to a person. So far so good. I take a deep breath and say to myself, "I'm going to meet this person." I approach the person and start talking. I get a little tense. That's OK, I expected that. I keep talking. Good. I'm doing much better.

There is no end to the types of mastery situations that can be imagined: getting a good grade on an exam; asking the boss for a raise; overcoming a smoking or eating habit. In each case a problem is met and realistically dealt with, resulting in a genuine and rewarding feeling of relaxation. When thinking about a mastery situation, it is often useful to include four steps (Meichenbaum, 1977):

1. *Anticipation.* Think about what happens before you meet the challenge. What thoughts do you have? How do you feel? What are you doing? Be sure to make your imagery realistic. Example: "It's the day before the exam. My anxiety is increasing. I realize it's normal to feel a little anxious. I'm doing all I realistically can to study. I have set aside an hour in the afternoon and an hour in the evening to review. I know exactly which chapters I will study."

2. *Confrontation.* Imagine you are now directly facing the challenge. Example: "I am now sitting in the classroom. The exams are being passed out. I feel a little panic. I take a deep breath, and slowly let it out while thinking, 'I'll do one item at a time, and skip those I don't know and return to them later. I know the material as well as I can.' "

3. *Involvement and possible setback.* You are now in the midst of the challenge. You proceed as realistically as possible. You handle po~sible setbacks calmly and maturely. Example: "I am in the middle of the exam. One question at a time. I start getting a little anxious. There are a lot of questions I don't know. Maybe I won't do as well as I had hoped. I think, 'Let's take this maturely. I studied as hard as I could. I'm doing a lot better than if I hadn't studied well, or if I had panicked. There will be other exams, and I can learn from my mistakes.' "

4. *Completion, relief, and reward.* The challenge is over. Imagine the good feelings of relief. Identify in what ways you displayed mastery. Reward yourself. Example: "Ah, the exam is over. That feels good. I feel so free. Sure, the exam wasn't perfect. But I did a good job of remaining calm. I studied better. I'm sure I got questions right I would have ordinarily missed. Yes, I'm improving. I deserve a pat on the back for this.' "

A somewhat different form of mastery theme involves imagining a desired end state, for example, physical fitness and health. The following illustrates such a health-directed theme:

> I am resting peacefully on an ocean beach. I do not have a care in the world, no obligations for the day, no pressing problems, nothing at all. My mind is free and unencumbered. My breathing is calm and relaxed, bringing energy and health to all parts of my body. I can feel the blood rushing through my veins, bringing strength and vitality. With every breath I let go of restraining tensions and let my body and mind move closer to the highest level of health and fitness that can be achieved at this moment.

Whatever images and phrases you pick, first take care to let them be realistic. Try not to think things such as "I can have anything I want," "I am all-powerful," "I am perfectly healthy in every way," or "I will find a girlfriend this week." If you think about it, these phrases reflect hopes that may be exaggerated or unfounded. Who says you can have absolutely everything you want? No mortal is all-powerful. Although most people can live healthier lives, few can achieve perfect health. And how can you guarantee that you will find a girlfriend *this* week? Select images that are realistic, unexaggerated, and yet relaxing.

Second, your imagery should have a positive direction and should be noncompetitive. Focus on what you want to achieve, not on what you are avoiding; and focus on yourself, not on how you compare with others. Avoid phrases like "I am not going to be so afraid" or "I am going to do better than so-and-so." Better ones would be "I feel secure" or "I simply do the best I can, nothing more."

Expression (RD 50)

Pleasure and meaning can be found in drawing, writing, singing, dancing, and a host of other self-expressive activities. In expressive imagery you entertain thoughts and descriptions of such activities. You imagine drawing a picture, writing a poem, singing a song, dancing, and so on. You can let yourself be as creative as you want. Remember: all imagery is in your mind. You can create anything you want without constraints. With expressive imagery there are no limits to what you can do.

Intuition (RD 51)

For themes of mastery and expression you are usually the creator and director of your imagery. When the theme is intuition, you assume a bit more passive role. As in mastery imagery, you begin with a problem, challenge, or question. However, at some point you sit back and take on the role of an observer and note how your mind, without your direct intervention, responds. For example, a student is trying to think of a topic for a term paper. In her mind's eye she lists all the topics she has already thought of. Then she imagines a blank screen and pictures herself asking the screen to list as many topics as possible. She simply observes the process.

Another student was curious about his future. As a way of stirring up ideas about how he might lead his life, he engaged in a bit of imagery. He pictured himself walking down a deep cave into a chamber with many doors. All the senses were involved—he could feel the cold air of uncertainty, see the shadows, and smell the musty odors. Suddenly he realized each door represented a different future. So, one by one he opened the doors and simply observed what his mind presented to him.

Intuitive exercises can mean as little or as much as you like. For some, they can be escapist fun and excitement, like an adventure movie. They can be aesthetically meaningful, like a touching novel. Some use such exercises to interact with and learn from a hidden "inner advisor." They even can verge on inner communion and prayer. However, it is not the goal of Relaxation Dynamics to tell you what should or should not be meaningful. This is your adventure.

All of the themes we have discussed involve in part imagining what you would see, hear, and feel in certain circumstances. The world of sensation can itself be the primary focus of imagery. It can be a source of deep relaxation. We conclude with the theme of sensation. The ideas presented for this theme can be tried alone or incorporated into all of the themes just described.

Sensation (RD 52)

Imagine being on a quiet beach. Can you see the clouds gently floating by? Hear the gentle splashing of the waves? Can you smell the ocean? How does the breeze feel? These are the sensations of relaxation. In sensation exercises you select a relaxing theme—resting on a beach, floating on a raft, sitting on a quiet hill, and so on. You try to experience the scene as a participant. Try thinking of a scene now. What do you see? What do you hear? Are there any fragrances, tastes, or feelings associated with the scene? Imagine you are watching a movie in your mind, and actually taking part. Notice the changes that take place. How does the scene evolve? Without trying to force yourself to experience anything, simply passively let the scene come to your mind. When your mind wanders or is distracted, quietly and gently return to the scene. Imagine the scene with all your senses.

Here are some examples of sensation themes:

Tropical island. You are on a quiet tropical island. A cool breeze is blowing. The sun is warm and comfortable. You can hear the grass and trees rustling and the birds singing.

Sunny beach. You are on a quiet, sunny beach. The ocean waves softly splash against the shore. You can smell the breeze. The sand feels warm and good.

Vacation room. You are away from home in a pleasant room. You are resting on a soft, comfortable sofa looking out of the huge window. In the room is everything you need for pleasurable relaxation.

When thinking of a scene, there are a number of guidelines you should follow. First, try to pick a scene that is familiar to you. Most people find it easier to picture something they know. Second, take care not to select a scene that might evoke distracting or disturbing thoughts. For example, if you are away from home, a scene of home might make you homesick. Finally, pick scenes in which you are passive, not trying to achieve some end or goal.

Enhancing Thematic Imagery

Thematic Deepening Suggestions (RD 53)

Here's a script of a brief thematic imagery exercise:

> Imagine you are resting on a large, soft cloud. The cloud is very comfortable, like a huge pillow. You can feel it pressing gently on your skin. You see the soft light filtering through. You can hear a gentle breeze flowing past. The air has a fresh fragrance to it. You become more and more relaxed. You are sinking deeper and deeper into the cloud . . . and the cloud is gently floating farther and farther away . . . carrying you away from all the cares and concerns of the world. You float into a deeper and more satisfying state of relaxation.

If you examine this script carefully, you should note two types of images. Some refer to simple sensations such as feeling the pillow, seeing soft light, or hearing a breeze. However, phrases like "sinking deeper and deeper" or "floating farther away" do not refer to sensations of external stimuli. Instead, they are suggestive of the increasing depth of relaxation experience. Such deepening suggestions can play an important part in thematic imagery. They can enhance the degree of focus, passivity, and receptivity experienced, increasing the quality of relaxation.

Deepening suggestions work by directly introducing pictures and phrases suggestive of focus, passivity, and receptivity. You could simply repeat the phrase "I am becoming more focused, passive, and receptive." However, as with all aspects of relaxation practice, different deepening thoughts seem to work better for different people. Here are some examples of deepening suggestions:

I sink into a deeper state of relaxation.

I become more and more still.

I become more centered.

I am letting go more and more.

I open up more and more to relaxing thoughts and images.

I become more aware and sensitive.

I put aside all my wishes and concerns.

There is nothing for me to do but attend to the exercise.

I become more and more transparent.

I become lighter and lighter.

I let thoughts and images come to me.

I become like a vessel and let relaxing thoughts fill me.

My mind becomes more focused.

My perception becomes increasingly clear.

I become absorbed with the object of my attention.

I understand more and more completely.

My mind becomes more lucid.

I merge more and more completely into relaxation.

This feels good and right.

After you have selected your deepening suggestions, select other images that are especially suggestive of these thoughts. For instance, if the phrase "I sink deeper and deeper into relaxation" works for you, you might want to think of riding an escalator down. If the phrase "I merge more and more completely into relaxation" feels right, you might want to imagine merging into a cool pond.

Some find it helpful to count backwards while repeating deepening suggestions. The next example illustrates how easily this can be done.

Ten. I am sinking deeper and deeper into a pleasant state of relaxation. Nine. With every count I gently float into a more profound state of relaxation. Eight. As I let go of my tensions I feel more and more relaxed. Seven. I become more completely immersed in relaxation as I sink farther and farther. Six. I let pleasant feelings of relaxation fill my entire being as I sink farther with every count. Five. I am becoming more and more relaxed. Four. I sink deeper within, farther and farther away from the cares of the world. Three. I am in my own deep inner world, outside cares and concerns seem distant and far away. Two. As I sink deeper and deeper I come close to a quiet inner place deep in the center of my being. One. I gently settle into the calm, still place of peace and relaxation, deep within.

One way of enhancing the effects of such a deepening countdown is to suggest a specific base level of relaxation for "Ten." Each count down becomes deeper than the suggested initial level. This is illustrated here:

Ten. I recall how relaxed I was last summer, especially when I was resting quietly on the lawn by the pond. I didn't have a care in the world. I felt completely at peace with myself. I let myself become, at this very moment, relaxed in a way that approaches my peaceful summer relaxation experience. I can feel the cool grass. I smell the fresh air. I hear the wind blowing past. Nine. I sink into a state of relaxation that is even deeper than this relaxing moment. Eight. With each count I become more and more relaxed.

Notice how the count "Ten" is anchored with a specific relaxation experience and how each subsequent count refers back to it.

Whatever deepening suggestions you think of, let yourself repeat them passively about once or twice a minute while doing thematic imagery. For still other ideas on enhancing imagery, see Samuels and Samuels (1975).

Generalized Thoughts About Yourself and the World: The "Three Rs" of Relaxation (RD 54)

We have seen that relaxing thought can touch upon a variety of specific themes—enjoying the world of the senses, mastering a challenge, enjoying one of life's pleasures, achieving self-expression through a creative activity, and experiencing the process of intuition. In many of the thematic exercises we have considered, we focused on specific events. It is from specific events that we develop overall understandings of what we and our world are like. These understandings can take a variety of forms. They can be as simple as a self-image or as pervasive as a philosophy of life. This process can be illustrated by a number of vignettes:

> John has spent some time appreciating the quiet beauty of a grassy field. He notices how peaceful everything seems. Eventually he finds himself thinking, "A calm serenity seems to underlie everything in the world."

This thought is a generalized understanding, a personal insight into the nature of things. And it is a thought that is especially calming in its own right. Let's take another example:

> Sue is entertaining in her mind a variety of mastery fantasies. In each one, she recalls an instance in which she met a challenge, small or large, and coped effectively. She thinks of the time she was overcharged in the store and assertively asked for her money back. She thinks of the time she called her boyfriend up for a date, rather than the other way around. She even recalls her last job interview which, although she didn't

get the job, did give her a good chance to practice interviewing. Eventually an image comes to her mind: "Sue—a competent woman. I may not always succeed, but I always give it a good try."

This is a generalized understanding Sue has acquired. It is realistic. It is not overstated. And it is a source of reassurance, of rest, to Sue.

We frequently have such general thoughts or understandings that represent overall views of ourselves and our world. Often these understandings take the form of internal self-talk or personal dialogues:

"It's important to put things in perspective."

"Deep inside, I'm a good person."

"Things might seem hard, but I can only do my best."

"I like the way I approach others."

"My friends still love me."

"God's will be done."

For some, such understandings can take the form of mental images or pictures. They can be embodied in images from art or passages from great literature. They can be of considerable eloquence, or utterly simple, like the phrase "I am calm" or "I can do it."

What are your implicit understandings of yourself and the world? What phrases or images do you find yourself repeating? Some of your understandings may actually be self-defeating or negative, but some are surely positive and affirming. Of these, the most important are those that are *relaxing,* yet in tune with *reason* and *reality*—the "Three Rs" of relaxation. Simply thinking such phrases and images is a very simple yet very important part of relaxation. When you practice the thematic exercises described in this lesson, or when you do any relaxation exercise, note the generalized thoughts about yourself and your world that fit the "Three Rs"— rest, reason, reality. These are thoughts worth repeating.

Focus, Passivity, and Receptivity in Unrestrictive Exercises

The unrestrictive exercises of somatic focusing and thematic imagery require a greater degree of attentional focus than do physical exercises. First, the object of our attention is more internal, our thoughts rather than overt action. In a sense the object of our attention, images and phrases, is more subtle. It is relatively easy to identify the sensations from actively squeezing or stretching, and even from breathing. It is a bit more difficult to sustain attention on a train of relaxing thought.

The mental exercises we have encountered involve a greater degree of passivity. Unlike isometric squeezing, stretching, or even breathing, absolutely no physical activity is involved; our bodies remain completely passive. When entertaining a relaxing scene or set of phrases, it is not important that we actively and deliberately attempt to achieve or "will" a desired end. It is often enough to passively dwell on certain selected relaxing thoughts.

Finally, mental exercises require a degree of receptivity, or tolerance of unfamiliar experiences. Of all thematic imagery exercises, those involving sensation, mastery, pleasure, and expression require the least amount of receptivity. Most of us already have some capacity for fantasy, or some ability to talk silently to ourselves. However, most people find the intuitive task of exploring questions passively and inwardly somewhat different from the usual mode of everyday problem solving. It's a way of thinking that can take some getting used to. Somatic focusing also can require a similar level of patient and trusting receptivity. As we have seen, passive thinking is not something we do every day. And relaxation may be taking place even when we do not feel the somatic changes that have been suggested.

Start Off Checklist

(Do before starting this week's exercises)

___ Have you selected practice times during which you are relatively unlikely to be distracted? Remember: it is often not a good idea to practice when you have some other duty that has to be performed.

___ Do you have a comfortable relaxation chair?

___ Do you have a quiet place in which to practice? If you are going to practice in a place where there are other people, try to make sure you won't be interrupted. Close the door to your room. Ask friends or family members not to interrupt while you are "resting." And it's OK to take the phone off the hook.

___ You should not take a nonprescription drug (marijuana, amphetamines, barbituates, psychedelic drugs) or alcohol for at least a day before practicing. Such drugs can make it more difficult to relax or focus attention on what you are doing. At the very least, they can limit the extent to which the effects of relaxation will generalize outside the session.

___ You should not have a drink containing caffeine (coffee, tea, cola) for at least 2 hours before practicing. Caffeine can make it more difficult to relax and focus attention on what you are doing.

___ You should not smoke tobacco for at least an hour before practicing.

___ You should not eat any food for at least an hour before practicing. If you are absolutely starving, eat a carrot.

___ Be sure to precede your practice with a physical quieting sequence.

___ When you are finished, come out of relaxation very slowly and gently. Arising too abruptly can be jarring and even make you feel dizzy. Take about 60 seconds to easily open your eyes all the way. Then stretch your arms to your sides and take a deep breath.

Thematic Imagery

Sensation Exercise (RD 52)

In this exercise we are going to relax by letting our minds dwell on a relaxing scene or setting.

PAUSE

Make sure you are seated upright in a comfortable position.

PAUSE

Are your feet flat on the floor?

PAUSE

Are your hands resting comfortably in your lap?

PAUSE

Now gently close your eyes and let yourself settle into a position that is comfortable.

PAUSE

For the next minute or so let your body become more and more quiet.

PAUSE 1 MINUTE

Let yourself begin to settle down and relax as you remain still.

PAUSE

And now attend to your body.

PAUSE

Let your breathing be calm and even.

PAUSE

Let every outgoing breath carry away any tension you might feel.

PAUSE

Let yourself feel more and more comfortably relaxed.

PAUSE

And now quietly ask yourself "What scene or setting is most relaxing to me at the moment?"

PAUSE 10 SECONDS

You might want to picture a quiet beach, or a grassy plain, or a cool mountain top, or a peaceful pond.

PAUSE 10 SECONDS

Whatever scene or setting is most relaxing to you, let it come to you in whatever way it wishes.

PAUSE 10 SECONDS

And now, quietly let your mind dwell on this scene for the next few seconds.

PAUSE 15 SECONDS

Let the scene become as vivid and real as possible.

PAUSE 10 SECONDS

How does it look?

PAUSE 10 SECONDS

Can you see the sky?

PAUSE

Can you feel the wind brushing against your skin?

PAUSE

Can you smell the gentle, cool air?

PAUSE

Can you feel the warm sunlight or perhaps the cool night air?

PAUSE

Involve all of your senses.

PAUSE

What do you see?

PAUSE

What do you hear?

PAUSE

What is touching your skin?

PAUSE

Can you taste or smell anything?

PAUSE

And let the scene grow in whatever way is most relaxing to you.

PAUSE 10 SECONDS

Perhaps words come to your mind that describe the scene.

PAUSE

If words or phrases come, simply let them repeat over and over like echoes.

PAUSE

Try not to force these words to change or make sense. Simply let them repeat over and over, very peacefully and quietly.

PAUSE

There is nothing for you to do except to quietly attend to your relaxing scene.

PAUSE

Let it change and evolve on its own.

PAUSE 15 SECONDS

If your mind wanders or is distracted, that's OK.

PAUSE

Quietly and gently return to your relaxing scene.

PAUSE 10 SECONDS

If you find yourself engaged in thinking about something or trying to figure something out, that's OK.

PAUSE

Quietly and gently return to your relaxing scene.

PAUSE 15 SECONDS

Let yourself sink deeper and deeper into a pleasant state of relaxation.

PAUSE

From time to time let yourself quietly repeat whatever words or pictures suggest deeper, more complete, and more satisfying relaxation.

PAUSE

You might think the words "I am sinking deeper and deeper," or "I am letting go more and more," or "There is nothing for me to do but let go," or "I am more fully aware."

PAUSE

Let the deepening suggestions come to you in whatever way feels most satisfying and relaxing.

PAUSE 10 SECONDS

Again and again, every time your mind wanders or is distracted, gently return to your pleasant, relaxing scene.

PAUSE

And now, continue attending to your scene for about 10 minutes. See where it leads you. See how it deepens. See how it grows and becomes more relaxing for the next 10 minutes.

PAUSE 10 MINUTES

And now, very gently let go of what you are attending to.

PAUSE 5 SECONDS

When you are ready, gently open your eyes.

PAUSE 5 SECONDS

Take a deep breath.

PAUSE 5 SECONDS

And stretch.

PAUSE 5 SECONDS

This completes the thematic imagery exercise.

Part V

Restrictive Mental Exercises

Lesson 12

Contemplation

In the preceding lessons we considered forms of imagery that are active and passive. With active imagery you are the director, choosing and guiding the course of your imagery. With passive imagery your role switches to that of observer. You do not decide upon the content of your experience. What you experience is determined by processes outside of your awareness and direct control. Contemplation is much like passive imagery; however, the focus of attention is more restricted and the goal more extensive.

In contemplation you select a relatively simple stimulus or topic and attend to it passively. Your intent is to acquire a deeper and richer appreciation of the stimulus, to get to know it better. You watch the object of your contemplation change and unfold on its own. Let's try a very simple exercise adapted from several suggested by Samuels and Samuels (1975):

> First, select a simple and interesting object nearby. It might be a plant, piece of fruit, jewelry, sculpture, or simply your hand. Now, quietly look at it. There is much more to this object than you can notice at any one time. More than you could analyze or figure out. Passively gaze at this object and note all the characteristics you see. How does the light strike the object? Notice the highlights, shadows, reflections, and range of colors and tones. Let your eyes wander over the outline of the object. Notice the sharp lines, soft lines, the total shape of the object, and the smaller shapes that comprise it. How is the object textured? Is it rough, smooth, dull, or shiny? Look at the color of the object. Is the color bright or

dull, faint or dark, uniform or varying? Be aware of the qualities of depth and perspective.

Now, look at the same object while slowly taking a number of different positions. Get behind it. Move up very close, so you almost touch it with your nose. Notice every little detail that is revealed as you examine it from a microscopic perspective. While still gazing at your object, slowly move away, as if you were in a plane or space ship. How does the object change when you change position? What new qualities do you notice?

Finally, look at the object from different mental points of view. What would you notice about the object if you were a small child? If you were the opposite sex? If you were an artist? An inventor? (Adapted from p. 115)

Contemplation is a way of understanding something more deeply and fully without using active and analytic thought. It's a type of experiencing you may already use while listening to music or appreciating art. Most people have a favorite piece of music, one they enjoy returning to again and again. Imagine you are quietly listening to this piece. There are many ways of appreciating it. You could analyze it and perhaps attempt to figure out for whom it was written or if the composer was trying to make a political point. Or you could simply put aside your analytic mind and let the music stir you as it will. The feelings you experience, whether they be love, reverence, or sadness, reflect a deeper, nonanalytic understanding of the music. It is an understanding that goes beyond the mere words of the piece (or the notes on the page). This is contemplation.

As another example, imagine your favorite work of art. A great artist puts far more into a painting than can be grasped at once, or than can be discovered through logical analysis. In fact, analytic thought can distract us from discovering, appreciating, and enjoying what is being communicated. When we contemplate on a piece of art, we put aside our thinking, analytical minds in order to understand more fully. We quietly attend and note what feelings and insights the painting reveals.

The idea underlying contemplation can be extended to all aspects of life. Anything we encounter—a person or a scene—has more qualities than we can ever list at once. Think, for example, of your best friend. What are all of his or her characteristics? You could probably spend hours analyzing and listing what you know, like, and dislike about this person. However, imagine you haven't seen this person for a while. He or she has been on a long vacation. Unexpectedly you see this person in the distance walking toward you. Suddenly you are filled with warmth, happiness, and excitement—feelings that summarize your experience of this person. These are feelings that go beyond words and logic. These are the kinds of felt meanings that can arise in the act of contemplation (Gendlin, 1981).

Whether the object of our contemplation is as simple as a painting or as complex as a friend, the act of contemplation is essentially the same. Instead of actively and purposefully analyzing and listing all you see and know, you sit back, attend, and quietly acknowledge the small portion of reality that unfolds before you this very moment. You continue attending and patiently wait for other aspects of this reality to emerge. A good work of art communicates far more than you could ever discover at any single moment. And there is more to the world of the senses than can be determined through thought alone.

Contemplation on Personal Strengths (RD 55)

In Lesson 2 we introduced the idea of contemplation with a relatively simple exercise, the contemplation on personal strengths. Here are the instructions again:

> Quietly and easily direct your attention to the question "What are my good points?" and without trying to deliberately figure out an answer, simply and quietly wait. See what comes to mind, what ideas this question stirs. However, whenever a thought does come to mind, do not pursue it. Simply note it (without evaluating or rejecting it) and return to quietly and easily attending to the question "What are my good points?" Your role is that of a passive observer, quietly noting thoughts and ideas that come to mind. Do not dwell upon or stay with any particular thoughts or ideas. Note them and let them float away, like clouds in the sky or echoes. Try this for 5 minutes.

What was this like? How did you feel at the end of the exercise? Did any new thoughts or feelings arise? Did you notice how this exercise differed from active imagery? Remember, the goal of all contemplation is to observe and note change. You permit images, words, thoughts, and feelings to arise on their own, stimulated and guided by what you are attending to. All you do is note each and return to the object of your attention.

Contemplation on Relaxation (RD 56)

A special form of contemplation involves attending to and exploring the experience of relaxation itself. This contemplation on relaxation is one of the most challenging forms of contemplation. However, it can be particularly rewarding.

In imagery you attended to specific thoughts and let relaxing feelings arise on their own. While deliberately focusing on a quiet meadow, feelings of peacefulness and serenity might have arisen. In the contemplation on relaxation you reverse the process. Instead of focusing on mental pictures and words that can suggest certain relaxed feelings, you will focus directly on feelings associated with relaxation, and let pictures and words come and go on their own.

We begin the exercise by asking "What feeling is restful to me at the moment?" (You might want to attend to how you felt right after doing the contemplation on personal strengths.) Without trying to analyze or hold on to the feeling, quietly and restfully attend and let words and images arise on their own. However, instead of dwelling on these words and images and holding them in your mind (as in imagery), acknowledge them when they arise, and then let them come and go, change, and evolve. Return to attending to what you feel. From time to time you may quietly ask, "What is most restful to me at this moment; what is the crux, the main thing about what feels most restful?" And then, without trying to figure out this question or construct an answer, quietly wait for your body or mind to respond. Gently acknowledge any pictures or words that arise, note how well they fit, and return again to attending to your feeling of relaxation. If you could see inside the mind of someone doing this form of contemplation, here is what you might notice:

What's Being Experienced	Interpretation
"What is relaxing to me at the moment?"	
"Hmmm . . . I feel kind of good . . . warm and mellow."	I now quietly attend to the "warm and mellow" feeling, without trying to figure it out, keep it, or push it away. I wait for pictures or words to come up that feel right in conveying the most important thing about this feeling.

"Warm and mellow . . ."

". . . Powerful?"

The word *powerful* just came to mind. I ask myself, "Does it fit how I feel?" It doesn't, so I return to attending to the warm and mellow feeling deep inside.

"Warm and mellow . . . warm and mellow . . ."

"Secure . . . does this word fit? Yes, that's it, that's just how I feel . . . nice and secure."

Now I attend to this somewhat new good feeling inside, the feeling "nice and secure," without trying to figure the feeling out, or keep it, or push it away. I continue to wait for pictures or words to come up that feel right and get at what is most important about the feeling.

"Nice and secure . . . nice and secure . . . feels good . . . nice and secure . . ."

Note several things about this exercise. First, words and pictures can come from feelings. Some words and pictures perfectly capture the gist or sense of feelings. They feel "just right" in saying what the feeling is. These are the words of poems and songs. When truly in love, the phrase "I love you" contains such words. Other words and pictures less clearly convey what is most important about the feeling. They feel less "right." In the scripted exercise, we quietly attend to how relaxation feels, and wait for words and pictures that feel "just right" in conveying the gist of what we experience.

The objective of this exercise is quite different from that of any previous exercise. You do not determine what you experience; you are the observer. You attend to a feeling of relaxation, and observe how the feeling changes and evolves without your intervention. You wait for words and pictures to emerge from the feeling, but you do not dwell upon them. Instead, you note if they fit with what you experience.

By doing this, you are observing a very important process. You are uncovering the many meanings of a feeling of relaxation, letting something deep within you uncover or reveal all the many facets of a state of relaxation. You are quietly watching a flower unfold, revealing its many colors. Any state of relaxation, whether it be a feeling of "calm," "warmth," or "peacefulness," is just the surface. In the contemplation on relaxation we begin to discover the hidden meanings of relaxation.

Choosing the Object of Your Contemplation

Clearly, the object of contemplation can be just about anything—art, music, literature, a photograph of a loved one, the quiet sky at night. The act of contemplation can be as simple as a brief moment of appreciation ("This sunset is beautiful; I think I'll just look at it a while"). Or it can be a regular and planned activity. For example, you might want to set time aside every day to contemplate passages from a book you find spiritually meaningful. Each day you might select a different passage and quietly let your mind dwell upon it. See what new meanings arise. What does the passage say to you? Similarly, you might direct your contemplation toward the "Three Rs thoughts" discussed in Lesson 11, quietly letting your mind dwell upon a phrase or image that summarizes how you see yourself and your world. See what associations arise. But do not dwell upon any particular association. Let them come and go.

Start Off Checklist

(Do before starting this week's exercises)

___ Have you selected practice times during which you are relatively unlikely to be distracted? Remember: it is often not a good idea to practice when you have some other duty that has to be performed.

___ Do you have a comfortable relaxation chair?

___ Do you have a quiet place in which to practice? If you are going to practice in a place where there are other people, try to make sure you won't be interrupted. Close the door to your room. Ask friends or family members not to interrupt while you are "resting." And it's OK to take the phone off the hook.

___ You should not take a nonprescription drug (marijuana, amphetamines, barbituates, psychedelic drugs) or alcohol for at least a day before practicing. Such drugs can make it more difficult to relax or focus attention on what you are doing. At the very least, they can limit the extent to which the effects of relaxation will generalize outside the session.

___ You should not have a drink containing caffeine (coffee, tea, cola) for at least 2 hours before practicing. Caffeine can make it more difficult to relax and focus attention on what you are doing.

___ You should not smoke tobacco for at least an hour before practicing.

___ You should not eat any food for at least an hour before practicing. If you are absolutely starving, eat a carrot.

___ Be sure to precede your practice with a physical quieting sequence.

___ When you are finished, come out of relaxation very slowly and gently. Arising too abruptly can be jarring and even make you feel dizzy. Take about 60 seconds to easily open your eyes all the way. Then stretch your arms to your sides and take a deep breath.

Contemplation

Contemplation on Relaxation (RD 56)

In this exercise we are going to quietly attend to the experience of relaxation itself.

PAUSE 5 SECONDS

Make sure you are seated upright in a comfortable position.

PAUSE 5 SECONDS

Gently close your eyes.

PAUSE 5 SECONDS

Are your feet flat on the floor?

PAUSE

Place your hands in your lap.

PAUSE 5 SECONDS

Now attend to your body.

PAUSE 5 SECONDS

Let your breathing be calm and even.

PAUSE 5 SECONDS

Let every outgoing breath carry away any tension you might feel.

PAUSE 5 SECONDS

Let yourself feel more and more comfortably relaxed.

PAUSE 5 SECONDS

Now let your attention turn inward. See how you feel now. See how you are at this moment.

PAUSE 10 SECONDS

You may feel a number of concerns or problems. They may seem important, as if they need immediate attention. However, for the next few minutes put these problems aside. You will have plenty of time to work on them later.

PAUSE

Now ask yourself "What good thoughts and feelings are inside? What is the most relaxing feeling that comes to me right now?" Is it a body sensation? A state of mind? The feeling doesn't have to be anything big. It might be nothing more than a little feeling of calm or relief or a pleasant feeling in the body. There is nothing for you to figure out. Simply stay quiet and listen. Try not to hold on to any feeling or put it into words. Simply attend to any relaxing feeling that comes to you right now.

PAUSE 5 SECONDS

If no good or relaxing feeling comes to mind, you might want to think of a recent experience in which you felt good and were relaxed. Pick an experience that is fairly fresh to you, one you can imagine clearly.

PAUSE 10 SECONDS

Imagine you are reexperiencing this pleasant and relaxing time.

PAUSE

What relaxing feeling comes to mind?

PAUSE 20 SECONDS

Now ask yourself "What is the crux, the main thing about this good feeling?" And without trying to deliberately come up with an answer, simply relax and wait. See what words or pictures come from the good feeling.

PAUSE 30 SECONDS

Gently and easily direct your attention to the good, relaxing feeling. If it changes or moves, let it do that. Whatever the feeling does, follow and pay attention to it.

PAUSE 10 SECONDS

Note any words or pictures that might arise, and again and again gently return to attending to the good feeling.

PAUSE 15 SECONDS

Now what is fresh or new in what you feel? What is the crux, the main thing about your relaxed feeling?

PAUSE 15 SECONDS

How are the words or pictures changing? Let them change whatever way they want. There is nothing for you to do but attend to what is restful to you, and note the movement and evolution of your words or pictures—and return to the feeling.

PAUSE 30 SECONDS

From time to time quietly check your words or pictures.

PAUSE 5 SECONDS

Ask inside "Is that right? Do the words or pictures fit?" And without trying to figure anything out, simply and restfully wait and attend.

PAUSE 15 SECONDS

There is nothing for you to do except let the words or pictures change until they feel just right in capturing the gist of what is restful to you.

PAUSE 1 MINUTE

Let the words and pictures move and evolve as you quietly attend to what feels restful to you.

PAUSE 5 MINUTES

And now, gently let go of what you are attending to. Slowly open your eyes.

PAUSE 5 SECONDS

Take a deep breath.

PAUSE 5 SECONDS

And stretch.

PAUSE 5 SECONDS

This completes our contemplation on relaxation.

Lesson 13

Centered and Open Focus Meditation

Meditative exercises have been around for thousands of years. They appear in just about every world culture. Some have deep ties with religion, while others are completely secular. All have one thing in common: the calm directing of attention toward a simple stimulus (Benson, 1975; Carrington, 1978; Kapleau, 1965; Naranjo & Ornstein, 1971; Shapiro, 1980).

In the previous lesson we learned that contemplation also involves attending to a simple stimulus. However, meditation goes one step beyond contemplation. The goal or "ulterior motive" of contemplation is to acquire a deeper or more comprehensive understanding of something. A work of art is contemplated so it can be seen in a new way. A philosophical passage is contemplated to discover new meanings and applications. But meditation on a stimulus is done with complete indifference, expecting nothing, desiring nothing. You simply attend and nothing else.

Often the first question people have when hearing this is "Why do it if you have no goal or intent?" It is perhaps best not to struggle with this question other than to acknowledge the large numbers of people who describe meditation as among the most profound of all approaches to relaxation (see Section II, Chapter 2). It might be useful to recall the notion of passive thinking introduced in our lesson on somatic focusing. Remember that when we tried to actively and deliberately *will* a somatic change, warm hands for example, little happened. However, when we simply let the phrase "hands are warm and heavy" repeat like an echo in the mind, our hands began to feel warm and heavy. Meditation

183

is something like that. While there is no goal or intent to the practice, there is for many a *result* of relaxation that can be more deeply rewarding than a soothing sense of warmth or heaviness. The paradox of meditation is that it often works best when done with much sincerity and respect, but with little desire or expectation. The willingness to accept this paradox requires a degree of receptivity.

Although you may not have been aware of it, you have already been taught a rudimentary form of meditation. The final integrative breathing exercise was in fact a simple meditation. Let's try this exercise again and see what we can learn from it:

> First, sit up straight in a comfortable position. Make sure your feet are flat on the floor. Close your eyes if you wish. Give yourself a few seconds to settle down. Scan your body for any sources of tension. Now, with every outgoing breath quietly and effortlessly think the word *one* or a relaxing word of your choice. Let the word repeat in your mind like an echo. That's all you have to do. And every time your mind wanders or is distracted, that's OK. Simply return to quietly thinking the word. Do this exercise for about 2 minutes.

Notice how simple your task was? Unlike contemplation, there is no intent to understand the word *one* more deeply. There is no expectation that the word *one* will change and unfold. It may change, but that is not important. All you need to do is attend, and only attend.

If you are like most beginning meditators, one of the most noteworthy aspects of your first meditation was probably all the distracting thoughts that came to mind. You may have actually attended to your meditation word for only a few brief seconds. Indeed, most of the time your mind may have wandered. You may have found yourself thinking about other things, or getting caught up with distracting sounds, thoughts, memories, or feelings. However, no matter how often your mind wandered, as long as you calmly returned to repeating the meditative word—even once—you were meditating.

Thus, meditation is not so much a focusing exercise as a returning exercise, a way of coming home. In fact, all you need to know in the way of instruction for meditation is this:

CALMLY ATTEND TO A SIMPLE STIMULUS.
AFTER EVERY DISTRACTION
CALMLY RETURN YOUR ATTENTION.

By patiently doing this, again and again and again, the mind is very gradually conditioned to attend for longer and longer periods of time. It is important to emphasize that this return of attention should be patient, easy, and gentle—not forced or strained. The goal is not to keep your mind vigilantly glued on the focal task, as if you were playing baseball or a video game. Instead, as calmly and restfully as possible, ease your attention back to the task. Let your mind wander. Every time your mind drifts from the task, you have another opportunity to calmly return your attention. It is only through such opportunities to *return* that you gradually condition your mind to attend to the focus. It is through distraction and diversion that the experience of meditation deepens and embraces more and more of the world.

Meditation tradition abounds with metaphors that describe this returning action of meditation. For example, meditation instructor Lawrence LeShan (1974) says:

> Give yourself permission to make constant slips from the directions. You will make them anyway and will be much more comfortable—and get along better with this exercise— if you give yourself permission in advance. Treat yourself as if you were a much-loved child that an adult was trying to keep walking on a narrow sidewalk. The child is full of energy and keeps running off to the fields on each side to pick flowers, feel the grass, climb a tree. Each time you are aware of the child leaving the path, you say in effect, "Oh, that's how children are. Okay, honey, back to the sidewalk," and bring yourself gently but firmly and alertly back to just looking. Again and again you will suddenly notice that you are thinking about something else or translating your perception into words or something of the sort. Each time, you should say the equivalent of "oh, that's where I am now; back to the work." (p. 54)

Another prominent meditation instructor, Patricia Carrington (1978), says:

> When meditating never *force* thoughts out of your mind. All kinds of thoughts may drift through your mind while you are meditating. Treat these thoughts just as you would treat clouds drifting across the sky. You don't push the clouds away—but you don't hold onto them either. You just watch them come and go. It's the same with thoughts during meditation, you just watch them, and then when it feels comfortable to do so, go back. (p. 25)

Elsewhere, Carrington advises against struggling against intruding thoughts when meditating. Such distractions are a natural part of everyone's meditative experience. Indeed, they are an important part of the meditative process and can even be signs that meditation is working.

She suggests greeting distracting thoughts "as you would a friend whom you like but with whom you do not have time to talk right now. Imagine that you are letting this friend walk alongside you, but that you are not becoming involved in conversation with him/her. In other words, flow *with* the thoughts that turn up during meditation and allow them full play, yet do not cling to them" (p. 20). Continue with your meditation, and let distractions come and go, and even dwell with you in the background.

Centered Focus Meditation (RD 57)

The "one" meditation we just demonstrated is actually a form of centered focus meditation. Other forms include transcendental meditation, beginning Zen exercises, and clinically standardized meditation. All forms involve quietly attending to a simple stimulus, like the word *one*. Once again, the intent is not to try to discover how the stimulus changes or unfolds; in fact, it is preferable that the object of centered focus meditation be simple and with little potential for change or deeper meaning. In the meditation to be taught here, the stimulus is a word or syllable to be repeated in the mind. This type of focus is called a *mantra*. (Actually, you could meditate on any relatively simple stimulus—a simple picture, the sound of your heartbeat, a candle flame, the sound of waves.) Your instructions are not to effortfully and deliberately think the mantra, but let it repeat on its own in your mind. There is nothing for you to do but quietly attend and, of course, return your attention every time your mind wanders. Put differently, you let the mantra go at its own pace and at its own volume. The mantra is like an echo in your mind. Dr. Carrington (1978) has a very nice description of mantra meditation.

> As you become a practiced meditator, the mantra will probably come to you automatically as you sit quietly in meditation, and it may well go away automatically. Simply let it come and go. Don't try to hold onto it. Don't try to repeat it consciously or force it to establish a rhythm. Don't try to stop it from doing these things. There is no need for any particular rhythm, or pronunciation, or inflection of the mantra. Let yourself find out what the mantra wants to do at any given moment when you allow it to have free rein. (p. 21)

What should you use as a mantra? You could use any smooth-sounding and relaxing word. However, a real word with some meaning might stir up distracting memories and associations. Thus, many meditation traditions suggest using a meaningless syllable or set of syllables. Here are some instructions for constructing your own mantra.

1. Make your mantra one or two syllables long.
2. For each syllable, select at least one vowel or vowel combination:

A E I O U AA OO OU etc.

3. If you wish, add any of the following smooth-sounding consonants to a mantra syllable:

H L M N R SH V W Y Z

4. You also may prefer to use one of the following ready-made mantras:

AUM
SHA-LOM
AAH-HAHM
A-RA-YEEM
SHOL
MOO-ROOM
A-ZEEN

5. Write your mantra on the following line:

_____

Open Focus Meditation (RD 58)

Open focus meditation (sometimes called *mindfulness* or *openness meditation*) does not make use of a mantra. Instead, you quietly and calmly attend to, note, and let go of every stimulus that impinges upon your awareness. You experience every thought, feeling, or sensation without trying to figure it out, think about it, push it away, or do anything. Simply let the stimulus come and go, then wait for the next one to appear.

You might picture yourself sitting in a quiet (and perfectly safe) glass dome at the bottom of a clear lake. You can see bubbles, seaweed, fish, and any of a number of unexpected inhabitants of the lake slowly and continuously rising, one by one. Each gently comes into sight, and then leaves. In open focus meditation you treat each thought, feeling, or sensation that comes to mind as a bubble that, on its own, drifts into view. All you have to do is acknowledge that it is there ("Yes, what an interesting thought, or feeling, or sensation"), and then let it drift away after a few seconds. You calmly wait for the next bubble.

Or you might want to imagine calmly resting in a tent in the woods at night. You feel peaceful and secure. There is nothing for you to do or figure out. You quietly listen to the sounds of the night, and hear the wind blowing through the trees. You acknowledge the sound of the wind, and without thinking about it or trying to figure it out, return to quietly listening once again. Silence. You notice the refreshing fragrance of the trees. You take note of it and return to a peacefully quiet and attentive stance. You hear a bird in the distance. You acknowledge the sound—"Oh, the sound of a bird"—and return to calmly listening again. You now feel the light, gentle wind. You take note, let go of what you are sensing, and return to a position of quiet inner acceptance.

It is tempting to do too much in this exercise. You don't have to figure out the connections between each stimulus. Often there will be none. There is no need for you to look for deeper understandings; that's not your job in this exercise. You don't have to attend to any thought, feeling, or sensation for any length of time. Indeed, you should dwell on any particular "bubble" or "sound of the night" for only several seconds—about the time it takes a real-life bubble to float in and out of sight, or the time it takes a gentle gust of wind to blow and settle into silence.

The object of your attention is indeed simple, every bit as simple as the object of centered focus meditation. However, instead of attending to one word or sound or sensation, you attend to the moment-to-moment flow of all stimuli. Instead of listening to the wind and only the wind, you take note of the wind, and then the fragrance of the trees, and then the unexpected song of a bird. Each moment offers its own simple stimulus. Each moment offers its own mantra. All you do is attend fully, let go, and attend again. You are like a mirror, or a clear pond, reflecting everything that comes and goes. You do nothing to interfere.

As in centered focus meditation, your mind will wander from its simple task. You will probably find yourself getting caught up with certain thoughts or distractions. You might pursue them, analyze them, try to push them away, worry about them, or become sidetracked by them. Here the instructions are exactly the same as for centered focus meditation: each time your attention is distracted, gently and easily return to your meditative task. Note the distraction ("Ah, a distraction—that's interesting") and gently and easily return to attending to whatever stimuli may drift past your awareness. Once again, remember: the key to meditation is the returning movement.

Distraction and Growth in Meditation

Masters of both centered and open focus meditation describe very poetically the growth that can come from meditative distraction. Some meditators liken distraction to silt at the bottom of a cool and quiet pond. This silt, when stirred, can cloud the waters. The return action of meditation is a way of clearing the mind of potential future distraction. Each meditative return is like a cleaning sweep along the bottom of the pond. Somewhat less poetically, by permitting distractions to come and go we might be releasing or discharging subtle inner tensions that might be a source of distraction.

In a slightly different light, the coming and going of distraction in meditation can be seen as a way of extending meditation's calming influence to larger and larger domains of experience. As one student described it: "When I see each distraction in the calm light of meditation, I see it differently. Problems seem less urgent. Frustrations seem less painful. And above all, at least in meditation, I am saying to myself that each distraction isn't as urgent as I might have thought. My meditation is more important. Intruding cares and concerns are secondary, at least during meditation."

Some distractions in meditation represent spontaneous attempts to deepen relaxation through approaches you may have learned. For example, you might start a meditation in a fairly tense mood. As your meditation progresses you might get in touch with your tension and find yourself thinking the somatic images "warm and heavy, I feel warm and heavy" as a way of soothing your tension. Or you might discover yourself attending to various muscle groups and quietly letting go (mental isometric relaxation). You might focus on the easy flow of breath (integrative breathing). All such distractions are normal and represent the integration of earlier techniques with meditation. However, as with all distractions, when you note your mind has wandered from your task, relax and gently return. If your body or mind requires further relaxation, you'll probably find yourself restfully distracted again.

Finally, you may find yourself distracted by a particularly pleasurable sensation or image and be tempted to pursue it. However, at moments such as these you have a unique opportunity to affirm what is perhaps the most important factor in making meditation successful: the extent to which you respect and value the meditative task. Every time you put aside a pleasurable distraction and return to the singular task of meditation you are in effect saying "At this moment, my meditation is more important than my pleasurable distraction."

Refocusing Using Images and Phrases

Images and suggestive phrases play an important part in every form of relaxation. From the previous discussion of distraction it might seem that all thoughts and images are to be considered distractions in meditation, but this is not entirely the case. Some phrases and images can actually help deal with mental distractions and wanderings. These are called *refocusing thoughts*.

What do you think when you discover your mind has wandered and you want to return to a task? Do you put yourself down? Do you tell yourself you must pay attention? Do you smile at your own distractibility? These are refocusing thoughts. They are what we say or picture in our minds when we want to return from a distraction to a task. Some refocusing thoughts only serve to upset us: "I'll never do this right, I'm so stupid." Some are simple self-reminders of what has to be done: "Ah, my mind wandered. Now what was I doing?" Meditation can often be made easier if, before beginning, you decide what refocusing phrases and images to entertain. This can reduce the likelihood of thinking thoughts that simply create more distractions.

Before starting meditation, decide what you will tell yourself or picture in your mind when you notice your mind wandering. Your refocusing thoughts should incorporate these ideas:

1. Distractions are normal and OK.
2. For the duration of the meditation session, your main task is to meditate and all other concerns are secondary.
3. Returning from a distraction is what meditation is all about.

Here are some examples of refocusing thoughts:

"Whenever I notice I am thinking about something unrelated to meditation, I picture myself letting go of this thought as if it were a butterfly I was holding and releasing."

"I give each distracting thought to my meditation, as if I were giving it a gift."

"I imagine dropping each distraction into a deep space, like dropping pebbles into a pond."

"Each time I find myself preoccupied with a train of thought unrelated to meditation, I surrender my thoughts. It's like I'm making a little offering or prayer."

Restriction and Openness in Meditation

Somatic focusing and thematic imagery exercises permit considerable latitude in constructing "inner movies." Both contemplation and meditation ask you to limit your attention to one stimulus. In addition, the tasks of contemplation, centered focus meditation, and open focus meditation are in themselves increasingly more restrictive. With contemplation you select a stimulus and observe it with the intent of watching it change and unfold. With centered focus meditation you again select a stimulus, but observe it without intent. With open focus meditation efforts at both selection and intention are put aside. You simply experience the stimuli that come to you.

Let's end our discussion of meditation with a thought often offered by meditators. Open focus meditation is the most restrictive of approaches, yet, paradoxically, it is also claimed by meditators to be the most open. Although the object of attention is the singular stimulus of the moment, that stimulus includes all that is. Open focus meditation is not just a technique. It is a way of seeing yourself and seeing the world. It is a way of living.

Start Off Checklist

(Do before starting this week's exercises)

___ Have you selected practice times during which you are relatively unlikely to be distracted? Remember: it is often not a good idea to practice when you have some other duty that has to be performed.

___ Do you have a comfortable relaxation chair?

___ Do you have a quiet place in which to practice? If you are going to practice in a place where there are other people, try to make sure you won't be interrupted. Close the door to your room. Ask friends or family members not to interrupt while you are "resting." And it's OK to take the phone off the hook.

___ You should not take a nonprescription drug (marijuana, amphetamines, barbituates, psychedelic drugs) or alcohol for at least a day before practicing. Such drugs can make it more difficult to relax or focus attention on what you are doing. At the very least, they can limit the extent to which the effects of relaxation will generalize outside the session.

___ You should not have a drink containing caffeine (coffee, tea, cola) for at least 2 hours before practicing. Caffeine can make it more difficult to relax and focus attention on what you are doing.

___ You should not smoke tobacco for at least an hour before practicing.

___ You should not eat any food for at least an hour before practicing. If you are absolutely starving, eat a carrot.

___ Be sure to precede your practice with a physical quieting sequence.

___ When you are finished, come out of relaxation very slowly and gently. Arising too abruptly can be jarring and even make you feel dizzy. Take about 60 seconds to easily open your eyes all the way. Then stretch your arms to your sides and take a deep breath.

Centered Focus Meditation (RD 57)

In this exercise we are going to relax by meditating on a mantra.

PAUSE

First, make sure you are seated upright in a comfortable position.

PAUSE 5 SECONDS

Are your feet flat on the floor?

PAUSE 5 SECONDS

Are your hands resting comfortably in your lap?

PAUSE 5 SECONDS

Now gently close your eyes, completely or part way.

PAUSE 5 SECONDS

How are you breathing?

PAUSE 5 SECONDS

Let your breathing become more calm and even and full.

PAUSE 5 SECONDS

Let yourself breathe in a manner that feels unhurried and relaxed.

PAUSE 10 SECONDS

There is nothing for you to do but attend to the gentle flow of breath, in and out.

PAUSE 10 SECONDS

Let each outgoing breath carry out the tensions of the day.

PAUSE 10 SECONDS

Let each incoming breath bring feelings of refreshing energy.

PAUSE 10 SECONDS

Now slowly let your mantra come to mind.

PAUSE

Let it come to you in whatever way it wishes.

PAUSE

Let it repeat, easily and effortlessly, like an echo, or clouds floating across the sky.

PAUSE 5 SECONDS

There is nothing for you to do but quietly attend to your mantra.

PAUSE 15 SECONDS

Every time your mind wanders or is distracted, that's OK. Gently and easily return to the mantra, again and again.

PAUSE 10 SECONDS

Let your mantra repeat effortlessly on its own for the next few minutes.

PAUSE 15 MINUTES

Now... slowly and easily let go of the mantra.

PAUSE 5 SECONDS

Gently and easily open your eyes. Do this very slowly, you have plenty of time.

PAUSE 10 SECONDS

And take a deep breath and stretch. This completes centered focus meditation.

Open Focus Meditation (RD 58)

In this exercise we are going to relax by attending to and noting all stimuli that come to mind.

PAUSE

First, make sure you are seated upright in a comfortable position.

PAUSE 5 SECONDS

Are your feet flat on the floor?

PAUSE 5 SECONDS

Are your hands resting comfortably in your lap?

PAUSE 5 SECONDS

Now gently close your eyes, completely or part way.

PAUSE 5 SECONDS

How are you breathing?

PAUSE 5 SECONDS

Let your breathing become more calm and even and full.

PAUSE 5 SECONDS

Let yourself breathe in a manner that feels unhurried and relaxed.

PAUSE 10 SECONDS

There is nothing for you to do but attend to the gentle flow of breath, in and out.

PAUSE 10 SECONDS

Let each outgoing breath carry out the tensions of the day.

PAUSE 10 SECONDS

Let each incoming breath bring feelings of refreshing energy.

PAUSE 10 SECONDS

Now easily attend to every stimulus that comes to mind.

PAUSE 5 SECONDS

Every time you hear, think, or feel something, quietly acknowledge what you experience.

PAUSE 5 SECONDS

And let go of what you have noted, and return to attending to whatever stimulus drifts into consciousness.

PAUSE 10 SECONDS

There is nothing for you to do or figure out.

PAUSE 10 SECONDS

Quietly wait, like a still pond, for the next sound or thought. Note the ripple it makes in the stillness of your mind. Let the ripple settle. And quietly attend again.

PAUSE 20 SECONDS

There is nothing else for you to do but observe the flow of stimuli that, like clouds in the sky, or sounds in the night, come and go.

PAUSE

Continue meditating this way for the next few minutes.

PAUSE 15 MINUTES

Now. . . slowly and easily let go.

PAUSE 5 SECONDS

Gently and easily open your eyes. Do this very slowly, you have plenty of time.

PAUSE 10 SECONDS

And take a deep breath and stretch. This completes open focus meditation.

Part VI

Putting It All Together

Lesson 14

Last and First Words

It is now time to step back and review the path we have taken. First, we have moved progressively inward. The focus of our attention has evolved and changed throughout this journey—from the relatively external skeletal muscles, inside to the lungs, to the heart, and then to the mind itself. In our minds we moved from thoughts about the skeletal muscles to the silent internal organs and then to relaxing images. With contemplation and meditation our inward journey took on a new and more subtle meaning. With these approaches we got "inside" the objects of our attention by understanding and appreciating them more deeply, fully, and clearly. We contemplated an object to understand the hidden meanings and nuances. With centered focus meditation we had an opportunity to appreciate a chosen object itself, without the distracting and distorting influence of our wishes and expectations. With open focus meditation we put aside all wishes and expectations, even our preconceptions of *what* we should attend to. We became like mirrors, reflecting clearly the flow of being.

We have focused on tasks of increasing simplicity. Isometric relaxation and yogaform stretching involved attending to many things—11 different muscle groups. In integrative breathing the object of our attention became more simple—processes related to breathing. In mental relaxation we attended to thoughts alone, first to "external" body sensations, then to the subtle activity of the deeper organs, and then to relaxing imagery. In contemplation we attended to a singular stimulus to appreciate more fully its many nuances. Meditation represented the ultimate in simplicity—a single stimulus, a stream of singular stimuli. In terms of simplicity of focus, meditation became again the final point of our journey through worlds of rest.

We have learned to put aside unnecessary effortful striving; we have become more passive. At the beginning of this program we stopped our busy involvement with everyday activities in order to do relaxation. This was our first step toward becoming more passive. In isometric relaxation we learned to tense up and let go. In yogaform exercises we passively let gravity (or antagonistic minor muscles) do the stretching. In breathing, we simply observed a process that can be utterly passive— the flow of breath itself. In the unrestrictive mental exercises we ceased all physical activity. In somatic focusing (and to some extent, thematic imagery) we encountered a new type of passivity; we repeated certain phrases or images and simply let relaxation happen.

In contemplation we ceased such activity and simply watched things with the intent of observing them change and unfold on their own. In meditation passivity evolved again. In centered focus meditation we selected a stimulus and observed it with no intent. In open focus meditation we did not even select the object of our attention. We put aside all goals, all intention, and quietly observed what each moment had to offer. In meditation, passivity evolved into what might be termed "detachment" or "letting be."

The main point of this book can be said in a few words: relaxation is putting to rest distraction. We first encountered this idea when we considered scanning, an exercise that involves looking for and letting go of unnecessary and wasteful tension. Indeed, all relaxation is a type of scanning. At each level of relaxation we learned to put to rest a different type of distraction and appreciate a potential new source of pleasure and meaning. In the isometric sequence we learned to keep one muscle group relaxed while tensing another. Residual tension became a source of distraction. Then, we discovered that not only residual tension, but also the act of tightening up and letting go could interfere with the task of achieving a satisfying, slow, and graceful stretch (it is difficult to tense and stretch at the same time). Likewise, stretching tension and effortful chest breathing were unnecessary for the task of quietly attending to and enjoying the gentle flow of breath. They were distractions to be put to rest.

For mental relaxation all physical movement became unnecessary. The complex scenes and fantasies of somatic focusing and thematic imagery presented us with the greatest leeway concerning what we could attend to. In contemplation, any attempt to direct or evoke images would have been distracting. We let them change on their own. Of all our exercises, meditation once again represented an end point in subtlety and refinement. In meditation, all thought, even all expectation of gain, could distract us from a centered awareness of the mantra or openness to the flow of all being.

In all relaxation, when tension is calmed, often something of lesser importance is set aside. A source of noise is stilled. And we can see with clearer perspective and act with greater honesty and freedom. By letting go of what is truly expendable, it is easier to find what really matters.

In this book I have attempted to present, in a fair and neutral fashion, a part of the worlds of relaxation. However, a psychology book can only go so far. What you discover in moments of still inner peace is perhaps better understood by poets, philosophers, and those with spiritual insight. It is a new universe for you to explore

Last and First Words

Lesson 15

Setting Up a Personalized Relaxation Program

Once you have learned one or more approaches to self-relaxation, you can combine various sequences of exercises into a personalized relaxation program. Below is a list of all the approaches and exercises taught in this book. Which have you learned?

Part I: Physical Exercises

Isometric Squeeze
1. Hand Squeeze
2. Arm Squeeze
3. Arm and Side Squeeze
4. Back Squeeze
5. Shoulder Squeeze
6. Back of Neck Squeeze
7. Face Squeeze
8. Front of Neck Squeeze
9. Stomach and Chest Squeeze
10. Leg Squeeze
11. Foot Squeeze

Yogaform Stretching
12. Hand Stretch
13. Arm Stretch
14. Arm and Side Stretch
15. Back Stretch
16. Shoulder Stretch

17. Back of Neck Stretch
18. Face Stretch
19. Front of Neck Stretch
20. Stomach and Chest Stretch
21. Leg Stretch
22. Foot Stretch

Integrative Breathing
23. Deep Breathing
24. Arm Swing Breathing
25. Body Arch Breathing
26. Breathing and Bowing
27. Bowing and Stretching
28. Stomach Squeeze Breathing
29. Active Diaphragmatic Breathing
30. Inhaling Through Nose
31. Exhaling Through Lips
32. Focused Breathing
33. Thinking the Word *One*
34. Thinking a Relaxing Word
35. Scanning

Part II: Unrestrictive Mental Exercises

Somatic Focusing (Beginning Exercises)
36. Breathing
37. Mental Isometric Relaxation
38. Mental Massage
39. Warmth and Heaviness

Somatic Focusing (Advanced Exercises)
40. Solar Plexis
41. Erect Spine
42. Heart
43. Base of Throat
44. Visual Phenomena
45. Somatic Deepening Suggestions

Thematic Imagery
46. Pleasure
47. Escape
48. Reminiscence
49. Mastery
50. Expression

You may have discovered that different exercises have different effects, and some may work better for you than others. Most important, you may have a better appreciation of the role of restful states in your life. But, although you may now know quite a number of specific relaxation exercises, your job is not finished. The goal of Relaxation Dynamics is not to impose a set of exercises on you, but to invite you to develop your own approach to relaxation.

Meta-Scanning

The simplest way to personalize relaxation is through an approach called *meta-scanning*. Recall that we discussed scanning in Lesson 9. The technique involved quietly checking the body for points of unnecessary tension and letting go with each outgoing breath. In meta-scanning we do not check for areas of tension. Instead we ask, "At this moment, what type of relaxation do I need to do?" And we do whatever exercise feels best for the moment. Let's try this technique:

> First, make sure you are in a comfortable position. For about
> 2 minutes simply sit quietly. Let yourself settle down. Now,
> ask yourself "How do I feel now, at this very moment? How
> do I feel tense? What relaxation exercise would I most like to
> do now? What exercise would feel most satisfying?" Then,
> without trying to analyze the question or deliberately for-
> mulate an answer, simply wait. Calmly and quietly attend to
> whatever answers might emerge. When a technique comes to
> mind that feels right, that's what you do.

That's all there is to it. Meta-scanning is nothing more than quietly getting in touch with how your body or mind needs to relax.

Free-Form Relaxation

Free-form relaxation is a slightly more complex version of meta-scanning. In this approach ask yourself "What exercise would feel best this moment?" every 4 or 5 minutes, and then do the exercise that comes to mind. For example, if you first feel like doing isometric squeeze relaxation, practice 4 or 5 minutes of complete isometric squeezes. Then settle into a position of restful quiet and ask the question again: "What exercise would now feel best?" If meditation or imagery comes to mind, that is your technique for the next 4 or 5 minutes. Continue asking and practicing for about 15 or 20 minutes. Free-form relaxation is highly unstructured. It can serve as a potent introduction to open focus meditation.

Personalized Relaxation Sequences

Many people find it useful to develop their own program of personalized relaxation sequences (Worksheet 19). In order to construct a personalized relaxation sequence, you need to address three questions:

1. What do I want from relaxation?
2. Which exercises seem to fit my goals?
3. In what order should I do these exercises?

First, what do you want from relaxation? You may have a wide variety of goals:

Recovering from the day's tensions at the end of the day

Preparing for sleep

Preparing for and recovering from a stressful event

Preparing for and recovering from sports and other physical activities

Preparing for and recovering from cognitive tasks (like studying)

Preparing for and recovering from emotional strain (like talking about an emotional issue)

Increasing creativity and solving problems

Doing for enjoyment

Using for personal growth and exploration

Preparing for meditation

Relaxing briefly (less than 5 minutes)

Preparing for a pleasurable or rewarding activity

Which exercises seem most appropriate for your relaxation goals? Are there any exercises you developed? What is the best order for the exercises you have selected? There is no simple way to construct a personalized relaxation sequence. Most people experiment with several. When they have decided upon a sequence that seems to fit a goal, they experiment further and fine tune and adjust their selection until it works best for them. Let's see some sequences others have developed.

Michael F.

Michael works as an insurance broker. His job is rewarding but extremely demanding. There are days he returns home utterly exhausted. What Michael wanted from relaxation was a simple way of unwinding at the end of the day, a "decompression" exercise to recover from the stress and strain of work. After experimenting with several sequences, he settled upon the following: "First I sit in my favorite chair. I settle down. Then I shrug my shoulders and neck together several times to squeeze out all the tension there [#5, Shoulder Squeeze; #6, Back of Neck Squeeze]. Next, I stretch my entire body, reaching up into the air and arching my torso [#14, Arm and Side Stretch]. I then bow over and reach up, while breathing fully and easily [#27, Bowing and Stretching]. I let my head hang in front of me, stretching my neck muscles more and more. I take my time on this one [#17, Back of Neck Stretch]. I let myself settle down and become quiet as I easily exhale through my lips, as if I were blowing at a candle flame [#31, Exhaling Through Lips]. I end by spending 15 minutes in my own private fantasy vacation spot [#47, Escape Imagery]. I think of resting on the beach. I hear the quiet waves on the shore, and feel the cool breeze and the warm sun. From time to time I let my body feel completely warm and heavy. I even repeat these words to myself to enhance the feeling [#39, Warmth and Heaviness]. After 25 minutes I am completely refreshed and ready for the night. This technique is better than watching TV, drinking a beer, or even taking a nap."

Kathi B.

Kathi is a college student majoring in music. She plays the piano and often performs in public. She developed the following sequence to do just before performing: "Sometimes when I play I get a bit nervous and don't do my best. Before I perform I now do a simple warmup exercise. Since I'm in public I can't be too conspicuous (and do big stretches). So I start by taking a deep breath and letting it out quietly through my lips [#31, Exhaling Through Lips]. I quietly attend to the flow of air in and out and let my breathing become more and more even and relaxed [#32, Focused Breathing]. I then slowly stretch and unstretch my fingers a few times [#12, Hand Stretch]. With every outgoing breath I let go of tension [#35, Scanning] and think to myself, 'I've done all I can do to do my best. If I make a few mistakes, most people won't notice or remember. Doing challenging performances like this improves my skill [#49, Mastery Imagery].' "

Marti W.

Marti is an occupational therapist who works with pain patients. Many of his patients are receiving chemotherapy for bone cancer. With each patient, Marti attempts to develop a personalized relaxation sequence to ease the pain. Here's one sequence he developed: "One of my patients suffers considerable pain in her arms and fingers. I first have her focus on the breathing process. I have her breathe as slowly and evenly as possible [#32, Focused Breathing]. She then imagines gentle fingers first massaging her hands and fingers, then moving all the way up her arms [#38, Mental Massage]. Finally, she imagines she is once again experiencing a pleasant boat ride she often took when young, recalling all the familiar sights she loved as a child [#48, Reminiscence Imagery]. The sun is bright and warms her skin [#39, Warmth and Heaviness]."

Rose M.

Rose is a deeply religious person. She is very active in her church and community, and prayer plays an important part in her life. She often finds it useful to explore different approaches. Here's a set of exercises she found particularly meaningful: "I start my prayer by settling down. I try to quiet the busy thoughts of my mind. I do a few beginning exercises like swinging my arms slowly in front of me while breathing out and slowly behind while breathing in [#24, Arm Swing Breathing]. I rest my hands in my lap and think the words of a hymn I find particularly beautiful and meaningful. I let the words come to me and I find myself singing joyfully in my mind [#50, Expression Imagery]. I then say a few words and quietly let my mind dwell upon one of the refrains of the song. Without trying to analyze it, I let thoughts and pictures come to mind to illuminate its meaning. I may come across new insights and understandings [Contemplation]. I then put all these new insights and ideas aside and simply sit in silent meditation. I meditate on the word *peace.* I am completely quiet as the word repeats in my mind like a soothing voice [#57, Centered Focus Meditation]."

Personalized relaxation sequences need not be long. Many students invent 5-minute mini-sequences of 3 or 4 exercises. Here are a few:

Mini-Sequence 1

1. Take a deep breath and let your breathing be even, slow, and full [#32, Focused Breathing].

2. Scan for and release tension [#35, Scanning].
3. Attend to your meditation mantra [#57, Centered Focus Meditation].

Mini-Sequence 2

1. Squeeze and stretch your shoulders [#5, Shoulder Squeeze; #16, Shoulder Stretch].
2. Pull in your stomach while exhaling, then inhale [#29, Active Diaphragmatic Breathing].
3. Gently breathe in through your nose and out through your lips [#30, Inhaling Through Nose; #31, Exhaling Through Lips].

Mini-Sequence 3

1. Take a deep breath and slowly exhale [#32, Focused Breathing].
2. While breathing, think the phrase "I am calm and settled" [#54, Generalized "Three R" Thoughts].

Creative Scripting

You might find it helpful to make your own relaxation tape. Tapes can be particularly useful for those who tend to rush through or forget parts of an exercise, and they can foster a degree of attentional focus for those who are easily distracted. Making a tape is a creative act: you must first write a script and then read it while taping.

Writing a Script

The preceding section discussed the steps in developing a personalized relaxation sequence. The process is fairly unstructured: you simply decide upon a relaxation goal and select and arrange exercises to meet this goal. The specifics of each exercise are either taken directly from the scripts presented in this book or improvised when the exercise is actually performed. For example, someone might choose to do isometric relaxation and then fantasize a quiet scene. That person could select isometric exercises from the book and construct an actual scene while doing the exercise. Writing a relaxation script leaves less up to chance.

There are six steps in writing a relaxation script:

1. Decide upon a relaxation goal.
2. Select exercises.
3. Elaborate upon unrestrictive mental exercises.
4. Determine exercise combinations.
5. Determine the sequence of exercises.
6. Determine pauses and silences.

Decide upon a relaxation goal. Why do you want to relax? When do you want to relax? How long do you want your relaxation exercise to last? These are the three questions you need to answer before beginning. Note how one person, Bill, approaches them.

> My relaxation goal is to enhance creativity. I am a writer and am constantly searching for new ideas. For example, at times I need to think of a topic for an article, one that is interesting and will sell. At other times I might be rewriting an article and must think of ideas on how to revise and improve what I have written. When and for how long do I want to relax? I have decided to set aside 30 minutes every other day. I think my best relaxation time would be around 10 a.m., since I am most productive in the morning.

Select exercises. Review the exercises in this book. Which seem most appropriate for your goal? Which did you enjoy most? Which seemed to foster the effects you desire? Once again, let's examine how Bill approaches these questions.

> Looking over my notes, it is clear that some sort of thematic imagery or meditation would work best for me. I particularly enjoyed the intuition exercise and centered focus meditation. The deepening exercises seemed to work well too. I also recall that mental exercises can be difficult for me, especially when I am tense and wound up, so perhaps I should include a physical exercise. I really enjoyed some of the active breathing exercises.

Elaborate upon unrestrictive mental exercises. Now, take a look at the mental exercises you have selected. If you picked an unrestrictive exercise (somatic focusing or thematic imagery), you will need to elaborate upon the details. You will need to write a script specifying all the details you want in your exercise. Write this script as if you were talking to someone, giving instructions, and noting what that person might be sensing, thinking, and feeling. Here is where you can be most creative. In fact, you might think of yourself as writing an imaginative story. Here is Bill's elaborated creative intuition exercise.

> You are strolling through a quiet and peaceful forest. The air is still. The warm sun filters through many layers of leaves. Occasionally a bird sings. You are far from any care or concern. Suddenly you come upon the opening to a cavern. It is clear that no one has ever been here before. Any mysteries the cavern holds are for you to discover. You slowly walk inside. The air is strangely cool and refreshing. A faint light

illuminates the walls. The cavern is deep. You begin walking, farther and farther. The entrance grows smaller and smaller in the distance. You are all alone. Eventually you come upon a very smooth and black portion of rock. It is so smooth it could almost be a window or mirror. You rest yourself comfortably and gaze quietly into the rock. You begin to realize that in this window/mirror are answers to questions you might have. All you need to do is quietly and peacefully gaze into its black depths, almost as if you were looking into the night sky. There is nothing for you to deliberately figure out, nothing for you to analyze. Indeed, there is only a simple, single task you need to perform in order to communicate with the mysteries of the rock. Quietly and silently let the word *one* repeat itself in your mind. This is your meditation for the next 20 minutes.

Bill also noted that he found the thematic deepening exercises useful. In order to elaborate upon them, he constructed a few phrases and sentences.

You begin counting backwards, starting with the number Ten. With every count you move deeper and deeper into relaxation. Your mind becomes more clear and still. You become more receptive to creative forces within you. Nine. You sink deeper and deeper. Eight. Your mind becomes more and more relaxed. Seven. You let thoughts and images come to you on their own. Do nothing to push them away. Six. There is nothing for you to do but sit quietly and peacefully. Five. With each count you become more and more completely relaxed. Four. With each count you become more and more completely open to creativity. Three. You sink deeper and deeper into a state of peaceful receptivity. Two. You become fully and thoroughly relaxed and open. And One. You are now firmly centered in a state of deep and receptive relaxation.

Determine exercise combinations. You now have all the pieces for a relaxation script. The next task is to combine any exercises that should be done simultaneously. For example, you would probably want to weave deepening and other thematic exercises together. Similarly, breathing exercises can be easily and effectively intermingled with other exercises. Here is how Bill combined his intuitive and thematic deepening exercises.

You are strolling through a quiet and peaceful forest. The air is still. The warm sun filters through many layers of leaves.

Occasionally a bird sings. You are far from any care or concern. Suddenly you come upon the opening to a cavern. It is clear that no one has ever been here before. Any mysteries the cavern holds are for you to discover. You slowly walk inside. The air is strangely cool and refreshing. A faint light illuminates the walls. The cavern is deep. You begin walking, farther and farther. The entrance grows smaller and smaller in the distance. You are all alone. Eventually you come upon a very smooth and black portion of rock. It is so smooth it could almost be a window or mirror. You rest yourself comfortably and gaze quietly into the rock.

You begin counting backwards, starting with the number Ten. With every count you move deeper and deeper into relaxation. Your mind becomes more clear and still. You become more receptive to creative forces within you. Nine. You sink deeper and deeper. Eight. Your mind becomes more and more relaxed. Seven. You let thoughts and images come to you on their own. Do nothing to push them away.

You begin to realize that in this window/mirror are answers to questions you might have. All you need to do is quietly and peacefully gaze into its black depths, almost as if you were looking into the night sky. •

Six. There is nothing for you to do but sit quietly and peacefully. Five. With each count you become more and more completely relaxed. Four. With each count you become more and more completely open to creativity. Three. You sink deeper and deeper into a state of peaceful receptivity. Two. You become fully and thoroughly relaxed and open. And One. You are now firmly centered in a state of deep and receptive relaxation.

There is nothing for you to deliberately figure out, nothing for you to analyze. Indeed, there is only a simple, single task you need to perform in order to communicate with the mysteries of the rock. Quietly and silently let the word *one* repeat itself in your mind. This is your meditation for the next 20 minutes.

Determine the sequence of exercises. Now you are about finished with your script. Each major component should be written out or located in this book. The next step is to determine the sequence of exercises. Here is what Bill did:

I begin with breathing exercises, specifically Bowing and Stretching and Exhaling Through Lips. I decided to use the scripts in the book. I follow the breathing sequence with my intuitive/deepening exercise.

Determine pauses and silences. A relaxation tape should include frequent pauses and periods of silence. It is at moments when nothing is being said that the effects of a tape can begin to take hold. When making your own tape, follow each idea with a pause lasting from 1 to 5 seconds. There also are times during an exercise that you might want to be left in silence, for example, during a meditation. In your script, write in instructions for pauses and periods of silence. Then, when you are making your tape and reach an instruction for pause or silence, simply stay quiet while the tape is running. Figure 2 is Bill's final script, complete with pauses and silences.

Reading a Script

When you have finished the script, you probably will want to record it. All you need for this is an inexpensive tape cassette recorder and an audio tape.

Begin by reading the script aloud several times before recording. This doesn't mean you have to give a virtuoso reading; it just allows you to decide what inflection you want for certain phrases and makes it less likely you will falter while recording.

When you are ready, record as you read the script slowly and naturally, just a little slower than you would normally speak in casual conversation. For each "PAUSE" in your script, wait 1 or 2 seconds, about as long as a slow breath. For longer pauses, such as "PAUSE 1 MINUTE," just stop talking as the tape continues.

To give you an idea of how to pace your script, Figure 3 (page 220) presents a practice exercise. Try reading it aloud. Speak softly. Time yourself. You should take about 60 seconds to finish reading. If you take less time, try again at a slower pace.

Remember that the tape is only meant to be a guide, a device to help you remember your original sequencing of exercises. If you find, after using your tape for a while, that you would prefer a different wording or would like to adjust the length of certain pauses, feel free to change it. And you may find, in time, that the tape is unnecessary for performing the sequence.

Evaluating Your Script

As you can see, there is no end to how you can use the exercises you have learned. This is your opportunity to be creative and go beyond this book. However, once you have written your script, you might want to go back and check it for possible problems.

Is your script too long or too short? Try reading it without a tape recorder. How long is it?

Are your instructions concrete and specific? Your script should include every detail. Very little should be left to the imagination (except in intuitive or contemplative segments). Remember that while listening to the tape you should be relaxed, and should not have to be concerned with filling in missing details or figuring out what the tape means. So instead of saying "Do some yoga stretching on your arm," say "Slowly, smoothly, and gently stretch and reach with your right arm." This instruction is far too vague: "Imagine a cool pond and relax." This one is better: "Picture yourself next to a clear, cool pond. There is barely a ripple. The water is blue. The sky is clear without a cloud. You can feel a calm wind."

Does your script contain any statements you might question or contradict? Avoid statements like the following:

"You will immediately recover from your cold."

"You will find the answer to your problem."

"You are at this moment more relaxed than you have ever been."

Frankly, you might not recover from your cold, find an answer to your problem, or become more relaxed than you have ever been. So avoid making promises you might not be able to keep. Remember the "Three Rs" of thematic imagery: make your suggestions restful, reasonable, and realistic.

Figure 2
Bill's Final Script

Before we begin, make sure you are seated upright in a comfortable position.

PAUSE

Rest your hands comfortably in your lap.

PAUSE

Make sure your feet are placed flat on the floor.

PAUSE

Now close your eyes and let yourself settle into a position that is comfortable.

PAUSE

For the next few minutes let your body become more and more quiet.

PAUSE

Let yourself begin to settle down and relax as you remain still.

PAUSE

Bowing and Stretching (RD 27)

Now, as you inhale, reach and stretch. Arch your back and gently circle both arms up toward the sky like the hands of a clock or the wings of a great bird. When you are ready to exhale, slowly circle your arms down so they are hanging heavily, and gently bow over, as before, squeezing out all the air. Let gravity pull your body down farther and farther. There is nothing for you to do. Continue breathing this way for a while. Breathe at whatever pace feels most comfortable. If you need to take a short breath from time to time, that's OK.

PAUSE

Continue breathing this way at your own pace. Reach up and breathe in; pause; and let go and bow over while breathing out. Do this very slowly and evenly, without hurrying and without rushing.

PAUSE 5 SECONDS

Make your movements very smooth and even.

PAUSE 10 SECONDS

Let yourself breathe deeply and fully, at your own pace.

PAUSE 10 SECONDS

Figure 2 (cont.)

Notice the easy flow of air as it moves in and out of your lungs.

PAUSE 5 SECONDS

Take your time, do not force yourself. Breathe comfortably and fully.

PAUSE 5 SECONDS

Now, as you sit up, place your hands in your lap. Stay in this position for a little while.

PAUSE

Let yourself breathe in a natural and easy way.

PAUSE 15 SECONDS

Attend to your stomach and chest.

PAUSE

How does it feel to breathe in a deep and relaxed manner?

PAUSE

You might want to think of a large, soft balloon that slowly fills, pauses, and empties of air.

PAUSE 5 SECONDS

Let each breath soothe your body, and make it more and more relaxed.

PAUSE 5 SECONDS

Exhaling Through Lips (RD 31)

Now take a slow deep breath and pause.

And breathe out slowly through your lips, as if you were blowing at a candle flame just enough to make it flicker, but not go out. Continue breathing out, emptying all the air from your stomach and chest.

PAUSE

Then breathe in through your nose.

PAUSE

Continue breathing this way, making the stream of air that passes through your lips as you exhale as smooth and gentle as possible.

PAUSE 5 SECONDS

Let the tension flow out with every breath.

PAUSE 5 SECONDS

Let the gentle movement of air dissolve any feelings of tension you might have.

PAUSE 10 SECONDS

Notice the easy flow of air as it relaxes and refreshes you.

PAUSE 10 SECONDS

Let each breath fill you with feelings of peaceful relaxation.

PAUSE 10 SECONDS

Notice the inner calm that comes with breathing in a way that is slow and full and even.

PAUSE 15 SECONDS

Creative Intuition Exercise

You are strolling through a quiet and peaceful forest. The air is still. The warm sun filters through many layers of leaves. Occasionally a bird sings. You are far from any care or concern.

PAUSE 5 SECONDS

Suddenly you come upon the opening to a cavern. It is clear that no one has ever been here before. Any mysteries the cavern holds are for you to discover.

PAUSE 5 SECONDS

You slowly walk inside. The air is strangely cool and refreshing. A faint light illuminates the walls. The cavern is deep. You begin walking, farther and farther.

PAUSE 5 SECONDS

The entrance grows smaller and smaller in the distance. You are all alone.

PAUSE 5 SECONDS

Eventually you come upon a very smooth and black portion of rock. It is so smooth it could almost be a window or mirror. You rest yourself comfortably and gaze quietly into the rock.

PAUSE 5 SECONDS

You begin counting backwards, starting with the number Ten. With every count you move deeper and deeper into relaxation.

PAUSE

Your mind becomes more clear and still.

Figure 2 (cont.)

PAUSE

You become more receptive to creative forces within you.

PAUSE

Nine. You sink deeper and deeper.

PAUSE 5 SECONDS

Eight. Your mind becomes more and more relaxed.

PAUSE 5 SECONDS

Seven. You let thoughts and images come to you on their own. Do nothing to push them away.

PAUSE

You begin to realize that in this window/mirror are answers to questions you might have. All you need to do is quietly and peacefully gaze into its black depths, almost as if you were looking into the night sky.

PAUSE 5 SECONDS

Six. There is nothing for you to do but sit quietly and peacefully.

PAUSE 5 SECONDS

Five. With each count you become more and more completely relaxed.

PAUSE 5 SECONDS

Four. With each count you become more and more completely open to creativity.

PAUSE 5 SECONDS

Three. You sink deeper and deeper into a state of peaceful receptivity.

PAUSE 5 SECONDS

Two. You become fully and thoroughly relaxed and open.

PAUSE 5 SECONDS

And One. You are now firmly centered in a state of deep and receptive relaxation.

PAUSE

There is nothing for you to deliberately figure out, nothing for you to analyze. Indeed, there is only a simple, single task you need to perform in order to communicate with the mysteries of the rock. Quietly and silently let the word *one* repeat itself in your mind. This is your meditation for the next 20 minutes.

PAUSE 20 MINUTES

Figure 3
Practice Exercise

Learning to relax is a very easy thing to do.
First sit up straight in a comfortable position.
Make sure your feet are flat on the floor.

PAUSE

Are your hands resting comfortably in your lap?

PAUSE

Now close your eyes, and give yourself a few seconds to settle down.

PAUSE 10 SECONDS

Now focus your attention on how your body feels.

PAUSE

If you feel tense in any part of your body, you might want to try shifting a bit so you are more comfortable.

PAUSE 10 SECONDS

Now take a deep breath and let it out.

PAUSE

Slowly open your eyes.
This ends the practice exercise.

Section II

The Instruction of Relaxation Dynamics

Chapter 1

Setting Up a Training Program

If you wish to learn or teach self-relaxation, you need a plan. This chapter presents schedules for five different Relaxation Dynamics training programs. All make use of the text material presented in Section I, relaxation scripts at the end of each lesson or relaxation tapes from the Relaxation Dynamics Cassette Series, and worksheets from the Appendix.

To follow any of the schedules presented, here is what you need to do:

1. Read the instructions for the program you have chosen that appear in this chapter. They will provide training objectives and assignments. Generally the assignments include lessons to read in Section I, a specific relaxation approach to practice, and written exercises to do

2. Read the assigned lesson.

3. Start practicing the assigned approach to relaxation. If you have audio taped instructions, play these each time you practice. You may make your own tapes using the scripts provided following each of the lessons (follow the instructions in "Reading a Script" from Lesson 15 of Section I), or use the tapes from the Relaxation Dynamics Cassette Series.

4. After practicing your approach, complete the assigned worksheets. These are found in the Appendix. Usually you will have to complete several copies of a single worksheet during the week. However, since only one copy of each is presented, you may make extra copies for your own use.

Before choosing a training program, be sure to read Lessons 1-3 in Section I. These lessons discuss the nature and goals of Relaxation Dynamics, guidelines, and medical and psychological precautions.

Self-relaxation training may be approached with a variety of goals, and different training formats will be appropriate for different goals. Five possible schedules are suggested here, with detailed instructions provided in the following pages.

The Complete 14-Week Training Program

Week 1: Orientation
Week 2: Measuring Stress and Relaxation
Week 3: Setting Time Aside for Rest
Week 4: Isometric Squeeze Relaxation
Week 5: Yogaform Stretching
Week 6: Integrative Breathing
Week 7: Consolidating, Experimenting, and Setting Up a Quieting Sequence
Week 8: Somatic Focusing (Beginning Exercises)
Week 9: Somatic Focusing (Advanced Exercises)
Week 10: Thematic Imagery
Week 11: Contemplation
Week 12: Centered Focus Meditation
Week 13: Open Focus Meditation
Week 14: Setting Up a Personalized Relaxation Program

The 5-Week Training Program

Week 1: Orientation and Isometric Squeeze Relaxation
Week 2: Yogaform Stretching
Week 3: Integrative Breathing
Week 4: Mental Relaxation: Thematic Imagery or Centered Focus Meditation
Week 5: Setting Up a Personalized Relaxation Program

The 4-Week Training Program

Week 1: Orientation and Isometric Squeeze Relaxation
Week 2: Yogaform Stretching or Integrative Breathing
Week 3: Mental Relaxation: Thematic Imagery or Centered Focus Meditation
Week 4: Setting Up a Personalized Relaxation Program

The 3-Week Training Program

Weeks 1-2: Orientation, Grand Tour, Review of All Approaches, and Practice of All Approaches

Week 3: Setting Up a Personalized Relaxation Program

The 2-Week Training Program

Week 1: Orientation, Grand Tour, Review of All Approaches, and Selection of Approach(es)
Week 2: Review and Fine-Tuning of Selected Approach(es)

The Complete 14-Week Training Program

This program follows Section I lesson by lesson. Each world approach is practiced for a week.

Week 1: Orientation

Objective
This week's goal is to introduce Relaxation Dynamics. Basic principles and medical and psychological precautions are covered. In addition, this week's readings describe the rewards of self-relaxation, with particular attention paid to stress management.

Assignment
- Read Lessons 1-4 in Section I.
- Play the Grand Tour tape (Tape 1, Side A).

Week 2: Measuring Stress and Relaxation

Objective
Before learning self-relaxation it can be useful to take stock of how you experience stress and relaxation. Learning inner signs of stress and relaxation is one of the first steps in self-relaxation training. These signs can serve as cues or reminders to relax, cues often ignored by the stress-prone individual. They can help you discover the impact of different exercises. Awareness and appreciation of the signs of stress and relaxation can sensitize you to and remind you of the potentials of relaxation training. This week's worksheet exercise is designed to enhance your awareness of stress and relaxation.

Assignment
- Review Lesson 4.
- Read Lesson 5.
- Complete at least three Day's End Questionnaires (Worksheet 1 in the Appendix).

Week 3: Setting Time Aside for Rest

Objective

The most difficult problem people have with relaxation training is learning to set aside a specific daily time for relaxation. Social pressures and stress addiction often combine to produce considerable resistance to the simple act of taking time off on a daily basis. A major goal of this week's lesson is to develop the healthy habit of taking a rest break every day. Warning: this is more difficult than you might think.

Assignment
- Read Lesson 6.
- Select a daily time-off period and practice a relaxation activity during this period every day. Evaluate the effects of your daily relaxation period by using *all* of the following worksheet exercises. This will give you practice with each of the types of exercises used throughout the program so you can decide which to use in future lessons.

Worksheet 2: First Session Questionnaire

Worksheet 3: Daily Log for Setting Time Aside for Rest

Worksheet 11: Final Assessment for Setting Time Aside for Rest

Worksheet 16: Personal Thoughts

Week 4: Isometric Squeeze Relaxation

Objectives

This week you will learn to relax by squeezing and letting go of major muscle groups. You will also have a chance to evaluate the effects of isometric squeeze relaxation by using your choice of worksheet exercises.

Assignment
- Read Lesson 7.
- Practice isometric squeeze relaxation at least once each day (Tape 1, Side B).
- Evaluate this approach by using any combination of the following worksheet exercises: 2, 4, 12, or 16.

If you are not sure which exercise(s) to select, reread "Appraising Your Progress" in Lesson 5.

Week 5: Yogaform Stretching

Objective

This week you will learn to relax by slowly, smoothly, and gently stretching and unstretching the same muscles you squeezed last week.

Assignment
- Read Lesson 8.
- Practice yogaform stretching at least once each day (Tape 2, Side A).
- Evaluate this approach by using any combination of the following worksheet exercises: 2, 5, 13, or 16.

Week 6: Integrative Breathing

Objectives

This week you will learn to relax by breathing in a way that is full, even, and unhurried. You will also learn to check for and release tension through a technique called scanning.

Assignment
- Read Lesson 9.
- Practice integrative breathing at least once each day (Tape 2, Side B).
- Evaluate this approach by using any combination of the following worksheet exercises: 2, 6, 14, or 16.

Week 7: Consolidating, Experimenting, and Setting Up a Quieting Sequence

Objectives

You have now completed all the physical approaches in Relaxation Dynamics. This week you will gain practice with these approaches and compare them in a variety of settings. Most important, you will construct your own quieting sequence, a set of physical "warmup" exercises to be done before approaches taught in later lessons.

Assignment
- Read and complete Worksheet 17: Rotational Practice and Trial Runs.
- Practice a different exercise a day, every day of the week.
- As described in Worksheet 17, practice at least one self-relaxation exercise before or after an activity you already find pleasurable or rewarding.

• Read and complete Worksheet 18: Setting Up a Quieting Sequence. This worksheet tells you how to experiment with and develop a quieting sequence.

Week 8: Somatic Focusing (Beginning Exercises)

Objective
  This week's beginning somatic focusing exercises involve attending to body sensations related to relaxation. You will think relaxing phrases and images that go with such sensations.

Assignment
  • Read Lesson 10 (pages 133–135 up to "Advanced Somatic Exercises" and page 137, "Quieting Sequences").
  • Practice the beginning somatic focusing exercises at least once each day (Tape 3, Side A). Precede each session with the physical quieting sequence you developed last week.
  • Do any of the following worksheet exercises: 2, 7, 15, 16.

Week 9: Somatic Focusing (Advanced Exercises)

Objective
  Advanced somatic focusing exercises are directed toward physical sensations that are more internal and subtle. Once again, you will think phrases and images that go with such sensations.

Assignment
  • Read Lesson 10 (pages 135–137).
  • Practice the advanced somatic focusing exercises at least once each day (Tape 3, Side A). Precede each session with a physical quieting sequence.
  • Do any of the following worksheet exercises: 2, 8, 15, 16.

Week 10: Thematic Imagery

Objective
  The goal of thematic imagery is to quietly think phrases or mental pictures associated with a specific relaxing theme. You may choose any theme you wish, although the lesson relaxation script and tape focus on the theme of sensation.

Assignment
  • Read Lesson 11.
  • Practice thematic imagery at least once each day (Tape 3, Side B). Precede each session with a physical quieting sequence.
  • Do any of the following worksheet exercises: 2, 9, 15, 16.

Week 11: Contemplation

Objective

In contemplation you will quietly attend to a stimulus in order to gain a greater appreciation of it.

Assignment

- Read Lesson 12.
- Practice contemplation at least once each day (Tape 4, Side A). Precede each session with a physical quieting sequence.
- Do any of the following worksheet exercises: 2, 10, 15, 16.

Week 12: Centered Focus Meditation

Objective

The goal of centered focus meditation is to quietly and restfully attend to a simple stimulus and learn to deal with distraction in a meditative way.

Assignment

- Read Lesson 13 (pages 183–187 up to "Open Focus Meditation," and pages 188–190 from "Distraction and Growth in Meditation" to "Restriction and Openness in Meditation").
- Practice open focus meditation at least once a day (Tape 4, Side B). Precede each session with a physical quieting sequence.
- Do any of the following worksheet exercises: 2, 10, 15, 16.

Week 13: Open Focus Meditation

Objective

The objective of open focus meditation is to quietly attend to all stimuli without dwelling upon any particular one.

Assignment

- Read Lesson 13 (pages 187–188, "Open Focus Meditation," and pages 190–191).
- Practice open focus meditation at least once a day (Tape 4, Side B).
- Precede each session with a physical quieting sequence.
- Do any of the following worksheet exercises: 2, 10, 15, 16.

Week 14: Setting Up a Personalized Relaxation Program

Objective

You have now completed your tour of nine major world approaches to self-relaxation. You have learned no fewer than 58 specific exercises. Your objective this week is to decide upon your relaxation goals, select exercises to meet these goals, and try these exercises. If you wish to increase your mastery of self-relaxation, you will need to continue practicing regularly, possibly under professional supervision.

Assignment
- Read Lessons 14 and 15.
- Do Worksheet 19.

The 5-Week Training Program

This program focuses on those components of the Complete 14-Week Training Program that beginning students of self-relaxation tend to find most useful.

Week 1: Orientation and Isometric Squeeze Relaxation

Objective
> This week's goal is to introduce Relaxation Dynamics and the first physical exercise, isometric squeeze relaxation. Basic principles and medical and psychological precautions are covered. In addition, this week's readings describe the rewards of self-relaxation, with particular attention paid to stress management.

Assignment for Day 1
- Read Lessons 1-6 in Section I. You do not need to do the exercises in Lesson 6.

Assignment for Days 2–7
- Read Lesson 7.
- Practice isometric squeeze relaxation at least once each day (Tape 1, Side B).
- Evaluate this approach by using any combination of the following worksheet exercises:

  Worksheet 2: First Session Questionnaire

  Worksheet 4: Daily Log for Isometric Squeeze Relaxation

  Worksheet 12: Final Assessment for Isometric Squeeze Relaxation

  Worksheet 16: Personal Thoughts

  If you are not sure which exercise(s) to select, reread "Appraising Your Progress" in Lesson 5.

Week 2: Yogaform Stretching

Objective
> This week's goal is to learn yogaform stretching.

Assignment
- Read Lesson 8.
- Practice yogaform stretching at least once each day (Tape 2, Side A).
- Evaluate this approach by using any combination of the following worksheet exercises: 2, 5, 13, 16.

Week 3: Integrative Breathing

Objective
> The goal this week is to learn integrative breathing.

Assignment
- Read Lesson 9.
- Practice integrative breathing at least once each day (Tape 2, Side B).
- Evaluate this approach by using any combination of the following worksheet exercises: 2, 6, 14, or 16.

Week 4: Mental Relaxation: Thematic Imagery or Centered Focus Meditation

Objective
> Two of the most popular mental exercises are thematic imagery and centered focus meditation. This week select and practice *one* of these approaches.

Assignment for Day 1
- Read Lessons 11 and 13.
- Decide whether to practice thematic imagery or centered focus meditation.
- Do Worksheet 18: Setting Up a Quieting Sequence. This worksheet tells you how to develop your own quieting sequence.

Assignment for Days 2–7
- Practice thematic imagery (Tape 3, Side B) or centered focus meditation (Tape 4, Side B) at least once each day. Precede each session with a physical quieting sequence.
- Do any of the following worksheet exercises: 2; 9 or 10; 15; or 16.

Week 5: Setting Up a Personalized Relaxation Program

Objective
> This week's goal is to develop a personalized relaxation program.

Assignment
- Read Lesson 15.
- Do Worksheet 19.

The 4-Week Training Program

Just like the 5-Week Training Program, this program also covers the most useful components of the 14-Week Training Program, but in a shorter time period.

Week 1: Orientation and Isometric Squeeze Relaxation

Objective

This week's goal is to introduce Relaxation Dynamics and the first physical exercise, isometric squeeze relaxation. Basic principles and medical and psychological precautions are covered. In addition, this week's readings describe the rewards of self-relaxation, with particular attention paid to stress management.

Assignment for Day 1

- Read Lessons 1-6 in Section I. You do not need to do the exercises in Lesson 6.

Assignment for Days 2–7

- Read Lesson 7.
- Practice isometric squeeze relaxation at least once each day (Tape 1, Side B).
- Evaluate this approach by using any combination of the following worksheet exercises:

Worksheet 2: First Session Questionnaire

Worksheet 4: Daily Log for Isometric Squeeze Relaxation

Worksheet 12: Final Assessment for Isometric Squeeze Relaxation

Worksheet 16: Personal Thoughts

If you are not sure which exercise(s) to select, reread "Appraising Your Progress" in Lesson 5.

Week 2: Yogaform Stretching or Integrative Breathing

Objective

This week's goal is to learn either yogaform stretching or integrative breathing.

Assignment for Day 1

- Read Lessons 8 and 9.
- Decide whether to practice yogaform stretching or integrative breathing.

Assignment for Days 2–7

- Practice yogaform stretching (Tape 2, Side A) or integrative breathing (Tape 2, Side B) at least once each day.
- Evaluate your approach by using any combination of the following worksheet exercises: 2; 5 or 6; 13 or 14; or 16.

Week 3: *Mental Relaxation: Thematic Imagery or Centered Focus Meditation*

Objectives

Two of the most popular mental exercises are thematic imagery and centered focus meditation. This week select and practice *one* of these approaches. You will also construct a physical quieting sequence, a set of physical "warmup" exercises to be done before any form of mental relaxation.

Assignment for Day 1
- Read Lessons 11 and 13.
- Decide whether to practice thematic imagery or centered focus meditation.
- Do Worksheet 18: Setting Up a Quieting Sequence. This worksheet tells you how to develop your own quieting sequence.

Assignment for Days 2–7
- Practice thematic imagery (Tape 3, Side B) or centered focus meditation (Tape 4, Side B) at least once each day. Precede each session with a physical quieting sequence.
- Do any of the following worksheet exercises: 2; 9 or 10; 15; or 16.

Week 4: *Setting Up a Personalized Relaxation Program*

Objective

This week's goal is to develop a personalized relaxation program.

Assignment
- Read Lesson 15.
- Do Worksheet 19.

The 3-Week Training Program

The 3-Week Training Program places special emphasis on reading and briefly sampling various approaches to relaxation.

Weeks 1-2: *Orientation, Grand Tour, Review of All Approaches, and Practice of All Approaches*

Objectives

Your objectives for the first 2 weeks are to acquire a basic introduction to Relaxation Dynamics and to sample each of the nine major world approaches to self-relaxation.

Assignment for Day 1
- Read all of Section I (this may be done as homework before beginning training).
- Play the Grand Tour tape (Tape 1, Side A).

Assignment for Days 2–10
- Practice a different relaxation approach at least once every day, starting with isometric squeeze relaxation. To evaluate each approach, use only Worksheet 2 (First Session Questionnaire). Complete this exercise each practice session.

Assignment for Days 11–14
- Practice again those exercises that seemed to be most effective.

Week 3: Setting Up a Personalized Relaxation Program

Objective
Now that all of the approaches have been attempted, you need to consider them all and choose those you want to integrate into a personalized relaxation program.

Assignment
- Review the approaches practiced. Develop a relaxation program using those that appear to be most effective on the basis of Worksheet 2.
- Read Lesson 15.
- Do Worksheet 19.

The 2-Week Training Program

This severely shortened and condensed program should be attempted only when a more extended program is not possible and when professional supervision is available.

**Week 1: Orientation, Grand Tour, Review of
All Approaches, and Selection of Approach(es)**

Objectives
The objectives for this week are to become acquainted with Relaxation Dynamics and the nine world approaches to self-relaxation, choose one or two approaches, and practice them.

Assignment Before Day 1
- Read all of Lessons 1-5 (and preferably all of Section I).

Assignment for Day 1
- Play the Grand Tour tape (Tape 1, Side A).

- With the instructor, choose one or two approaches to practice. Regardless of which are chosen, they should be preceded by the Preparatory Breathing sequence (pages 68–69).

Assignment for Days 2–7
- Read the lesson(s) corresponding to the chosen approach(es).
- Practice your selection at least once each day. If you chose two approaches, alternate your practice between them.

Week 2: Review and Fine-Tuning of Selected Approach(es)

Objective

During this week you will consider your practice experiences and decide how you might alter or combine the exercises you have learned.

Assignment
- Appraise the approach(es) you have tried by asking yourself these questions:

Which exercises did I like best?

Which exercises would I consider dropping?

Which exercises could I combine?

Then revise your relaxation sequence accordingly.

- Practice your revised relaxation sequence at least once each day.

Teaching Relaxation to Others

Relaxation is best taught by qualified health professionals. (Those who are not trained professionals should not attempt teaching others for the reasons given in Section I, Lesson 3.) In teaching self-relaxation, numerous formats are possible. However, a good relaxation program should have at least two components: (1) a *training phase,* in which specific exercises are taught and student preferences determined; (2) a *mastery phase,* in which the student continues practicing and masters the selected exercises in depth. (The training programs listed in the preceding section include outlines *only* for the training phase.)

Training Phase

Preliminary assessment. A number of preliminary questions should be answered before a decision to teach self-relaxation is made. Does the prospective student have any medical conditions that could interfere with training (see Section I, Lesson 3)? If self-relaxation is to be used clinically, is it appropriate for this client's problems? This second question is beyond the scope of this book. When used clinically, self-relaxation should be a component of a more encompassing approach. Thus, the appropriateness of self-relaxation is mainly a function of the appropriateness of the general clinical strategy it is part of (classical desensitization, stress inoculation training, etc.).

Introduction and rationale. Self-relaxation should be clearly and honestly explained before taught. An effective introduction and rationale can foster motivation to practice and sensitize the student to the effects of specific exercises. Particular care should be taken not to encourage unrealistic hopes and expectations.

It also is important to discuss the student's existing understandings of the techniques to be taught. Many students have serious misconceptions concerning the nature of relaxation training. Some may have had unfortunate experiences with various popular relaxation-based programs or with inept or inexperienced trainers. It is important to identify how Relaxation Dynamics differs from what the student might be expecting.

In addition, the rationale presented should be consistent with the student's beliefs and values. For example, for a religious student, self-relaxation can be presented as a spiritual exercise. For some, an emphasis on empirical research is more appropriate. Relaxation can also be taught as a tool for "consciousness expansion" or self-exploration. The instructor should be sensitive to what interests the student and tailor the rationale accordingly.

Initial instruction. For any approach, instruction should begin with an explanation of the specific exercises to be taught, followed by demonstration and modeling of each one. Each exercise should be attempted with the student (or the student's practice should be observed). Following this, there should be an assessment of the success of the exercise, leading to a decision to either revise the practiced exercise or continue with the next one. For example, an instructor might begin isometric squeeze relaxation by explaining, demonstrating, and modeling the right hand squeeze. Here is a transcript of such a training session.

> In this sequence we will be doing 11 squeeze exercises. First, let me demonstrate the hand squeeze. I focus my attention on my right hand. I now make a tight fist. I squeeze the fingers together in a way that feels pleasurable and complete. I let the tension build completely while keeping·the rest of my body relaxed. I notice the tension . . . and **let go.** I let myself relax. I let the tension go. I focus on my hand as it begins to relax

more and more. I attend to the good feelings as the momentum of relaxation begins to carry the tension away.

Now, let's try this same exercise together. Focus your attention on your right hand. Make a fist **now**. Squeeze the fingers together in whatever way feels most pleasurable and complete. Let the tension build completely. Notice the tension . . . and **let go.** Let yourself relax. Let the tension go. Focus on your hand as it begins to relax more and more. Attend to the good feelings as the momentum of relaxation begins to carry the tension away.

How did that go? Could you feel the tension build? Did you notice the difference between tension and relaxation? How did it feel to let go of your tension?

In this example, if the student had had difficulty or had been unable to relax, the exercise would have been repeated, revised according to the rules presented in Relaxation Dynamics, or omitted as the instructor moved on to the next exercise. The student should be given positive feedback ("good") if the exercise is successful.

Dress rehearsal. After all exercises in a sequence have been demonstrated and the student knows each exercise, the entire sequence should be attempted without interruption. Instructions are either presented orally by the instructor as the student practices, or played from a tape for both instructor and student. It can be very useful for the student to make a home-practice tape during this session.

At the end of this dress rehearsal, the student should again be asked if there were any difficulties and the success of each specific exercise should be assessed. This is the time for any last-minute alterations. Once again, a successful session should end with appropriate reinforcement.

Daily practice. The student is ready to practice the sequence of exercises at home in accordance with the guidelines presented in this book. If practice logs and other worksheets from the Appendix are to be used, they should be distributed and explained.

Follow-up. The instructor and student should meet for further training no more than 1 week after dress rehearsal. The effects of the approach practiced at home should be discussed.

Mastery Phase

Once the student has completed a training program and selected a sequence of preferred exercises, the mastery phase of instruction can begin. The student should meet with the instructor once a week and practice the selected sequence. If problems concerning practice arose during the week, they should be addressed. The instructor should assess the level of relaxation attained, determine if any revisions or additions are needed, and reinforce the student for any progress made.

The objective of this phase of training is for the student to attain a level of proficiency at self-relaxation appropriate to the overall goals of the training program. For example, if self-relaxation were being taught as a component of classical desensitization, it would be desirable for the student to learn to relax deeply and quickly even when faced with potentially threatening stimuli. To achieve this degree of proficiency, up to 10 weeks of practice might be required. In contrast, if self-relaxation were being taught for nonclinical purposes (for example, as preparation for study, work, or sports, or as a way of resting at the end of the day), a lesser degree of mastery might be required. Often only 5 weeks of practice are sufficient. However, if no time is devoted to posttraining mastery practice, it cannot be assumed that the student has mastered self-relaxation. At best, the student will have received an introduction to relaxation.

Chapter 2

Research and Relaxation Training

Relaxation literature gives an abundance of advice on the benefits and shortcomings of different types of relaxation training—perhaps too much. Research on relaxation exercises is still in its infancy and it is premature to make empirically based prescriptions. However, this book would be incomplete without at least mentioning the speculations, hypotheses, and preliminary findings of seasoned clinicians and scientists. In this chapter four general topics will be considered:

Selecting an Approach

Understanding Distraction and the Process of Relaxation

Dealing with Common Sources of Disruption in Relaxation

Assessing Progress

The chapter will conclude with a developmental model of relaxation.

If you are a student of relaxation, you might want to test some of these ideas out on yourself. If you are a professional scientist, the following ideas provide fertile ground for research.

Selecting an Approach

Single Technique vs. Multi-Technique Programs

One of the first decisions that has to be made when setting up a program is whether to focus exclusively on one technique to relaxation or to master several and develop a personalized approach. It might be argued that the traditional strategy of focusing on just one or two techniques maximizes the degree of mastery of relaxation skills. However, in my opinion, multi-technique programs can be mastered equally well when sufficient time is devoted to the training and mastery phases. In addition, there are numerous advantages to multi-technique programs. First, the student is provided with a wide range of choices, maximizing the possibility that satisfying and effective techniques will be found. Second, although the student may not fully master all techniques, it is highly likely a few will be mastered in a short time. These may well become part of a personalized relaxation program. Third, although the student changes techniques from week to week, basic self-relaxation skills are still being developed. The student acquires greater proficiency at attending to a simple, internal stimulus while maintaining a stance of passivity and receptivity. These skills, perhaps more than proficiency at a specific technique, are what self-relaxation is all about. Further, I believe the ability to relax is more likely to generalize outside the training setting if a variety of strategies is attempted. Fourth, exposure to many techniques makes self-relaxation an interesting adventure rather than a health chore. Motivation and involvement are enhanced, and students are less likely to drop out or practice irregularly. In my clinical experience, the dropout rate for multi-technique training is roughly half that for single-technique training. Fifth, at the end of training, the student chooses the techniques to be mastered. Thus the element of choice and self-control, which may be a therapeutic component central to all self-relaxation, is maximized in the Relaxation Dynamics multi-technique program.

Although multi-technique training appears to be more effective than single-technique, there are at times legitimate reasons for teaching only one or two techniques. There may not be enough time for more than one or two, or the student may have a strong initial interest in one technique or another. Single techniques also can be taught with Relaxation Dynamics, as each technique has a corresponding lesson.

Appropriateness of Relaxation for Presenting Problem

Before an approach to relaxation is selected, it is important to consider if relaxation or a relaxation-based treatment is even appropriate. Numerous clinical treatments, both insight-oriented and behavioral, do make use of various forms of relaxation training; however, such clinical decisions should be left to qualified health professionals.

Often students learn self-relaxation in hopes of finding a way of dealing with depression, anger, low self-esteem, lack of assertiveness, shyness, loneliness, or other problems. Relaxation training may be helpful to a few people with these problems, but when presented alone, it is not the treatment of choice for such problems.

Absence of Physical Limitations

Relaxation exercises should be selected on the basis of what the student is capable of doing safely and comfortably. Recent surgery, certain physical deformities, and injury to the skin, skeletal muscles, bones, or ligaments can limit the practice of physical exercises. If necessary, it might be useful to attempt abbreviated versions of some physical exercises, deleting those specific ones that may pose some risk.

Absence of Negative History With Relaxation Training

It can be useful to ask about previous experiences a student may have had with relaxation exercises before teaching relaxation. At times students report adverse experiences, often concerning techniques taught in quasi-religious cults or by inept professionals. Meditative and imagery-based approaches often pose the greatest problem. A negative history with specific relaxation approaches can interfere with training, particularly if similar approaches are to be taught. Potentially troublesome techniques may be omitted if it appears they may generate adverse associations. At the very least, the Relaxation Dynamics approach should be differentiated from others that may have been encountered.

Familiarity Hypothesis

In my experience, students are more likely to stay with and benefit from approaches that resemble activities familiar to them. Often students who have had positive experiences with meditation or yoga prefer trying similar approaches in Relaxation Dynamics. Similarly, students who enjoy lifting weights often like isometric squeeze relaxation; dancers, yogaform stretching; professional singers, integrative breathing; and artists, imagery, contemplation, or meditation.

Locus of Control Hypothesis

Locus of control (Lefcourt, 1976; Rotter, 1966) refers to the generalized beliefs people have concerning the source of life's fortunes and misfortunes. Individuals characterized as having an *internal locus of control* generally believe they are the masters of their fate and can have considerable impact on how things go for them. Those with an *external locus of control* believe their lives are generally influenced by outside factors such as fate, God, or society.

It might be expected that those with an external locus of control would respond better to forms of relaxation that involve considerable externally imposeu structure, attention to external stimuli, and external instructions, while those with an internal locus of control would respond better to internal structure, stimuli, and instructions. However, the evidence for this proposition is somewhat mixed. Beiman, Johnson, Puente, Majestic, and Graham (1984) found, as expected, that those with an internal locus of control respond better to transcendental meditation, an internally focused approach. In contrast, Curtis (1984) found locus of control does not predict either continuation or success with clinically standardized meditation. Di Nardo and Raymond (1979) offer what is perhaps the clearest evidence for the locus of control hypothesis. They found that internals have more successful and less distracted meditation sessions than do externals. Furthermore, externals do better when asked to direct attention externally to a candle flame than internally to an imagined image of a candle flame.

It seems likely that people with an external locus of control find themselves less able to attend to an internal focal stimulus and more distracted by intrusive thoughts. As a result, they are more likely to discontinue an internally focused technique.

Cognitive-Somatic Specific Effects Hypothesis

Davidson and Schwartz (1976) have proposed that cognitive relaxation treatments should work best for cognitive symptoms such as excessive worry, physical treatments for physical symptoms, and so on. As we have seen, physical exercises have a significant cognitive component to the extent that they involve the skills of focusing, passivity, and receptivity. And cognitive techniques such as somatic focusing and meditation can incorporate physical relaxation strategies (deep breathing, isometric "letting go," etc.). For this reason, the cognitive-somatic hypothesis may have limited value (Carrington, 1984; Lehrer & Woolfolk, 1984). Indeed, Schwartz, Davidson, and Goleman (1978) have since revised the specificity hypothesis and have stated that the specific effects of various relaxation techniques may be superimposed on a general relaxation response elicited by most approaches to relaxation training.

It does seem true that somatic symptoms may interfere with internal, passive, and cognitive approaches to relaxation. As a person's attention is directed inward, it is perhaps more likely that that person will detect and become preoccupied with somatic symptoms. Rivers and Spanos (1981) found that subjects with more psychosomatic complaints tend to drop out of meditation. Similarly, Curtis (1984) found that beginning meditators who are initially high on somatic anxiety are most likely to experience intruding thoughts during meditation and practice less or drop out.

First-Order Physical Symptom Specificity Hypothesis

Clinicians frequently apply relaxation exercises on the basis of specific muscle groups, organ systems, or symptom content (Lehrer & Woolfolk, 1984), that is, on what Smith and his students (Smith & Seidel, 1982; Smith & Siebert, 1984) have termed *first-order physical symptoms.* If this idea were followed, a person with tense shoulder muscles would do best with an isometric shoulder exercise, irregular breathers with breathing exercises, and so on. Such specificity is based on the assumptions that physical stress symptoms do not form a general somatic factor, but are independent, and that different exercises work for different symptoms. Research is currently testing both hypotheses.

Second-Order Physical Symptom Specificity Hypothesis

Smith and Siebert (1984), starting with research that examined 1,500 physical stress symptoms, found that most symptoms define four second-order factors: Factor I, the Complex Stress Arousal Pattern (diffuse autonomic and skeletal arousal with a significant cognitive component); Factor II, the Indirect Stress Symptom Pattern (delayed and indirect symptoms such as fatigue, headaches, backaches, and skin problems); Factor III, the Simple Stress Arousal Pattern (a simple manifestation of the "fight-or-flight" response); and Factor IV, Gastric Distress. These same researchers have proposed that self-relaxation techniques should be particularly effective for Factor III reactions and less effective for the remaining reaction patterns.

Somatic Focusing and the Autonomic Specificity Hypothesis

It has been claimed that the content of somatic imagery has a specific impact on the targeted organ system. Thus, thinking "hands are warm and heavy" or "heartbeat is slow and regular" should result in changes in blood flow to the hands and a slower and more regular heartbeat (Luthe, 1963, 1977). Likewise, imagery of active and effective sensitized lymphocytes has been argued to improve the response of the immune system to cancer (Simonton, Matthews-Simonton, & Creighton, 1978). Evidence for such extreme versions of the autonomic specificity hypothesis is weak.

Hierarchy of Relaxation Techniques

Some claim that all relaxation techniques are functionally equivalent, that they all produce the same relaxation response (Benson, 1975). Others argue that different techniques have different effects. Ironically, the most frequently applied specificity hypothesis is the one least frequently acknowledged. It is that different approaches to relaxation form a hierarchy in terms of difficulty, and that easy techniques prepare the user for those that are more difficult. Put differently, those best suited for advanced approaches are those who have mastered the more basic approaches. This notion has been stated most explicitly in yogic tradition, unfortunately with considerable religious and ritualistic excess baggage. In yoga the student usually is taught stretching first, then breathing, then centered focus meditation, and then (if at all) open focus meditation. Similarly, the student of Zen is taught centered focus meditation before open focus meditation. Usually without explaining why, Western relaxation programs that combine techniques utilize a similar sequence. Table 2 summarizes the sequence of approaches emphasized by several popular Eastern and Western systems (approaches that are included in the method but not emphasized have been omitted).

Careful examination of this table reveals that in almost every case relaxation exercises are presented in an order consistent with the order of presentation in this book. Isometric squeeze relaxation, when it is taught, is taught first. Meditation is taught last. Imagery, both thematic and somatic, is presented in the middle of training. Western instructors rarely, if ever, provide a rationale for their ordering of techniques. At most they suggest that physical exercises can prepare students for meditation by reducing potentially distracting somatic anxiety (Davidson & Schwartz, 1984). However, the pattern presented in the table suggests that the order is not completely random. Seasoned relaxation instructors probably have an unstated sense of which techniques are easy and difficult.

Let me venture two hypotheses concerning the proper ordering of techniques: (1) the approaches presented in Relaxation Dynamics define a hierarchy in terms of required attentional focus, passivity, and receptivity; (2) exercises presented early in the hierarchy prepare the student for those presented later. These hypotheses imply that approaches near the top of the hierarchy (contemplation and meditation) are relatively difficult and perhaps should not be taught to beginners. They also imply that exercises lower in the hierarchy should be taught first in a relaxation program. If a student does not succeed at one level of the hierarchy, it is reasonable to try an easier approach. Those who don't enjoy yoga might try isometric squeeze relaxation; those who find thematic imagery frustrating might try integrative breathing.

Table 2
Exercise Sequences of
Popular Approaches to Self-Relaxation*

Autogenic Training (Luthe, 1977)
Somatic Focusing (Beginning Exercises)
Somatic Focusing (Advanced Exercises)
Thematic Imagery
Centered Focus Meditation (unclear if actually represented)

Benson's Meditation Method (Benson, 1975)
Somatic Focusing (Beginning Exercises)
Integrative Breathing
Centered Focus Meditation

Progressive Relaxation (Bernstein & Borkovec, 1973)
Isometric Squeeze Relaxation
Somatic Focusing (Beginning Exercises)

Progressive Relaxation (Rosen, 1977)
Isometric Squeeze Relaxation
Thematic Imagery

Quieting Reflex Training (Stroebel, 1983)
Integrative Breathing
Isometric Squeeze Relaxation
Somatic Focusing (Beginning Exercises)
Somatic Focusing (Advanced Exercises)
Thematic Imagery

Relaxation Training Program (Budzynski, 1974)
Isometric Squeeze Relaxation
Integrative Breathing
Somatic Focusing (Beginning Exercises)
Thematic Imagery

Relaxation Training Sequence (Charlesworth & Nathan, 1982)
Isometric Squeeze Relaxation
Integrative Breathing
Somatic Focusing (Beginning Exercises)
Somatic Focusing (Advanced Exercises)
Thematic Imagery

Yoga (Iyengar, 1965; Rama et al., 1976)
Yogaform Stretching
Integrative Breathing
Centered Focus Meditation

Yoga Therapy (Patel, 1984)
Integrative Breathing
Somatic Focusing (Beginning Exercises)
Centered Focus Meditation

Zen Meditation Training (Kapleau, 1965)
Integrative Breathing
Centered Focus Meditation
Open Focus Meditation

---

*Exercise sequences are listed in terms of the specific Relaxation Dynamics approach represented. For example, the instructions for what Luthe has termed "autogenic meditation" correspond to what I have termed "thematic imagery." Similarly, the first phase of Benson's meditation method involves attending to skeletal muscle groups and mentally releasing any tension that may be present. I have termed this "mental isometric relaxation," one of the beginning somatic focusing exercises.

245

Skills of Focusing, Passivity, and
Receptivity as Predictors of Outcome

A corollary of the preceding hypotheses is that the skills of focusing, passivity, and receptivity should be most predictive of outcome for exercises high on the hierarchy (meditation and contemplation) and least predictive for exercises low on the hierarchy (isometric squeeze relaxation and yogaform stretching). Once again, *focusing* refers to the ability to attend to simple stimuli for an extended period of time, *passivity* is the ability to stop unnecessary goal-directed or analytic activity, and *receptivity* is the ability to tolerate new and unfamiliar experiences. Operationally, focusing would appear to be tapped by such measures as the Tellegen Absorption Scale, particularly the factors of Reality and Fantasy Absorption (Tellegen & Atkinson, 1974), the Van Nuys (1971) Intrusion measure, and the Sizothymia or Factor A scale on the Sixteen Personality Factor Questionnaire (16 PF) (Cattell, Eber, & Tatsouka, 1970). As would be expected, preliminary research suggests a relationship between these measures and success in meditation (Davidson, Goleman, & Schwartz, 1976; Smith, 1978; Van Nuys, 1973). Individuals displaying little skill at focusing probably would do better at isometric or yogaform relaxation. Passivity would appear to be the opposite of Type A coronary-prone behavior (Friedman & Rosenman, 1974), particularly the propensity toward hypercontrol identified by Glass (1977), and possibly behavior displayed by obsessive-compulsives. Thus, those with Type A behavior and obsessive-compulsive individuals might well have the most trouble with meditation and the easiest time with isometric squeeze relaxation. Finally, receptivity to new and unfamiliar experiences appears to be central to Autia or Factor M on the 16 PF, Absorption (the Openness to Experiences as well as the Devotion and Trust dimensions of the Tellegen Absorption Scale), skill at "focusing" as defined by Gendlin, and creativity. The converse of such openness is anxiety concerning such experiences. And again, each of these variables has been tentatively linked with outcomes in meditation. Individuals scoring low on such dimensions would probably once again do better with more physical exercises.

Understanding Distraction and the
Process of Relaxation

Students at all levels of relaxation training report a wide range of distracting experiences, including somatic sensations, changes in perception, vivid emotions, thoughts, and images. Most schools of relaxation training make much of such distractions. Teachers of autogenic training have referred to them as *autogenic discharges* (Luthe, 1977). In hypnosis they have been described as *abreactive* or *uncovering reactions* (Reyher, 1964). In transcendental meditation they have been viewed as signs of *unstressing, normalization,* and *stress release* (Kanellakos & Lukas, 1974). Carrington (1977, 1978) has described them as *tension-release side effects.* A common theme is that the body somehow effortlessly and automatically relieves itself of sources of tension, and indeed pathology, during relaxation. However, such conceptualizations of distraction often lack precision and at times border on the mystical.

To understand distraction, it is important to understand how relaxation works. In the most general terms, the process of relaxation is cyclical, with alternating phases of decreased and increased physical and cognitive arousal. In terms of the constructs used in this book, the relaxer experiences an "inward stroke" of increased focus of attention, passivity, and receptivity followed by an "outward stroke" of diverted attention, greater effort and activity, and reduced receptivity. The inward and outward strokes of this cycle must both occur for relaxation to deepen. Increased focus of attention, passivity, and receptivity unearth new sources of distraction. New distractions present the student with an opportunity to acquire even greater proficiency at maintaining focused attention, passivity, and receptivity. Part of the "work" of self-relaxation is learning to deal with distraction by refocusing on the relaxation task while maintaining a stance of passivity and receptivity. Let's first examine the processes that contribute to the inward stroke of relaxation.

Processes Contributing to the Deepening of Relaxation: The "Inward Stroke"

Selective attention. By simply diverting attention from outside stimuli and tasks, as well as thought and worry, the relaxer removes an important source of distraction and arousal. He is simply less likely to think about stimuli that do not occupy the center of attention (Ellis, 1984).

Deliberate reductions in muscular activity. We have seen that a number of deliberate physical activities directly contribute to relaxation. These include ceasing physical activity, tensing and letting go, stretching, and deliberately breathing in a slow, full, and even manner. As muscles relax, less proprioceptive stimulation reaches the brain. Cognitive activity is less likely to be aroused. The mind becomes more relaxed. Similarly, as cognitive activity decreases, cortical stimulation to the rest of the body is reduced, further enhancing physical relaxation.

Desensitization. Distractions once associated with tension and excitement eventually become linked with relaxation and are less likely to be disruptive (Goleman, 1977). This process is most likely to work for minor disruptions rather than major emotional problems (Shapiro, 1980). For example, thoughts like "I need to wash the car" or "I really like my new dress" might ordinarily be experienced with a degree of upset or excitement. However, when they emerge again and again in the calm of the relaxation setting, they lose their emotional charge and become neutral thoughts that come and go.

Extinction. Behavior that is rewarded is likely to persist. Behavior that is ignored or not reinforced tends to cease or *extinguish*. Distractions that are effortfully pursued during relaxation are rewarded through the attention they receive. However, returning to the task of relaxation deprives distracting thoughts of attention. Eventually, through simple extinction, they are less likely to occur, deepening relaxation (Heide & Borkovec, 1984).

Habituation. The brain tends to cease to react to stimuli appraised as unimportant, continuous, and unchanging. This phenomenon is called *habituation* and it explains why we tune out the constant drone of air conditioners, passing trains, and a variety of sources of discomfort. The distractions facing the student of relaxation are often of trivial importance, continuous, and unchanging. As long as the student does not interrupt the session and change the environment, reactions to such distracting stimuli usually habituate.

Ornstein (1972) has proposed that deeper forms of relaxation may be associated with more pervasive forms of habituation. Relaxation may contribute to a "shutting down" or restful deactivation of parts of the brain likely to be associated with distracting analytic and discursive thought. He takes as an analogy the experience of "blank-out" reported in certain perception experiments in which attention is restricted to a continuous, unchanging stimulus. For example, by placing halved ping-pong balls over the eyes, an unchanging visual field can be created. All that is seen is white, like a snowstorm in Antarctica. When this occurs there may be a prolonged burst of alpha activity in the brain and a radical reduction of discursive, analytic (left-hemisphere) thought. Similarly, the focus of attention during relaxation is on a relatively restricted stimulus, perhaps also establishing a relatively unchanging stimulus field and thus decreasing cognitive activity and increasing relaxation.

Relaxation-enhancing appraisal processes. Relaxation is enhanced when the relaxation task as well as potentially disruptive stimuli are relabeled in a manner consistent with focusing, passivity, and receptivity. The following examples illustrate how such appraisals often underlie all of the deepening processes mentioned so far.

A student of relaxation has trouble starting a practice session. She finds herself thinking, "Do I really want to learn how to relax? How important is it to me?" After a few seconds of thought, she concludes, "I have decided to learn this important skill. I want very much to control my hypertension without relying so heavily on medication. Also, I think there are some very important insights I can gain through relaxation." This reappraisal enables her to begin the session motivated to master the skills of focusing, passivity, and receptivity.

While practicing, she is disrupted by the thought "I want a hamburger." She appraises this thought as unimportant or a thought that can be tended to after the relaxation session, and easily selectively attends to the task of relaxation.

She notices she is tapping her foot, and that this restless act is distracting. The appraisal "It's OK to let go and simply be quiet during relaxation" facilitates reductions in muscular activity.

While relaxing, an urgent thought repeatedly comes to mind: "I forgot to dust today, the apartment looks a mess." She relabels the situation—"The apartment may be a bit dusty, but it's not the end of the world"—and thereby removes some of its emotional charge. She has contributed to the process of desensitization.

Similarly, she repeatedly has the urge to terminate the session and check the mail. By thinking "No, I will not reward this urge by giving in to it now," she facilitates the process of extinction.

Finally, she notices the constant drone of the air conditioner in the background. By thinking "Oh, this is nothing new, just the same old sound from the air conditioner," she appraises the stimulus as a constant and contributes to habituation.

Processes Contributing to Distraction in Relaxation: The "Outward Stroke"

At every level of relaxation distractions can emerge. Indeed, many of the very processes that contribute to relaxation eventually contribute to distraction.

External stimuli and demands. Obviously the environment can be a source of considerable distraction. However, the demand characteristics of a relaxation setting form a more subtle source of distraction. For example, a setting richly appointed with mysterious and esoteric trappings may well evoke bizarre and intense imagery. A setting defined as "hypnotic" or "religious" may stir a variety of related distracting associations.

Physiological processes. Six physiological processes, many associated with relaxation, can also be a source of distraction.

1. The physical effort associated with tensing, letting go, and stretching can lead to muscular discomfort and even cramps. The effort of deliberate deep breathing can make inhalation and exhalation a self-conscious and labored exercise.

2. Skeletal muscle relaxation can trigger spontaneous muscular-skeletal events such as tics, twitches, spasms, and jerks.

3. Increased oxygenation associated with some stretching and breathing exercises can contribute to mild symptoms of hyperventilation (feeling dizzy, faint, etc.).

4. The shift to parasympathetic dominance associated with relaxation can be accompanied by vasodilation in the extremities (feelings of warmth, heaviness, and tingling), decreased heart rate, and palmar perspiration.

5. Paradoxical and brief increments in central and sympathetic nervous system activity (Shapiro, 1980) may be associated with temporary arousal symptoms (sweaty hands, quickened breathing, racing heart, intense emotional states, racing thoughts).

6. The postulated reduction of left-hemisphere dominance (Ornstein, 1972) may be associated with an increase in right-hemisphere activity (visual and auditory imagery, changes in body image, vivid and emotional recollections, nonverbal insight).

Attentional processes. The restriction of attention and associated reduction in distracting cognitive and physical arousal can lead to the detection of new sources of distraction. By directing attention inward, the relaxer is more likely to notice stimuli previously missed. New sources of discomfort may be discovered. In addition, reduced arousal may contribute to increased awareness and sensitivity, enhancing the distracting potential of stimuli that are detected.

Associations to relaxation. The state of relaxation can stir a rich variety of associations. Sleep, reverie, and sexual expression are often linked with relaxation in everyday life. It is not surprising that the student of relaxation often encounters drowsiness, daydreaming, and feelings of sexual arousal while practicing a relaxation exercise. Similarly, stimuli that accompany relaxation may resemble stimuli linked with other experiences (exhaustion, drug experiences, alcohol intoxication, illness) and trigger related associations.

Stress appraisal processes. Stress is experienced when one appraises (1) a situation as a threat to well-being, and (2) external and internal coping resources to be unavailable or ineffective (Lazarus & Folkman, 1984). Any of the previously mentioned sources of distraction can be appraised this way and become a source of distracting stress arousal and worry. Somatic signs of parasympathetic dominance can be labeled as "strange" or as symptoms of underlying illness. Relaxation experiences may be taken as signs of "going crazy" or "dying." Even the act of directing attention inward can be viewed as a threatening confrontation with negatively appraised personal thoughts or feelings (frightening and embarrassing memories, unwanted impulses, etc.).

In addition, relaxation-related experiences may be upsetting when they are felt to threaten beliefs of being effective and in control, of having the resources to cope. According to some (Heide & Borkovec, 1984), such appraisals form an important component of relaxation-induced stress and anxiety. To an extent, popular culture reinforces the link between relaxation and helplessness. The hypnotist is all too often seen as completely controlling the client. Mystical states linked with yoga and Zen are sometimes casually associated with drug-related and even psychotic states. At a more mundane level, society often tells us that desired ends are achieved through active effort. Relaxation is at best a reward for working hard or a way of preparing for future efforts. At worst, it signifies laziness, self-indulgence, weakness, or a lack of will power. But it is an error to equate relaxation with helplessness. The person capable of achieving a state of relaxed passivity is displaying what is perhaps a higher level of control. And such a person always has the choice of terminating relaxation. The relaxer is very much in control.

Lazarus and Folkman (1984) have identified a third level of stress appraisal. The stressed individual can *reappraise* initial assessments of threat and helplessness. Such *tertiary appraisal* can lead to a reassessment of a formerly stressful situation as benign. However, it can also compound the experience of stress if the reassessment is negative. The relaxer may well display an "aversion to the experience of anxiety" (Heide & Borkovec, 1984), a fear of feeling anxious during relaxation. Put differently, the experience of relaxation-induced stress and anxiety can itself be viewed as a threat ("Oh no! I'm so anxious I must be crazy!") and a sign of helplessness ("I'm afraid I won't be able to calm myself down, I might be overwhelmed by my anxiety!").

Dealing with Common Sources of Disruption in Relaxation

Distraction and disruption are often an important part of relaxation, possibly contributing to the development of basic relaxation skills. However, at times disruption requires special attention. Here are some suggestions on how some of the problems can be dealt with.

Problems with external distractions. Students may complain that it is difficult to practice because of external distractions. Since relaxation can increase sensitivity to external stimuli, a degree of distraction should be expected. Indeed, as suggested earlier, part of the "work" of relaxation involves practice at putting distraction aside and returning to the relaxation task. However, if concerns about distraction continue, it might be useful to reexamine the relaxation setting. (Is the place as quiet as possible? Has the student selected a time in which other concerns might be pressing?) Often it is useful to review the points made in Lesson 6 (Learning to Set Time Aside for Rest).

Distracting muscular-skeletal events. Students often experience a variety of manifestations of muscle tension, including cramps, twitches, myoclonic jerks, tics, spasms, and restless movement. Such problems are more frequently associated with physical exercises, that is, isometric relaxation, yogaform stretching, and integrative breathing, than mental exercises.

A disruptive form of muscle tension is the cramp. A cramped muscle should be left alone and not tensed or stretched again until the cramp goes away. The instructor should show sensitivity and concern, but not a sense of urgency, as excessive concern can increase the student's anxiety and prolong the problem. Most students discover effective ways of dealing with cramps on their own. If the problem does not go away in a few minutes, the instructor can suggest that the student gently massage the muscle. Above all, the instructor should reassure the student and calmly advise him to "take your time . . . the problem should go away in a few minutes."

Breathing-related difficulties. Some students report problems associated with respiration. Such problems are more likely to occur with integrative breathing than with other approaches. Breathing can feel labored or uncomfortable. Students occasionally experience a conflict between the need to control inhalation and exhalation and the need to relax. When this occurs, breathing exercises are best omitted. An alternative is to avoid making breathing the center of attention (as is the case in integrative breathing) by weaving breathing-related exercises as secondary and incidental suggestions into other approaches ("focus your attention on squeezing your shoulder muscles together, then let go as you breathe out and relax... let tension dissolve as your breathing becomes more even"). Stretching exercises that automatically affect respiration (RD 24, 25, 26, and 27) can be performed without mentioning breathing. Finally, imagery highly suggestive of calm, even, full, and slow breathing might be suggested ("Picture the waves of the ocean, slowly splashing against the shore, carrying away the tensions of the day"). Such imagery can be particularly effective when done in pace with the instructor's own breathing (slowly breathe out while saying "slowly splashing against the shore").

At times students may feel dizzy, faint, or lightheaded while practicing breathing-related exercises. Here it is usually sufficient to shorten exercises and recommend that they be performed less vigorously.

Drowsiness. A number of students may report feeling drowsy while practicing. Some may actually fall asleep. Such experiences usually are normal and probably indicate a physiological need for sleep. If drowsiness occurs in spite of a lack of need for sleep, a number of other factors should be checked. Is the student practicing in bed or in a place associated with sleep? Is the student practicing right after eating? Is the practice site adequately ventilated? On occasion drowsiness can be a symptom of stress, or underlying emotional or physical pathology. In such cases professional guidance should be sought.

Frequently drowsiness occurs because of the association many students have made between relaxation and sleep. Indeed, some have experienced relaxation only while going to sleep. For such individuals, an important initial goal of relaxation training is learning to differentiate sleepiness from relaxation. It is important not to reinforce the failure to differentiate the two by permitting the student to sleep during a relaxation period. It is better to treat feelings of drowsiness as minor distractions or, if the feelings persist, to leave the relaxation site and take a nap.

Mild relaxation-related experiences. Many students are simply unfamiliar with experiences associated with deliberate physical relaxation, maintenance of attentional focus, and passivity. They may report sensations of floating, sinking, heaviness, warmth, coolness, increased clarity of perception, increased body awareness, and all of the experiences noted in the Checklist of Rest-Related States (Appendix, Worksheet 1). It can be useful to reassure students that such experiences are normal and often indicate that relaxation is taking place. However, such experiences should not be described as a goal of relaxation training; in fact, they are often distractions. A person can be deeply relaxed without such experiences. If a student is unable to tolerate a relaxation-related experience, the instructor should consider the suggestions that are offered in later sections on conflicts over relinquishing control and relaxation-induced anxiety.

Vivid relaxation-related experiences. Some relaxation-related experiences can be fairly dramatic. These include body sensations of growing, shrinking, moving, and leaving one's body; dramatic increases or decreases in sensitivity to outside stimuli; and vivid memories, emotional states, and imagery. Once again, students should be reassured that such experiences usually are normal indices of relaxation, but should not be pursued. If the experiences are too disruptive, the suggestions concerning conflicts over control and relaxation-induced anxiety should be considered.

"Paranormal" experiences. Not infrequently students of relaxation report a wide range of "paranormal" experiences, including seeing into the past or future, reading thoughts, and perceiving stimuli at great distances. A few students believe very deeply in the validity of such experiences; others find them perplexing or upsetting. On occasion, such experiences can indicate underlying pathology. Generally it is useful to avoid either reinforcing or challenging such experiences. In the context of relaxation training, the experience of the paranormal has the same status as other distractions, whether they be sexual fantasies, worry about work, or the desire for a hot dog. Distractions provide the student with an opportunity to further develop skill at focusing attention while maintaining a stance of passivity and receptivity.

Conflicts over relinquishing control. The experience of relaxation can be threatening to those who feel a need to maintain active control over their environment. The sense of "letting go" can be uncomfortable and at times even frightening. Fears can range from "I might be too relaxed to go back to work after relaxation" to "I'm afraid of going crazy" or "I might die." Psychological reasons for such conflicts may well be complex. The instructor should take care to determine if these fears are indicative of emotional problems that might require professional attention. It can be helpful to remind the student that she is always in control and can stop an exercise whenever desired. Also, the student might be reminded that it is she, not a tape recorder or instructor, who is producing the experience of relaxation. The more active and familiar exercises (isometric squeeze, yogaform stretching, thematic imagery) are somewhat less likely to trigger fears of loss of control. If it appears desirable to continue an exercise in spite of such fears, the exercise can be shortened, made more complex and active, or practiced with the eyes partially open (directed toward the ground 3 or 4 feet ahead). Students might try practicing with others or with soothing background music.

Relaxation-induced anxiety. Virtually every form of relaxation has been claimed to have the potential for generating anxiety (Heide & Borkovec, 1984). Researchers have said that physical relaxation, particularly progressive relaxation (Lehrer & Woolfolk, 1984), is less likely to have this impact. For instance, it has been suggested (Lehrer & Woolfolk, 1984) that if relaxation-produced anxiety becomes troublesome for a student of cognitive relaxation, progressive relaxation (isometric squeeze relaxation) can be attempted as a substitute.

We have seen that relaxation-induced anxiety may be due to conflicts over relinquishing control or a number of other factors. If any of the previously mentioned factors appears to be the cause, the instructor need only treat the anxiety as yet another relaxation-related experience, and so reassure the student. It can be useful to emphasize that the student remains in control even while relaxing. And, as with the student experiencing conflicts over control, it can be useful to substitute a more active and familiar exercise, shorten the practice session, make the exercise more complex and active, or recommend practicing with eyes open, with others, or while playing soothing background music.

However, those who teach imagery, autogenic training, and meditation (Carrington, 1977; Luthe, 1977; Reyher, 1964) warn that relaxation-produced anxiety may be symptomatic of underlying pathology or conflict. It has been argued that relaxation training can temporarily ease defenses against such internal threats. Indeed, cognitive relaxation techniques are at times used in therapy to unearth hidden problems. If there is any suspicion that anxiety is more than a temporary discomfort with an unfamiliar technique, psychotherapeutic intervention should be considered.

Relaxation as avoidance. Some students use relaxation to avoid confronting and coping with stressful situations. For example, a nonassertive person who objects to another person's behavior might engage in relaxation rather than deal directly with the problem. This might be appropriate if relaxation facilitated an appropriate and assertive encounter. However, relaxation might well divert attention from the problem and reduce motivation to act. In addition, overemphasis on the value of relaxation can reinforce self-defeating avoidance appraisals, such as "It is better to let things be rather than make waves; things will work out on their own." The relaxation instructor must be sensitive to the possible misuse of relaxation. However, remember that in some circumstances avoidance and denial may well be an appropriate reaction to a stressor

(Lazarus & Folkman, 1984). For example, immediately after heart surgery, the avoidance of arousing situations may be desired, even if this involves diverting attention from actual problems.

Assessing Progress

How does an instructor know if an approach to relaxation is working? A popular answer to this question is one I hesitate to recommend: "The approach you are practicing works for everyone. If it doesn't seem to work for you, keep at it. The effects take time to become apparent." Different techniques work for different people, and in my experience it takes from 1 day to 2 months to tell if any specific technique is worth continuing. Here are some of the signs to look for.

Absence of adverse effects. If a physical approach is having an adverse physical effect (cramping, dizziness, physical discomfort), it may not be working. Psychological negative effects (anxiety, depression, boredom) are more difficult to evaluate and they need to be weighed against technique benefits.

Negative reinforcement. If self-relaxation reduces a student's physical or mental problems, it is negatively reinforcing. Indeed, relaxation techniques are most frequently evaluated in terms of their potential for negative reinforcement. Symptom improvement (especially self-reported physical symptoms) can occur during the first session of training, and for some students the degree of first session improvement can be an excellent predictor of subsequent long-term improvement.

Positive reinforcement. Frequently ignored by relaxation instructors is self-relaxation's potential for positive reinforcement. If an approach is pleasurable or meaningful, it is working. The Checklist of Rest-Related States (Appendix, Worksheet 1) presents those words used most frequently by my students to describe the positive reinforcement value of self-relaxation exercises.

Ease of practice. If a relaxation technique is working, it is easier to practice. Students may report less resistance in setting time aside for relaxation and less time spent to achieve a satisfying level of relaxation. Often, as a student becomes more adept at relaxation, beginning techniques are experienced as too active and unnecessarily complicated. For example, isometric squeeze relaxation may become a strain to practice. The student may comment on the ease and simplicity of more meditative approaches.

Skill development. As claimed throughout this book, successful self-relaxation depends on the skills of focusing, passivity, and receptivity. To the extent an approach to relaxation fosters these skills, it is working. While a student of relaxation may not experience symptom relief or pleasure from a technique, training is indeed working if that student learns to practice with less distraction, increased passivity, and a greater willingness to tolerate unfamiliar rest-related states.

The relaxation deepening cycle. One effect of relaxation often mislabeled as an adverse reaction can actually be a sign of improvement. As discussed earlier, proficiency at relaxation may well unearth new sources of distraction. The range of distraction can vary considerably, including somatic sensations, emotional states, recollections, imagery, experiences that may seem paranormal, and increased alertness and sensitivity to external stimuli (see Checklist of Rest-Related States, Appendix, Worksheet 1). Such phases of increased distraction are most common in meditation, although they can occur in other approaches.

Such distractions may be part of the relaxation deepening cycle. If so, they may indicate that the student is honing skills of maintaining attentional focus, passivity, and receptivity. Part of the "work" of self-relaxation involves learning to deal with distraction by refocusing on a relaxation task while maintaining a stance of passivity and receptivity.

It is not easy to distinguish a genuinely adverse reaction from a distraction phase. Generally, if cognitive or affective intrusions are clearly linked with underlying pathology, they should be considered adverse reactions and treated accordingly. In addition, the following guidelines are somewhat useful.

1. Phases of distraction are generally characterized by experiences that most people find tolerable. Intruding thoughts and feelings are usually not particularly upsetting. Typically students describe their distractions as a nuisance. They may be perplexed that a once pleasurable or meaningful approach is now boring.

2. Phases of distraction are temporary, usually lasting no longer than 2 weeks.

3. Phases of distraction follow periods of practice that are particularly rewarding, periods in which the student displays increased skill at focusing and maintaining passivity and receptivity.

4. If a student reports that previous periods of distraction were followed by periods of deeper relaxation, the deepening cycle is most likely at work.

5. If distractions represent experiences new to the student, they may indicate that the student has acquired greater proficiency at focusing, passivity, and receptivity and is capable of experiencing deeper states of relaxation.

Research   257

Relaxation and Life: A Developmental Model

The most extensive way of evaluating relaxation's impact is to examine its place in the rest of life's activities. Rather than offer yet another questionnaire or checklist, here I will sketch a tentative and somewhat speculative developmental model of relaxation.

As a student becomes more proficient at self-relaxation, the experience of relaxation becomes differentiated and integrated. The student can identify a greater diversity of rest-related states and such states become integrated with the rest of life's activities. This process can occur on at least four levels.

Relaxation as a health chore or tranquilizer. At the first level self-relaxation is an externally prescribed activity done for its presumed benefits to health and well-being. For example, the student may be a heart patient who urgently wants to do whatever is possible to facilitate recovery. Practice is externally maintained, often through group or peer pressure or admonitions from therapists or physicians. Even the perceived benefits tend to be external. A student may continue practicing because of objectively measured improvements in symptomatology (for example, reductions in blood pressure) or signs of success provided by biofeedback equipment.

Relaxation as a valued activity. At this level, relaxation is done for its own sake. The student has internal signs of improvement such as symptom reduction and pleasurable rest-related states. Relaxation becomes a daily habit, at times a "healthy addiction." It is something to look forward to. If a practice session is missed, the student may feel the day is somehow incomplete.

For students at this level, relaxation may acquire an identity of its own. A set of exercises may begin to be valued like a friend or a special place. At this level, comments such as the following are not uncommon:

"Every time I do my exercises, it is like I am spending time with a special friend."

"I treasure my exercises, like I would a child. I try to guard them from the noisy intrusions of the day."

"When I sit to relax, it is as if I were returning to a special place, a sort of private vacation spot."

"Doing my relaxation is like coming home after a long departure."

"In my relaxation I am communing with a very special part of myself."

Relaxation as a part of life. Here, rest-related experiences generalize to outside the practice session. The student may unthinkingly squeeze or stretch at a moment of tension or fatigue. She may, in a quiet moment, drift into a pleasurable state of relaxation. In addition, the student may begin to identify underlying commonalities among different rest-related experiences. Students may have feelings about relaxation such as these:

> "When I put aside my petty concerns and see things in perspective, I feel a sense of serenity. This can happen while I practice my technique, or almost any other time."

> "When deep in contemplation I am reminded of those special moments in life when everything seems right, everything is in order. I felt this once while watching a beautiful sunset. This is how I feel when listening to certain music, or after making love. It's the same feeling."

> "Whether I am listening to peaceful music or contemplating a painting, I somehow feel in touch with things."

> "I seem to be most at peace when I am content with myself. I feel this at different times—when practicing yoga, taking a quiet walk, or spending time with a close friend."

Relaxation and the meaning of life. In moments of utter stillness and freedom from distraction, students may encounter insights of a philosophical or spiritual nature. Such moments are most profound when they provide meaning, structure, and guidance to all of life, even during times of pressure and tension. At this level, psychology has relatively little to say other than to acknowledge with respect the depth and diversity of human experience.

Chapter 3

Technical Notes

The following section describes some of the thinking that went into the development of Relaxation Dynamics. Here I will say a few words about the origin of each approach and how traditional instructions have been altered.

Lessons 1–5

A New Perspective on Relaxation Training

Much of traditional relaxation training (at least in the West) is unidimensional or unimodal. It is based on the assumption that all approaches have the same effect, the generation of a nonspecific physiological hypometabolic state (Benson, 1975). Potential cognitive or emotional differences between approaches are not addressed. Relaxation Dynamics takes a new perspective on relaxation training. It is based on the following premises: different approaches can have different effects and work differently for different people; it is better to combine several approaches than teach one alone; and subjective effects are to be taken seriously. These notions are supported by recent research and thinking on relaxation training (Bernstein & Borkovec, 1973; Engel, Glasgow, & Gaarder, 1983; Glasgow, Gaarder, & Engel, 1982; Lehrer & Woolfolk, 1984; Ornstein, 1972; Patel, 1984; Schwartz et al., 1978; Smith, 1977, 1978; Smith & Seidel, 1982; Smith & Siebert, 1984; Vahia et al., 1973).

Nine Major World Approaches to Relaxation

The nine major world approaches to relaxation represent approaches that appear frequently in the clinical and empirical literature. I am often

261

asked about a variety of approaches I have omitted, most notably biofeedback, hypnosis, jogging, dancing, swimming, and a large number of lesser-known techniques. Biofeedback and hypnosis are forms of *assisted relaxation* since they rely considerably on external equipment or guidance. Self-relaxation requires a minimum of such assistance. Activities such as jogging, dancing, or swimming are active and complex forms of recreation. Such recreation may indeed be relaxing, but for the sake of economy and consistency I chose to include only exercises that require a certain degree of passivity and withdrawal from the external world. Relaxation Dynamics begins when active involvement with outside pressures and demands ceases. Finally, some students may question the omission of certain relatively unknown personal favorites. Devotees of kriya yoga, Sufi teachings, shum yoga, Silva mind control, Benson's method, Simonton's method, and prayer of the heart may initially feel slighted that I have made no mention of approaches they may find quite meaningful. However, I firmly believe that the essence of each of these techniques is embodied in the Relaxation Dynamics framework. I may not provide a specific "healing fantasy," magic mantra, or prayer, but the raw materials are all here. Ultimately the student must invent, explore, and discover for herself.

It should be noted that many of the exercises presented here are also represented in various spiritual traditions. Relaxation Dynamics treats all such traditions with neutrality and respect. While the exercises presented here can be incorporated into a variety of programs of spiritual exploration, such a move is up to the reader.

Benefits of Self-Relaxation

The various individual approaches that comprise Relaxation Dynamics have at one time or another been claimed to prevent or alleviate illness, stress symptoms, insomnia, anxiety, performance anxiety, pain, burnout, and sexual difficulties; enhance creativity and performance; facilitate learning and retention; enrich pleasurable activity; and contribute to spiritual growth (Benson, 1975; Budzynski, 1974; Carrington, 1977; Charlesworth & Nathan, 1982; Davidson & Schwartz, 1984; Engel et al., 1983; Iyengar, 1965; Kriyananda, 1967; Lehrer & Woolfolk, 1984; Luthe, 1963, 1965, 1977; Masters & Houston, 1972; McCaffery, 1979; Meichenbaum & Jaremko, 1982; Naranjo & Ornstein, 1971; Patel, 1984; Pelletier, 1977; Quick & Quick, 1984; Rama et al., 1976; Reyher, 1964; Rosen, 1977; Samuels & Samuels, 1975; Shapiro, 1980; Shapiro & Walsh, 1984; Simonton et al., 1978; Turk et al., 1983; Vahia et al., 1973; Woolfolk & Lehrer, 1984). Although many students of Relaxation Dynamics have claimed these and other benefits, there are still serious empirical questions to be answered. For example, although progressive relaxation has been frequently used with considerable success in stress management, the use of contemplation has been relatively untested. Rigid prescription of one approach over another is not justified at this time. Instead, the most prudent approach is to note that different people react to different approaches in different ways. The instructor and student of self-relaxation can be invited to experiment and try with an open mind.

Assessment of Stress and Relaxation

The general stress symptoms described in Lesson 5 are derived from Stress Inventories 6 and 7 (Smith, 1980, 1982; Smith & Seidel, 1982; Smith & Sheridan, 1983; Smith & Siebert, 1984). The emotions listed as general stress symptoms are derived from Izard's (1977) factor analytic research on fundamental human emotions.

Lesson 6

The effects of casual self-relaxation are often underestimated. Such activities as reading for pleasure, daydreaming, listening to music, and sitting quietly can in certain circumstances be as helpful as formal single-technique approaches (Beiman et al., 1978; Boswell & Murray, 1979; Fenwick et al., 1977; Marlatt et al., 1984; Michaels et al., 1976; Puente & Beiman, 1980; Smith, 1976; Travis et al., 1976). The relaxing effects of casual approaches may be due to expectation of relief or an increased sense of self-control. Or perhaps setting time aside on a daily basis for quiet and restful activity provides a therapeutic diversion from stressful concerns and pressures. Whatever the value of unimodal approaches, casual or otherwise, combination approaches appear to be more effective (see the preceding section, "A New Perspective on Relaxation Training").

Lesson 7

Isometric squeeze exercises are derived in part from progressive relaxation, but they differ in a number of important ways. The strategy of tensing up and letting go of various muscle groups is fundamental to all schools of progressive relaxation. Yet, in spite of this stated objective, most manuals of progressive relaxation (including the classics listed later) introduce an occasional quick stretch, thereby confounding the effects of isometric relaxation with those of yogaform stretching. In addition, all major manuals further confound training by incorporating a variety of breathing and imagery exercises. The isometric exercises in Relaxation Dynamics are all purely isometric in nature. Other exercises are incorporated to enhance awareness of the effects of isometric relaxation. This enables the student to differentiate the effects of isometric tension and tension-release from the effects of other techniques.

Most traditional approaches instruct the student to abruptly generate a great deal of tension and then suddenly release the tension. Tension must be released immediately, as if "turning off a light switch" or "cutting the strings of a puppet." It is argued that this approach trains the student to detect muscle tension, discriminate between different sources of tension, and set into motion a tension-release rebound ("the momentum of letting go") that deepens relaxation. Unfortunately, in my experience this approach is counterproductive. It may explain why some studies find subjects practice and enjoy progressive relaxation less than other techniques (Carrington, 1977; Lehrer & Woolfolk, 1984). Here is my reasoning.

Traditional approaches to progressive relaxation give the student an aversive appraisal of sensations related to deliberate muscle constriction. When the student deliberately tightens up a muscle group, the resulting sensations are labeled "tension," and are described as a deliberate and somewhat exaggerated form of everyday nervous muscle tension. I suspect this aversive labeling tends to generalize to progressive relaxation as a whole: the technique ceases to be fun and becomes something of a health chore.

Isometric squeeze relaxation provides the student with three ways of appraising deliberate constriction as pleasurable. The "squeeze" action can be experienced as pleasing in and of itself, as something akin to a massage. The buildup and release of tension also can be enjoyable (like climbing a diving board and diving). Or the neuromuscular self-control demonstrated by tensing and relaxing specific muscle groups can be a source of reinforcement. Muscle constriction is not intrinsically unpleasant; only when it is chronic, excessive, and out of control does it become aversive. In isometric squeeze relaxation the student learns to control the duration and intensity of tension.

Making progressive relaxation fun does not detract from its effectiveness. The essential elements are still intact: muscle tension is generated and released; discrimination of tension from relaxation is learned; the ability to tense up and relax smaller and smaller muscle groups (differential relaxation) is developed; and attention is diverted from the worries of the world to a pleasurable and relaxing task. However, students also learn an important new skill, that of discriminating tension that is chronic, excessive, and out of control from tension that is deliberate and pleasurable. They learn how to generate tension in a way that is interesting and pleasant.

Finally, the Relaxation Dynamics program emphasizes that isometric relaxation is under the student's own control. I agree with Turk et al. (1983) that such an emphasis is important to enhancing generalization. More so than with any other approach to relaxation, the experience of self-control and mastery (especially in generating tension in isolated muscle groups) is part of what makes isometric relaxation fun. However, in later approaches we deemphasize control because it tends to conflict with the enhancement of passivity.

Those interested in traditional approaches to progressive relaxation should consult Bernstein and Borkovec (1973), Borkovec (1976), Jacobson (1938), Turk et al. (1983), and Wolpe (1958).

Lesson 8

Just as manuals of progressive relaxation frequently mix isometric and stretching exercises, yoga manuals mix a variety of approaches, including isometric, stretching, breathing, imagery, and meditative exercises. However, the basic yoga exercises place primary emphasis on the simple stretching of major muscle groups. The yogaform stretching sequence in Relaxation Dynamics is based purely on this strategy. Once again, the goal is to enable the student to differentiate the effects of yogaform stretching from the effects of other relaxation strategies. To facilitate comparisons with isometric relaxation, the stretching exercises presented here have been carefully developed to be parallel with the previous isometric exercises. The same muscle groups are involved, and both sequences are equally long and complex.

Yoga instructors may question my exclusive emphasis on stretching muscles, ligaments, and joints. Traditional yoga also incorporates exercises claimed to stimulate the glands, clean the alimentary canal and nasal passages, redistribute blood flow, infuse one with the life force, and so on. Such exercises are not included in Relaxation Dynamics because (1) they are difficult and possibly dangerous (as admitted even by their proponents); (2) their rationales are questionable; and (3) they appear with relative infrequency in broad-based yoga programs.

For extended discussion of yoga exercises and concepts, consult Eliade (1969), Funderburk (1977), Goleman (1977), Iyengar (1965), Kriyananda (1967), and Rama et al. (1976).

Lesson 9

Breathing exercises have a long and varied tradition. Some involve active and vigorous stretching; others involve more passive movement, such as breathing while pursing the lips. Some breathing exercises emphasize the importance of imagery, while others are nearly meditative in their simplicity. Relaxation Dynamics incorporates the full range of breathing exercises. It should be noted that a number of breathing exercises that appear routinely in yoga texts (such as alternate nostril breathing) have been omitted here because in my experience they are poorly received by students.

Every physical exercise in Relaxation Dynamics is preceded by a brief preparatory breathing exercise. This is a traditional practice in some forms of yoga. In my experience, a brief initial breathing sequence helps quiet potentially distracting tension and sensitize the student to the potential benefits of the exercise to follow.

The full range of breathing exercises is represented in the works of Charlesworth and Nathan (1982), Iyengar (1981), Jencks (1977), and Rama et al. (1979). Although the scanning exercise presented here closely resembles exercises that appear elsewhere (Bernstein & Borkovec, 1973; Budzynski, 1974; Charlesworth & Nathan, 1982; Paul, 1966), it is most properly described as a variant of mental isometric relaxation (RD 37).

Lesson 10

Exercises presented here derive in part from autogenic training, kundalini yoga, and Zen meditation. However, because of the quasi- and outright mysticism of these approaches, their record for generating research of dubious quality, and their propensity to mix and thus alter the effects of relaxation strategies, a more descriptive title was chosen for this sequence. Somatic focusing targets two levels of somatic sensations associated with relaxation. Beginning somatic exercises focus on sensations that are easier to detect, under greater voluntary control, and to some extent more external. Sensations of tingling, warmth, and heaviness are associated with the external skeletal muscles and skin. They are indirectly under voluntary control in that they often result from deliberately massaging, tensing, and stretching muscles. Breathing, of course, is also under partial voluntary control. And at least some of the sensations associated with relaxed breathing (flow of breath through the nostrils and outer nasal passages, movement of the chest muscles) are external.

It should be noted that, although I have retained the traditional warmth and heaviness suggestions, I believe that the student should be permitted to select whatever thoughts work best. Indeed, in some circumstances (a warm setting, an overweight student) a focus on warmth and heaviness could be aversive. The phrases and images students associate with relaxation processes differ considerably. For example, the dilation of peripheral blood vessels may for most trigger associations of "heaviness," but for a few trigger associations of "lightness." The student should be permitted to select whatever thoughts work best.

My students most frequently choose among the following:

Cool	Mellow
Elastic	Melting
Floating	Sedate
Fluid	Sensuous
Glowing	Slack
Heavy	Smooth
In control	Soft
Invigorated	Soothing
Light	Strong
Limber	Supple
Liquid	Throbbing
Listless	Touched
Loose	Warm
Massaged	

The second level of somatic focusing parallels the more advanced autogenic, Zen, and kundalini yoga exercises. Here, autogenic training focuses on the solar plexis and heart. Kundalini exercises identify imagined energy focal points or *chakras* identical to these areas. Additional chakras are located at the base of the throat and in an area between and slightly above the eyes. Kundalini yoga also places considerable importance on maintenance of an erect spine and on sensations imagined to represent "energy" flowing up the spine. All such sensations are ordinarily not either under voluntary control or indirect consequences of deliberate physical action. Such sensations are also more difficult to detect and are generally associated with deep internal organ systems.

It should be noted that my conceptualization of beginning and advanced somatic exercises is somewhat divergent from traditional accounts. Usually all somatic exercises are lumped together and treated as autonomically mediated. I argue that this is not entirely the case and that beginning exercises should be distinguished from those that are more advanced.

For further discussion of traditional accounts see Jencks (1977), Luthe (1963, 1965, 1977), Norris and Fahrion (1984), and Rama et al. (1976).

Lesson 11

Relaxation programs provide us with countless imagery exercises. Typically a preformulated image is imposed on all students. Relaxation Dynamics emphasizes not so much the content of imagery as the process of forming images. In my experience, students respond more favorably when given the opportunity to formulate their own imagery.

Relaxation Dynamics also focuses on theme over modality. Unlike most imagery-based programs, this program does not emphasize producing mental pictures that are vivid and life-like. Such a focus would be contrary to the spirit of passivity (the cessation of goal-directed striving) central to deeply rewarding self-relaxation. In addition, some students do not enjoy visual imagery. For this reason, Relaxation Dynamics presents visual imagery instructions side-by-side with verbal imagery (or association) exercises.

What is important is the theme of mental relaxation. Students are provided with seven potential general themes and are encouraged to develop their own.

A potential area of confusion merits attention. *Mastery imagery* as described in Relaxation Dynamics closely parallels the notion of *coping imagery* introduced by Meichenbaum and others. Coping imagery traditionally involves picturing the process of becoming anxious in a stressful situation, and then eventually coping with difficulties that might arise. What might be confusing is that others use the phrase *mastery imagery* in a different way. *Mastery imagery* has been used to refer to picturing oneself successfully dealing with a problem situation. Put differently, coping imagery incorporates experiences related to the *process* of dealing with a threat, whereas traditional mastery imagery focuses more on the *outcome,* the actual experience of success. Indeed, it might be better to term these two types of imagery "process imagery" and "outcome imagery."

I have chosen to use the term *mastery* to refer to all facets of successful coping—both the process of meeting a challenge, and the pleasurable and rewarding outcome of success. I have found that the term *coping* often suggests confrontation and struggle, making do or barely getting by (as when one responds "I'm coping" when asked "How are you doing?"). These connotations are hardly the stuff of deeply pleasurable fantasy. In contrast, *mastery* suggests the full range of pleasures that derive from actually meeting and overcoming a challenge. It has a connotation of self-affirmation and internal locus of control ("I am the master of my fate" vs. "I cope") central to successful thematic imagery. For further discussion of thematic exercises see Kroger and Fezler (1976), Masters and Houston (1972), McCaffery (1979), Meichenbaum (1971), and Samuels and Samuels (1975).

Lesson 12

Gendlin (1981) has introduced a psychotherapeutic technique called *focusing*. This technique involves directing attention toward a felt problem and in a nonanalytic and nondiscursive fashion exploring and experiencing the "felt meanings" associated with the problem. Put simply, it is a technique for getting in touch with hidden painful feelings associated with a problem area.

Gendlin makes it clear that the full range of life's experiences have felt meanings that are often hidden. Relaxation Dynamics' "Contemplation on Relaxation" exercise applies Gendlin's strategy, not to a problem, but to the experience of relaxation. It is a technique that acknowledges that there is often more to the experience of rest than meets the eye, recognizing the diversity and complexity of rest-related states. As such, it is an exercise that clearly displays the thinking underlying the entire Relaxation Dynamics program.

Lesson 13

Most trainers and scholars of meditation identify two broad schools of meditation technique: concentrative and mindfulness (or openness) meditation. Examples of concentrative meditation include transcendental meditation, clinically standardized meditation, and Benson's technique. Mindfulness meditations include advanced Zen exercises and a variety of "techniqueless" approaches such as that of Krishnamurti (1956). I have tried to construct exercises true to these contrasting traditions. However, the terms *concentrative* and *mindfulness* tend to be confusing to students. All too often concentrative is seen as meaning the effortful deployment of attention, while mindfulness draws blank, noncomprehending stares. I have taken the liberty to rename these approaches *centered focus* and *open focus* meditation. Open focus meditation should not be confused with Fehmi's "open focus" training, an advanced somatic focusing exercise that involves imagining the spatial characteristics of various regions of the body (Fehmi & Fritz, 1980; Fritz & Fehmi, 1982).

For a further discussion of meditation see Carrington (1978), Deikman (1982), Eliade (1969), Goleman (1977), Kapleau (1965), Krishnamurti (1956), LeShan (1974), Naranjo and Ornstein (1971), Ornstein (1972), Shapiro (1980), Shapiro and Walsh (1984), and Smith (in press).

Appendix

Worksheet Exercises

The following are worksheet exercises designed to facilitate and enhance the learning and use of self-relaxation. Some of them provide instructions on new ways of testing out and using relaxation techniques. Others ask you to think about and evaluate approaches you have learned. All of them require that you carefully report your thoughts and feelings in writing.

Whether you learn a single approach or the entire Relaxation Dynamics sequence of nine approaches, written exercises are an important part of Relaxation Dynamics. They can sensitize you to the often fleeting and subtle effects of certain exercises. They also can help you sort out and identify relaxation goals, compare and contrast techniques, and develop your own approach to relaxation.

This appendix contains 19 worksheet exercises to be used with the Relaxation Dynamics training programs described in Chapter 1 of Section II. Each program uses a different set of worksheets. Before starting a training program, follow the program's instructions for selecting and assembling the necessary worksheets. If you are an instructor, please be aware that students may require the Checklist of General Stress Symptoms and the Checklist of Rest-Related States found in Worksheet 1 in order to complete the Daily Log and Final Assessment worksheets.

Worksheet 1

DAY'S END QUESTIONNAIRE

Stress

Stress can have many meanings and no single meaning fits everyone. In this inventory you will be asked various questions about stress in your life. Try to answer honestly and openly. There are no right or wrong answers, since nearly everyone can experience stress in one form or another.

Stress can be caused by many different kinds of situations and events. These situations and events are called *stressors*. What created stress for you today? Below are a number of blanks. In these spaces list three or four of today's stressors.

1. _____

2. _____

3. _____

4. _____

Now, which of the above stressors is the best example of stress for you? That is, which one best illustrates what you are like under stress? (Please exclude those that are rare or unusual for you.) In the space below, describe this stressor again, this time in detail. Include where and when it happened, who was involved, what you did, and what happened to you. Make your description as specific and precise as possible.

Today's Typical Stressor

Now, imagine you are in the situation or event described above. What kinds of experiences did you have? How did you act? What did you think and feel? On the following Checklist of General Stress Symptoms check those words that fit how you felt today.

275

Checklist of General Stress Symptoms

Basic Physical Stress Symptoms

___ My heart beat fast, hard, or irregularly.
___ My breathing felt hurried, shallow, or uneven.
___ My muscles felt tight, tense, or clenched up.
___ I felt restless and fidgety.

Secondary Physical Stress Symptoms

___ I felt tense or self-conscious when I said or did something.
___ I perspired too much or felt too warm.
___ I felt the need to go to the rest room even when I didn't have to.
___ I felt uncoordinated.
___ My mouth felt dry.

Physical Stress Aftereffects

___ I felt tired, fatigued, worn out, or exhausted.
___ I had a headache.
___ I felt unfit or heavy.
___ My back ached.
___ My shoulders, neck, or back felt tense.
___ The condition of my skin seemed worse (too oily, blemishes).
___ My eyes watered or were teary.

Digestive Tract Symptoms

___ My stomach was nervous and uncomfortable.
___ I lost my appetite.

Cognitive Stress

___ I worried too much about not having what it takes to handle things.
___ I worried too much about how difficult or punishing my tasks are.
___ I worried too much about the outside demands and pressures in my way.
___ I worried too much about how complicated things are.
___ I worried too much about not knowing where I stand.
___ I worried too much about my frustrations.
___ I took things too seriously and did not see things in perspective.
___ I was burdened by my thoughts and worries.

Emotional Stress

___ I felt too distressed (discouraged, downhearted, or sad).
___ I felt too irritated or angry (annoyed, provoked, mad, or defiant).
___ I felt too much contempt.
___ I felt too much distaste or disgust.
___ I felt too shy or sheepish.
___ I felt too fearful.
___ I felt too depressed.
___ I felt too anxious.

Worksheet 1

Relaxation

When were you most relaxed today? What were you doing? Where were you? Were you with anyone? In the space below describe what you were doing when you were most relaxed today.

Today's Most Relaxing Moment

How did you feel when you were relaxed? What kinds of experiences did you have? On the following Checklist of Rest-Related States check those words that fit or describe what things were like for you when you were most relaxed. Try not to make this a chore. There is no need to slave over each word and make fine and perfect distinctions. Simply browse over the terms, as if you were in a bookstore, and check those that fit.

Checklist of Rest-Related States

__ Able	__ Concentrated	__ Fascinated
__ Absorbed	__ Confident	__ Feeling
__ Accepting	__ Conscious	__ Flexible
__ Actualized	__ Contemplative	__ Floating
__ Adjusted	__ Contented	__ Flowering
__ Agreeable	__ Controlled	__ Flowing
__ Alert	__ Cool	__ Fluid
__ Alive	__ Coordinated	__ Focused
__ Amazed	__ Coping	__ Fortified
__ Amused	__ Cosmic	__ Free
__ Animated	__ Cozy	__ Fresh
__ Answered	__ Creative	__ Full
__ Assertive	__ Daydreaming	__ Fun
__ Assured	__ Deep	__ Funny
__ At ease	__ Delighted	__ Gentle
__ At home	__ Detached	__ Giggly
__ At one	__ Devoted	__ Glorious
__ Athletic	__ Discharged	__ Glowing
__ Attentive	__ Discovering	__ Good
__ Attuned	__ Discriminating	__ Gratified
__ Awake	__ Dissolving	__ Great
__ Aware	__ Distant	__ Happy
__ Balanced	__ Dreamy	__ Harmonious
__ Beaming	__ Drowsy	__ Healing
__ Beautiful	__ Dynamic	__ Healthy
__ Belonging	__ Easy	__ Heavy
__ Beneficial	__ Easygoing	__ High
__ Blessed	__ Ecstatic	__ Hopeful
__ Blissful	__ Effective	__ Imaginative
__ Boundless	__ Elastic	__ Immense
__ Bright	__ Elated	__ Immortal
__ Calm	__ Encouraged	__ Immune
__ Capable	__ Energized	__ In control
__ Captivated	__ Engaging	__ In touch
__ Carefree	__ Engrossed	__ Indifferent
__ Caressed	__ Enlivened	__ Inexhaustible
__ Caring	__ Enraptured	__ Infinite
__ Casual	__ Enthusiastic	__ Innocent
__ Centered	__ Entranced	__ Insightful
__ Cheerful	__ Equanimous	__ Inspired
__ Childlike	__ Escaped	__ Integrated
__ Cleansed	__ Eternal	__ Interested
__ Clear	__ Even	__ Intuitive
__ Collected	__ Exalted	__ Invigorated
__ Comfortable	__ Excited	__ Jolly
__ Competent	__ Expansive	__ Joyful
__ Complete	__ Far away	__ Knowing
__ Composed	__ Far off	__ Laid back

___ Leisurely
___ Lethargic
___ Letting be
___ Letting go
___ Liberated
___ Light
___ Lightheaded
___ Lighthearted
___ Limber
___ Limp
___ Liquid
___ Listless
___ Lively
___ Loose
___ Loving
___ Loyal

___ Lucid
___ Luminous
___ Massaged
___ Meaningful
___ Meditative
___ Mellow
___ Melting
___ Motionless
___ Moved
___ Natural
___ Noiseless
___ Nonchalant
___ Open
___ Optimistic
___ Ordered
___ Pacified

___ Passive
___ Patient
___ Pausing
___ Peaceful
___ Perceptive
___ Placid
___ Playful
___ Pleasant
___ Pleased
___ Pleasured
___ Poised
___ Positive
___ Potent
___ Prayerful
___ Productive

___ Profound
___ Pure
___ Quiet
___ Radiant
___ Ready
___ Real
___ Realized
___ Reassured
___ Reborn
___ Receptive
___ Recovered
___ Refined
___ Refreshed
___ Rejoicing
___ Rejuvenated
___ Relaxed

___ Released
___ Relieved
___ Remote
___ Removed
___ Renewed
___ Reposed
___ Resolved
___ Rested
___ Restored
___ Reverent
___ Right
___ Safe
___ Satisfied
___ Secure
___ Sedate
___ Sensitized

___ Sensuous
___ Serene
___ Settled
___ Sexy
___ Sharp
___ Silent
___ Simple
___ Slack
___ Sleepy
___ Slow
___ Smooth
___ Soaring
___ Social
___ Soft
___ Soothing

___ Speechless
___ Spirited
___ Spiritual
___ Spontaneous
___ Stable
___ Steady
___ Still
___ Stimulated
___ Strengthened
___ Strong
___ Supple
___ Surprised
___ Sustained
___ Thankful
___ Thrilled
___ Throbbing

___ Tickled
___ Timeless
___ Tingling
___ Touched
___ Tranquil
___ Transcendent
___ Transparent
___ Unaffected
___ Unbothered
___ Unburdened
___ Unconstrained
___ Understanding
___ Undistracted
___ Unflappable
___ Unhurried
___ Unified

___ Uninhibited
___ Unruffled
___ Unworried
___ Vigorous
___ Vitalized
___ Void
___ Warm
___ Warmhearted
___ Whole
___ Wholesome
___ Wise
___ Wonderful
___ Wordless
___ Worshipful
___ Other Rest-
Related States:

Worksheet 2

FIRST SESSION QUESTIONNAIRE

1. **Fill out the first two checklists before practicing.** Before practicing this week's technique for the first time, describe how you feel right now, at this very moment, by checking the stress symptoms and rest-related states that fit you best. Try not to make this a chore. There is no need to slave over each word and make fine and perfect distinctions. Simply browse through the items, as if you were in a bookstore, and check those that fit.

2. **After filling out the checklists, practice this week's technique.** Practice for 20-30 minutes.

3. **Fill out the second two checklists after practicing.** You have now finished practicing your technique for this week. How do you feel at this time, this very moment? Once again, check the stress symptoms and rest-related states that fit you best.

4. **Fill out the Summary.** Compare your stress symptoms and rest-related states from before and after your practice.

Checklist of General Stress Symptoms

Basic Physical Stress Symptoms

___ My heart beats fast, hard, or irregularly.
___ My breathing feels hurried, shallow, or uneven.
___ My muscles feel tight, tense, or clenched up.
___ I feel restless and fidgety.

Secondary Physical Stress Symptoms

___ I feel tense or self-conscious when I say or do something.
___ I perspire too much or feel too warm.
___ I feel the need to go to the rest room even when I don't have to.
___ I feel uncoordinated.
___ My mouth feels dry.

Physical Stress Aftereffects

___ I feel tired, fatigued, worn out, or exhausted.
___ I have a headache.
___ I feel unfit or heavy.
___ My back aches.
___ My shoulders, neck, or back feels tense.
___ The condition of my skin seems worse (too oily, blemishes).
___ My eyes are watering or teary.

Digestive Tract Symptoms

___ My stomach is nervous and uncomfortable.
___ I have lost my appetite.

Cognitive Stress

___ I worry too much about not having what it takes to handle things.
___ I worry too much about how difficult or punishing my tasks are.
___ I worry too much about the outside demands and pressures in my way.
___ I worry too much about how complicated things are.
___ I worry too much about not knowing where I stand.
___ I worry too much about my frustrations.
___ I take things too seriously and do not see things in perspective.
___ I am burdened by my thoughts and worries.

Emotional Stress

___ I feel too distressed (discouraged, downhearted, or sad).
___ I feel too irritated or angry (annoyed, provoked, mad, or defiant).
___ I feel too much contempt.
___ I feel too much distaste or disgust.
___ I feel too shy or sheepish.
___ I feel too fearful.
___ I feel too depressed.
___ I feel too anxious.

Worksheet 2

Checklist of Rest-Related States

___ Able
___ Absorbed
___ Accepting
___ Actualized
___ Adjusted
___ Agreeable
___ Alert
___ Alive
___ Amazed
___ Amused
___ Animated
___ Answered
___ Assertive
___ Assured
___ At ease
___ At home

___ At one
___ Athletic
___ Attentive
___ Attuned
___ Awake
___ Aware
___ Balanced
___ Beaming
___ Beautiful
___ Belonging
___ Beneficial
___ Blessed
___ Blissful
___ Boundless
___ Bright
___ Calm

___ Capable
___ Captivated
___ Carefree
___ Caressed
___ Caring
___ Casual
___ Centered
___ Cheerful
___ Childlike
___ Cleansed
___ Clear
___ Collected
___ Comfortable
___ Competent
___ Complete
___ Composed

___ Concentrated
___ Confident
___ Conscious
___ Contemplative
___ Contented
___ Controlled
___ Cool
___ Coordinated
___ Coping
___ Cosmic
___ Cozy
___ Creative
___ Daydreaming
___ Deep
___ Delighted
___ Detached

___ Devoted
___ Discharged
___ Discovering
___ Discriminating
___ Dissolving
___ Distant
___ Dreamy
___ Drowsy
___ Dynamic
___ Easy
___ Easygoing
___ Ecstatic
___ Effective
___ Elastic
___ Elated
___ Encouraged

___ Energized
___ Engaging
___ Engrossed
___ Enlivened
___ Enraptured
___ Enthusiastic
___ Entranced
___ Equanimous
___ Escaped
___ Eternal
___ Even
___ Exalted
___ Excited
___ Expansive
___ Far away
___ Far off

___ Fascinated
___ Feeling
___ Flexible
___ Floating
___ Flowering
___ Flowing
___ Fluid
___ Focused
___ Fortified
___ Free
___ Fresh
___ Full
___ Fun
___ Funny
___ Gentle
___ Giggly

___ Glorious
___ Glowing
___ Good
___ Gratified
___ Great
___ Happy
___ Harmonious
___ Healing
___ Healthy
___ Heavy
___ High
___ Hopeful
___ Imaginative
___ Immense
___ Immortal
___ Immune

___ In control
___ In touch
___ Indifferent
___ Inexhaustible
___ Infinite
___ Innocent
___ Insightful
___ Inspired
___ Integrated
___ Interested
___ Intuitive
___ Invigorated
___ Jolly
___ Joyful
___ Knowing
___ Laid back

___ Leisurely
___ Lethargic
___ Letting be
___ Letting go
___ Liberated
___ Light
___ Lightheaded
___ Lighthearted
___ Limber
___ Limp
___ Liquid
___ Listless
___ Lively
___ Loose
___ Loving
___ Loyal

___ Lucid
___ Luminous
___ Massaged
___ Meaningful
___ Meditative
___ Mellow
___ Melting
___ Motionless
___ Moved
___ Natural
___ Noiseless
___ Nonchalant
___ Open
___ Optimistic
___ Ordered
___ Pacified

___ Passive
___ Patient
___ Pausing
___ Peaceful
___ Perceptive
___ Placid
___ Playful
___ Pleasant
___ Pleased
___ Pleasured
___ Poised
___ Positive
___ Potent
___ Prayerful
___ Productive

___ Profound
___ Pure
___ Quiet
___ Radiant
___ Ready
___ Real
___ Realized
___ Reassured
___ Reborn
___ Receptive
___ Recovered
___ Refined
___ Refreshed
___ Rejoicing
___ Rejuvenated
___ Relaxed

___ Released
___ Relieved
___ Remote
___ Removed
___ Renewed
___ Reposed
___ Resolved
___ Rested
___ Restored
___ Reverent
___ Right
___ Safe
___ Satisfied
___ Secure
___ Sedate
___ Sensitized

___ Sensuous
___ Serene
___ Settled
___ Sexy
___ Sharp
___ Silent
___ Simple
___ Slack
___ Sleepy
___ Slow
___ Smooth
___ Soaring
___ Social
___ Soft
___ Soothing

___ Speechless
___ Spirited
___ Spiritual
___ Spontaneous
___ Stable
___ Steady
___ Still
___ Stimulated
___ Strengthened
___ Strong
___ Supple
___ Surprised
___ Sustained
___ Thankful
___ Thrilled
___ Throbbing

___ Tickled
___ Timeless
___ Tingling
___ Touched
___ Tranquil
___ Transcendent
___ Transparent
___ Unaffected
___ Unbothered
___ Unburdened
___ Unconstrained
___ Understanding
___ Undistracted
___ Unflappable
___ Unhurried
___ Unified

___ Uninhibited
___ Unruffled
___ Unworried
___ Vigorous
___ Vitalized
___ Void
___ Warm
___ Warmhearted
___ Whole
___ Wholesome
___ Wise
___ Wonderful
___ Wordless
___ Worshipful
___ Other Rest-
    Related States:

Worksheet 2

Checklist of General Stress Symptoms

Basic Physical Stress Symptoms

___ My heart beats fast, hard, or irregularly.
___ My breathing feels hurried, shallow, or uneven.
___ My muscles feel tight, tense, or clenched up.
___ I feel restless and fidgety.

Secondary Physical Stress Symptoms

___ I feel tense or self-conscious when I say or do something.
___ I perspire too much or feel too warm.
___ I feel the need to go to the rest room even when I don't have to.
___ I feel uncoordinated.
___ My mouth feels dry.

Physical Stress Aftereffects

___ I feel tired, fatigued, worn out, or exhausted.
___ I have a headache.
___ I feel unfit or heavy.
___ My back aches.
___ My shoulders, neck, or back feels tense.
___ The condition of my skin seems worse (too oily, blemishes).
___ My eyes are watering or teary.

Digestive Tract Symptoms

___ My stomach is nervous and uncomfortable.
___ I have lost my appetite.

Cognitive Stress

___ I worry too much about not having what it takes to handle things.
___ I worry too much about how difficult or punishing my tasks are.
___ I worry too much about the outside demands and pressures in my way.
___ I worry too much about how complicated things are.
___ I worry too much about not knowing where I stand.
___ I worry too much about my frustrations.
___ I take things too seriously and do not see things in perspective.
___ I am burdened by my thoughts and worries.

Emotional Stress

___ I feel too distressed (discouraged, downhearted, or sad).
___ I feel too irritated or angry (annoyed, provoked, mad, or defiant).
___ I feel too much contempt.
___ I feel too much distaste or disgust.
___ I feel too shy or sheepish.
___ I feel too fearful.
___ I feel too depressed.
___ I feel too anxious.

Worksheet 2

Checklist of Rest-Related States

___ Able
___ Absorbed
___ Accepting
___ Actualized
___ Adjusted
___ Agreeable
___ Alert
___ Alive
___ Amazed
___ Amused
___ Animated
___ Answered
___ Assertive
___ Assured
___ At ease
___ At home

___ At one
___ Athletic
___ Attentive
___ Attuned
___ Awake
___ Aware
___ Balanced
___ Beaming
___ Beautiful
___ Belonging
___ Beneficial
___ Blessed
___ Blissful
___ Boundless
___ Bright
___ Calm

___ Capable
___ Captivated
___ Carefree
___ Caressed
___ Caring
___ Casual
___ Centered
___ Cheerful
___ Childlike
___ Cleansed
___ Clear
___ Collected
___ Comfortable
___ Competent
___ Complete
___ Composed

___ Concentrated
___ Confident
___ Conscious
___ Contemplative
___ Contented
___ Controlled
___ Cool
___ Coordinated
___ Coping
___ Cosmic
___ Cozy
___ Creative
___ Daydreaming
___ Deep
___ Delighted
___ Detached

___ Devoted
___ Discharged
___ Discovering
___ Discriminating
___ Dissolving
___ Distant
___ Dreamy
___ Drowsy
___ Dynamic
___ Easy
___ Easygoing
___ Ecstatic
___ Effective
___ Elastic
___ Elated
___ Encouraged

___ Energized
___ Engaging
___ Engrossed
___ Enlivened
___ Enraptured
___ Enthusiastic
___ Entranced
___ Equanimous
___ Escaped
___ Eternal
___ Even
___ Exalted
___ Excited
___ Expansive
___ Far away
___ Far off

___ Fascinated
___ Feeling
___ Flexible
___ Floating
___ Flowering
___ Flowing
___ Fluid
___ Focused
___ Fortified
___ Free
___ Fresh
___ Full
___ Fun
___ Funny
___ Gentle
___ Giggly

___ Glorious
___ Glowing
___ Good
___ Gratified
___ Great
___ Happy
___ Harmonious
___ Healing
___ Healthy
___ Heavy
___ High
___ Hopeful
___ Imaginative
___ Immense
___ Immortal
___ Immune

___ In control
___ In touch
___ Indifferent
___ Inexhaustible
___ Infinite
___ Innocent
___ Insightful
___ Inspired
___ Integrated
___ Interested
___ Intuitive
___ Invigorated
___ Jolly
___ Joyful
___ Knowing
___ Laid back

___ Leisurely
___ Lethargic
___ Letting be
___ Letting go
___ Liberated
___ Light
___ Lightheaded
___ Lighthearted
___ Limber
___ Limp
___ Liquid
___ Listless
___ Lively
___ Loose
___ Loving
___ Loyal

___ Lucid
___ Luminous
___ Massaged
___ Meaningful
___ Meditative
___ Mellow
___ Melting
___ Motionless
___ Moved
___ Natural
___ Noiseless
___ Nonchalant
___ Open
___ Optimistic
___ Ordered
___ Pacified

___ Passive
___ Patient
___ Pausing
___ Peaceful
___ Perceptive
___ Placid
___ Playful
___ Pleasant
___ Pleased
___ Pleasured
___ Poised
___ Positive
___ Potent
___ Prayerful
___ Productive

___ Profound
___ Pure
___ Quiet
___ Radiant
___ Ready
___ Real
___ Realized
___ Reassured
___ Reborn
___ Receptive
___ Recovered
___ Refined
___ Refreshed
___ Rejoicing
___ Rejuvenated
___ Relaxed

___ Released
___ Relieved
___ Remote
___ Removed
___ Renewed
___ Reposed
___ Resolved
___ Rested
___ Restored
___ Reverent
___ Right
___ Safe
___ Satisfied
___ Secure
___ Sedate
___ Sensitized

___ Sensuous
___ Serene
___ Settled
___ Sexy
___ Sharp
___ Silent
___ Simple
___ Slack
___ Sleepy
___ Slow
___ Smooth
___ Soaring
___ Social
___ Soft
___ Soothing

___ Speechless
___ Spirited
___ Spiritual
___ Spontaneous
___ Stable
___ Steady
___ Still
___ Stimulated
___ Strengthened
___ Strong
___ Supple
___ Surprised
___ Sustained
___ Thankful
___ Thrilled
___ Throbbing

___ Tickled
___ Timeless
___ Tingling
___ Touched
___ Tranquil
___ Transcendent
___ Transparent
___ Unaffected
___ Unbothered
___ Unburdened
___ Unconstrained
___ Understanding
___ Undistracted
___ Unflappable
___ Unhurried
___ Unified

___ Uninhibited
___ Unruffled
___ Unworried
___ Vigorous
___ Vitalized
___ Void
___ Warm
___ Warmhearted
___ Whole
___ Wholesome
___ Wise
___ Wonderful
___ Wordless
___ Worshipful
___ Other Rest-
      Related States:

Summary

Now compare your two Checklists of General Stress Symptoms. Did any symptoms decrease after practicing? Did any increase?

How do your two Checklists of Rest-Related States compare? How would you describe the quality of relaxation you experienced this session?

Worksheet 2

Worksheet 3

DAILY LOG FOR SETTING TIME ASIDE FOR REST

On the following page is your daily log for this week. Indicate the effects of this week's technique every day.

In the first space, describe your relaxation time-off activity for the day.

In the second space rate your level of tension before practicing and in the third space rate your level of tension after practicing. Use the following scale, in which:

  3 = Very tense
  2 = Moderately tense
  1 = Slightly tense
  0 = Not at all tense, completely relaxed

Then, going to the Checklist of General Stress Symptoms (p. 276), list the types of stress reduced most. Indicate whether the technique worked best for physical, cognitive, or emotional stress, and be sure to specify the type of stress that was reduced. For example, if your headache was lessened (a physical symptom), state that in the space provided. If you felt less afraid (an emotional stress symptom), indicate that in the space provided.

Next, going to the Checklist of Rest-Related States (p. 278), select the relaxation words that fit your technique best for the day. Write these words in the space provided.

Finally, describe any rest-related states you experienced at other times during the day.

Setting Time Aside for Rest

	Day 1	Day 2	Day 3	Day 4	Day 5	Day 6	Day 7
Time-Off Relaxation Activity							
Tension Level Before Practice							
Tension Level After Practice							
Types of Stress Reduced Most							
Relaxation States Produced							
Other Restful States							

Worksheet 4

DAILY LOG FOR ISOMETRIC SQUEEZE RELAXATION

On the following page is your daily log for this week. Indicate the effects of this week's technique every day.

In the first space rate your level of tension before practicing, and in the second space rate your level of tension after practicing. Use the following scale, in which:

3 = Very tense
2 = Moderately tense
1 = Slightly tense
0 = Not at all tense, completely relaxed

In the split spaces that follow, evaluate the degree of muscle tension you experienced in each of the 11 muscle groups before and after you practiced your exercises for that day (before\after).

Then, going to the Checklist of General Stress Symptoms (p. 276), list the types of stress reduced most. Indicate whether the technique worked best for physical, cognitive, or emotional stress, and be sure to indicate the type of stress that was reduced. For example, if your headache was lessened (a physical symptom), state that in the space provided. If you felt less afraid (an emotional stress symptom), indicate that in the space provided.

Next, going to the Checklist of Rest-Related States (p. 278), select the relaxation words that fit your technique best for the day. Write these words in the space provided.

Following that, describe any muscle groups that needed special attention (needed to be "squeeze-relaxed" more than twice, or needed to be divided into components).

Then describe the exercises you preferred, as well as any you developed or altered. If you divided a muscle group into components, describe how you relaxed each component. If you used a different technique to relax any muscle group, describe the technique.

Finally, describe any rest-related states you experienced at other times during the day.

Isometric Squeeze Relaxation

	Day 1	Day 2	Day 3	Day 4	Day 5	Day 6	Day 7
Tension Level Before Practice							
Tension Level After Practice							
Hands	✓	✓	✓	✓	✓	✓	✓
Arms	✓	✓	✓	✓	✓	✓	✓
Arms & Sides	✓	✓	✓	✓	✓	✓	✓
Back	✓	✓	✓	✓	✓	✓	✓
Shoulders	✓	✓	✓	✓	✓	✓	✓
Back of Neck	✓	✓	✓	✓	✓	✓	✓
Face	✓	✓	✓	✓	✓	✓	✓
Front of Neck	✓	✓	✓	✓	✓	✓	✓
Stomach & Chest	✓	✓	✓	✓	✓	✓	✓
Legs	✓	✓	✓	✓	✓	✓	✓
Feet	✓	✓	✓	✓	✓	✓	✓

Worksheet 4

Types of Stress Reduced Most	Relaxation States Produced	Areas Needing Special Attention	Special & Revised Exercises	Other Restful States

Worksheet 5
DAILY LOG FOR YOGAFORM STRETCHING

On the following page is your daily log for this week. Indicate the effects of this week's technique every day.

In the first space rate your level of tension before practicing, and in the second space rate your level of tension after practicing. Use the following scale, in which:

3 = Very tense
2 = Moderately tense
1 = Slightly tense
0 = Not at all tense, completely relaxed

In the split spaces that follow evaluate the degree of muscle tension you experienced in each of the 11 muscle groups before and after you practiced your exercises for that day (before\after).

Then, going to the Checklist of General Stress Symptoms (p. 276), list the types of stress reduced most. Indicate whether the technique worked best for physical, cognitive, or emotional stress, and be sure to indicate the type of stress that was reduced. For example, if your headache was lessened (a physical symptom), state that in the space provided. If you felt less afraid (an emotional stress symptom), indicate that in the space provided.

Next, going to the Checklist of Rest-Related States (p. 278), select the relaxation words that fit your technique best for the day. Write these words in the space provided.

Following that, describe any muscle groups that needed special attention (needed to be stretched more than twice, or needed to be divided into components).

Then describe the exercises you preferred, as well as any you developed or altered. If you divided a muscle group into components, describe how you relaxed each component. If you used a different technique to relax any muscle group, describe the technique.

Finally, describe any rest-related states you experienced at other times during the day.

295

Yogaform Stretching

	Day 1	Day 2	Day 3	Day 4	Day 5	Day 6	Day 7
Tension Level Before Practice							
Tension Level After Practice							
Hands	✓	✓	✓	✓	✓	✓	✓
Arms	✓	✓	✓	✓	✓	✓	✓
Arms & Sides	✓	✓	✓	✓	✓	✓	✓
Back	✓	✓	✓	✓	✓	✓	✓
Shoulders	✓	✓	✓	✓	✓	✓	✓
Back of Neck	✓	✓	✓	✓	✓	✓	✓
Face	✓	✓	✓	✓	✓	✓	✓
Front of Neck	✓	✓	✓	✓	✓	✓	✓
Stomach & Chest	✓	✓	✓	✓	✓	✓	✓
Legs	✓	✓	✓	✓	✓	✓	✓
Feet	✓	✓	✓	✓	✓	✓	✓

Worksheet 5

Types of Stress Reduced Most	Relaxation States Produced	Areas Needing Special Attention	Special & Revised Exercises	Other Restful States

Worksheet 6

DAILY LOG FOR INTEGRATIVE BREATHING

On the following page is your daily log for this week. Indicate the effects of this week's technique every day.

In the first space rate your level of tension before practicing, and in the second space rate your level of tension after practicing. Use the following scale, in which:

3 = Very tense
2 = Moderately tense
1 = Slightly tense
0 = Not at all tense, completely relaxed

Following that, you will find a space for each of this week's exercises. Put a plus sign (+) in the spaces for the exercises you found generally positive, helpful, or enjoyable. Put a minus sign (−) in the spaces for the exercises that were not positive, helpful, or enjoyable. Also, note any special feelings or experiences associated with each exercise.

Then, going to the Checklist of General Stress Symptoms (p. 276), list the types of stress reduced most. Indicate whether the technique worked best for physical, cognitive, or emotional stress, and be sure to indicate the type of stress that was reduced. For example, if your headache was lessened (a physical symptom), state that in the space provided. If you felt less afraid (an emotional stress symptom), indicate that in the space provided.

Next, going to the Checklist of Rest-Related States (p. 278), select the relaxation words that fit your technique best for the day. Write these words in the space provided.

In the following space, describe any exercises you developed, altered, or combined.

After that, indicate the scanning cues you used each day.

Finally, describe any rest-related states you experienced at other times during the day.

Integrative Breathing

	Day 1	Day 2	Day 3	Day 4	Day 5	Day 6	Day 7
Tension Level Before Practice							
Tension Level After Practice							
Deep Breathing							
Arm Swing							
Body Arch							
Breathing/Bowing							
Bowing/Stretching							
Stomach Squeeze							
Diaphragmatic							
Inhaling: Nose							
Exhaling: Lips							
Focused Breathing							
Thinking One							
Thinking Word							

Types of Stress Reduced Most	Relaxation States Produced	Special, Revised, & Combined Exercises	Scanning Cues Used	Other Restful States

Worksheet 7

DAILY LOG FOR SOMATIC FOCUSING (BEGINNING EXERCISES)

On the following page is your daily log for this week. Indicate the effects of this week's technique every day.

In the first space rate your level of tension before practicing, and in the second space rate your level of tension after practicing. Use the following scale, in which:

3 = Very tense
2 = Moderately tense
1 = Slightly tense
0 = Not at all tense, completely relaxed

Following that, you will find two spaces for each of this week's exercises. Put a plus sign (+) in the first space for the exercises you found generally positive, helpful, or enjoyable. Put a minus sign (−) in the first space for the exercises that were not positive, helpful, or enjoyable. In the second space describe the supporting and deepening images and/or phrases you found most helpful.

Then, going to the Checklist of General Stress Symptoms (p. 276), list the types of stress reduced most. Indicate whether the technique worked best for physical, cognitive, or emotional stress, and be sure to indicate the type of stress that was reduced. For example, if your headache was lessened (a physical symptom), state that in the space provided. If you felt less afraid (an emotional stress symptom), indicate that in the space provided.

Next, going to the Checklist of Rest-Related States (p. 278), select the relaxation words that fit your technique best for the day. Write these words in the space provided.

In the following space, describe any exercises you developed, altered, or combined.

In the space after that, describe and rate (+ or −) the quieting sequences you used.

Finally, describe any rest-related states you experienced at other times during the day.

303

Somatic Focusing (Beginning Exercises)

	Day 1	Day 2	Day 3	Day 4	Day 5	Day 6	Day 7
Tension Level Before Practice							
Tension Level After Practice							
Breathing							
Images/Phrases							
Isometric							
Images/Phrases							
Massage							
Images/Phrases							
Warm/Heavy							
Images/Phrases							

Types of Stress Reduced Most	Relaxation States Produced	Special, Revised, & Combined Exercises	Quieting Sequences Tried	Other Restful States

Worksheet 8

DAILY LOG FOR SOMATIC FOCUSING (ADVANCED EXERCISES)

On the following page is your daily log for this week. Indicate the effects of this week's technique every day.

In the first space rate your level of tension before practicing, and in the second space rate your level of tension after practicing. Use the following scale, in which:

3 = Very tense
2 = Moderately tense
1 = Slightly tense
0 = Not at all tense, completely relaxed

Following that, you will find two spaces for each of this week's exercises. Put a plus sign (+) in the first space for the exercises you found generally positive, helpful, or enjoyable. Put a minus sign (−) in the first space for the exercises that were not positive, helpful, or enjoyable. In the second space describe the supporting and deepening images and/or phrases you found most helpful.

Then, going to the Checklist of General Stress Symptoms (p. 276), list the types of stress reduced most. Indicate whether the technique worked best for physical, cognitive, or emotional stress, and be sure to indicate the type of stress that was reduced. For example, if your headache was lessened (a physical symptom), state that in the space provided. If you felt less afraid (an emotional stress symptom), indicate that in the space provided.

Next, going to the Checklist of Rest-Related States (p. 278), select the relaxation words that fit your technique best for the day. Write these words in the space provided.

In the following space, describe any exercises you developed, altered, or combined.

In the space after that, describe and rate (+ or −) the quieting sequences you used.

Finally, describe any rest-related states you experienced at other times during the day.

Somatic Focusing (Advanced Exercises)

	Day 1	Day 2	Day 3	Day 4	Day 5	Day 6	Day 7
Tension Level Before Practice							
Tension Level After Practice							
Solar Plexus							
Images/Phrases							
Spine							
Images/Phrases							
Heart							
Images/Phrases							
Throat							
Images/Phrases							
Visual							
Images/Phrases							

Types of Stress Reduced Most	Relaxation States Produced	Special, Revised, & Combined Exercises	Quieting Sequences Tried	Other Restful States

Worksheet 8

Worksheet 9

DAILY LOG FOR THEMATIC IMAGERY

On the following page is your daily log for this week. Indicate the effects of this week's technique every day.

In the first space, describe the type of thematic imagery you used.

In the second space rate your level of tension before practicing, and in the third space rate your level of tension after practicing. Use the following scale, in which:

3 = Very tense
2 = Moderately tense
1 = Slightly tense
0 = Not at all tense, completely relaxed

Then, going to the Checklist of General Stress Symptoms (p. 276), list the types of stress reduced most. Indicate whether the technique worked best for physical, cognitive, or emotional stress, and be sure to indicate the type of stress that was reduced. For example, if your headache was lessened (a physical symptom), state that in the space provided. If you felt less afraid (an emotional stress symptom), indicate that in the space provided.

Next, going to the Checklist of Rest-Related States (p. 278), select the relaxation words that fit your technique best for the day. Write these words in the space provided.

In the following space, describe any exercises you developed, altered, or combined.

In the space after that, describe the deepening exercises and Three R thoughts you incorporated.

Next, describe and rate (+ or −) the overall effects of the exercise you have chosen.

Then describe and rate (+ or −) the quieting sequences you used.

Finally, describe any rest-related states you experienced at other times during the day.

Thematic Imagery

	Day 1	Day 2	Day 3	Day 4	Day 5	Day 6	Day 7
Exercise Used							
Tension Level Before Practice							
Tension Level After Practice							
Types of Stress Reduced Most							
Relaxation States Produced							

Special, Revised, & Combined Exercises	Deepening Exercises & Three R Thoughts	Overall Effects	Quieting Sequences Tried	Other Restful States

Worksheet 10

DAILY LOG FOR RESTRICTIVE MENTAL EXERCISES

Check approach used:
— Contemplation
— Centered focus meditation
— Open focus meditation

On the following page is your daily log for this week. Indicate the effects of this week's technique every day.

In the first space, describe the type of restrictive mental exercise you used.

In the second space rate your level of tension before practicing, and in the third space rate your level of tension after practicing. Use the following scale, in which:

3 = Very tense
2 = Moderately tense
1 = Slightly tense
0 = Not at all tense, completely relaxed

Then, going to the Checklist of General Stress Symptoms (p. 276), list the types of stress reduced most. Indicate whether the technique worked best for physical, cognitive, or emotional stress, and be sure to indicate the type of stress that was reduced. For example, if your headache was lessened (a physical symptom), state that in the space provided. If you felt less afraid (an emotional stress symptom), indicate that in the space provided.

Next, going to the Checklist of Rest-Related States (p. 278), select the relaxation words that fit your technique best for the day. Write these words in the space provided.

In the following space, describe and rate (+ or −) the overall effects of the exercise you have chosen.

Then describe and rate (+ or −) the quieting sequences you used.

Finally, describe any rest-related states you experienced at other times during the day.

315

Restrictive Mental Exercises

	Day 1	Day 2	Day 3	Day 4	Day 5	Day 6	Day 7
Exercise Used							
Tension Level Before Practice							
Tension Level After Practice							
Types of Stress Reduced Most							
Relaxation States Produced							

Overall Effects	Quieting Sequences Tried	Other Restful States

Worksheet 10

Worksheet 11

FINAL ASSESSMENT FOR SETTING TIME ASIDE FOR REST

You are now ready to evaluate the effects of setting time aside for rest on a regular basis. What are the strengths and weaknesses of this approach? What are its special effects?

Let's begin with stress symptoms. What stress symptoms seem to be most affected by this approach? Describe these symptoms in detail, if possible. If you completed other worksheets for this approach, feel free to refer to them.

Now, what types of relaxation seem to be most associated with this technique? You might want to refer to the Checklist of Rest-Related States (p. 278).

Which of the following do you think this approach would be best for? Check those that apply.

_____ Waking up at the start of the day?

_____ Recovering from tensions at the end of the day?

_____ Preparing for sleep?

_____ Preparing for a stressful activity?

_____ Recovering from a stressful activity?

_____ Before work or study?

_____ After work or study?

_____ Increasing creativity and solving problems?

_____ Doing for fun?

_____ Using for personal growth and development?

_____ Other: _____

Describe any drawbacks, problems, or limitations that may be associated with this approach.

Did this approach have a different effect on different days or at different times? Explain.

Describe any activities you would give an overall positive evaluation and might use again.

Worksheet 12

FINAL ASSESSMENT FOR ISOMETRIC SQUEEZE RELAXATION

You are now ready to evaluate the effects of isometric squeeze relaxation. What are the strengths and weaknesses of this approach? What are its special effects?

Let's begin with stress symptoms. What stress symptoms seem to be most affected by this approach? Describe these symptoms in detail, if possible. If you completed other worksheets for this approach, feel free to refer to them.

Now, what types of relaxation seem to be most associated with this technique? You might want to refer to the Checklist of Rest-Related States (p. 278).

Which of the following do you think this approach would be best for? Check those that apply.

_____ Waking up at the start of the day?

_____ Recovering from tensions at the end of the day?

_____ Preparing for sleep?

_____ Preparing for a stressful activity?

_____ Recovering from a stressful activity?

_____ Before work or study?

_____ After work or study?

_____ Increasing creativity and solving problems?

_____ Doing for fun?

_____ Using for personal growth and development?

_____ Other: _____

Describe any muscle groups that needed special attention.

Which of the squeeze exercises seemed most valuable?

Which seemed least valuable?

Which squeeze exercises might you combine into larger, simpler exercises?

Describe any ways in which you revised or improved upon exercises.

Describe any drawbacks, problems, or limitations that may be associated with this approach.

Did this approach have a different effect on different days or at different times? Explain.

Worksheet 13

FINAL ASSESSMENT FOR YOGAFORM STRETCHING

You are now ready to evaluate the effects of yogaform stretching. What are the strengths and weaknesses of this approach? What are its special effects?

Let's begin with stress symptoms. What stress symptoms seem to be most affected by this approach? Describe these symptoms in detail, if possible. If you completed other worksheets for this approach, feel free to refer to them.

Now, what types of relaxation seem to be most associated with this technique? You might want to refer to the Checklist of Rest-Related States (p. 278).

Which of the following do you think this approach would be best for? Check those that apply.

_____ Waking up at the start of the day?

_____ Recovering from tensions at the end of the day?

_____ Preparing for sleep?

_____ Preparing for a stressful activity?

_____ Recovering from a stressful activity?

_____ Before work or study?

_____ After work or study?

_____ Increasing creativity and solving problems?

_____ Doing for fun?

_____ Using for personal growth and development?

_____ Other: _____

Describe any muscle groups that needed special attention.

Which of the stretching exercises seemed most valuable?

Which seemed least valuable?

Which stretching exercises might you combine into larger, simpler exercises?

Describe any ways in which you revised or improved upon exercises.

Describe any drawbacks, problems, or limitations that may be associated with this approach.

Did this approach have a different effect on different days or at different times? Explain.

Worksheet 14

FINAL ASSESSMENT FOR INTEGRATIVE BREATHING

You are now ready to evaluate the effects of integrative breathing. What are the strengths and weaknesses of this approach? What are its special effects?

Let's begin with stress symptoms. What stress symptoms seem to be most affected by this approach? Describe these symptoms in detail, if possible. If you completed other worksheets for this approach, feel free to refer to them.

Now, what types of relaxation seem to be most associated with this technique? You might want to refer to the Checklist of Rest-Related States (p. 278).

Which of the following do you think this approach would be best for? Check those that apply.

_____ Waking up at the start of the day?

_____ Recovering from tensions at the end of the day?

_____ Preparing for sleep?

_____ Preparing for a stressful activity?

_____ Recovering from a stressful activity?

_____ Before work or study?

_____ After work or study?

_____ Increasing creativity and solving problems?

_____ Doing for fun?

_____ Using for personal growth and development?

_____ Other: _____

Which of the breathing exercises seemed most valuable?

Which seemed least valuable?

Which breathing exercises might you combine into larger, simpler exercises?

Describe any ways in which you revised or improved upon exercises.

Describe any drawbacks, problems, or limitations that may be associated with this approach.

Did this approach have a different effect on different days or at different times? Explain.

Worksheet 15

FINAL ASSESSMENT FOR MENTAL EXERCISES

Check approach used:
___ Somatic focusing (beginning) ___ Somatic focusing (advanced)
___ Thematic imagery ___ Contemplation
___ Centered focus meditation ___ Open focus meditation

You are now ready to evaluate the effects of the mental exercise you have been practicing. What are the strengths and weaknesses of this approach? What are its special effects?

Let's begin with stress symptoms. What stress symptoms seem to be most affected by this approach? Describe these symptoms in detail, if possible. If you completed other worksheets for this approach, feel free to refer to them.

Now, what types of relaxation seem to be most associated with this technique? You might want to refer to the Checklist of Rest-Related States (p. 278).

Which of the following do you think this approach would be best for? Check those that apply.
_____ Waking up at the start of the day?
_____ Recovering from tensions at the end of the day?
_____ Preparing for sleep?
_____ Preparing for a stressful activity?
_____ Recovering from a stressful activity?
_____ Before work or study?
_____ After work or study?
_____ Increasing creativity and solving problems?
_____ Doing for fun?
_____ Using for personal growth and development?
_____ Other: _____

327

What are the strengths and weaknesses of this approach?

Which quieting sequence seemed to be best for this approach?

Describe any ways in which you revised or improved upon exercises.

Describe any drawbacks, problems, or limitations that may be associated with this approach.

Did this approach have a different effect on different days or at different times? Explain.

Worksheet 16
PERSONAL THOUGHTS

Name of Approach: _____

What is your overall impression of what you did this week for relaxation? How would you describe its essence, its most important characteristics, to a close friend? Answer this question in any way you wish. You might write an essay, poem, or letter; create a drawing; or keep a relaxation diary. Express yourself in whatever way seems most meaningful.

Worksheet 17

ROTATIONAL PRACTICE AND TRIAL RUNS

Rotational Practice

The goal of this exercise is to give you more experience with those approaches you have been practicing. Before proceeding further, list these approaches in the blanks below:

Approaches Practiced

_____

_____

_____

_____

For the time assigned by your instructor or suggested in the program instructions, practice a different approach each day. Rotate your exercise sequences. For example, if you have practiced isometric squeeze relaxation, yogaform stretching, and integrative breathing, practice isometric relaxation today, yogaform stretching tomorrow, and integrative breathing the next day. This should help sensitize you to their differing effects while providing you with additional practice experience. Remember, it takes time and practice for the effects of self-relaxation to become fully apparent.

Trial Runs

Often the effects and potentials of self-relaxation become more apparent when we experiment with practicing at different times and in different situations. You may be surprised at what can happen when you do a relaxation exercise before giving a talk, participating in sports, dancing, reading, making love, and so on. Try scheduling special relaxation exercise sessions immediately before or immediately after other activities. These special sessions are called *trial runs*.

It is important to plan your trial runs for activities that are pleasurable and rewarding. For instance, you might practice a sequence of isometric squeeze exercises before playing golf or taking a walk. You might try a session of yogaform stretching before going out to dinner, or integrative breathing before dancing or listening to music. Whatever you do, avoid practicing relaxation before or after a stressful activity. This advice may seem strange, since relaxation exercises are often promoted as tools for stress management. However, most people need practice at self-relaxation before they are ready to put it to use in stress management. Superficial training in self-relaxation usually isn't enough to counter the effects of stress.

More importantly, when self-relaxation is used prematurely, its effects can be distorted or limited by stress. If you consistently associate integrative breathing with a stressful activity, integrative breathing may itself take on stressful qualities. This effect of conditioning through association is often subtle and very powerful. We cringe when we see lightning because lightning is usually followed by a thunderclap. Children learn to dislike food that has at one time caused a stomachache because "bad" food is followed by discomfort. Fortunately, conditioning also teaches children not to touch hot stoves, for touching the stove is followed by a painful burn. But when relaxation is deliberately placed before a tense and threatening activity, relaxation also can become something to be avoided. Perhaps this is one of the reasons why many people who learn self-relaxation in stress clinics quit practicing in a few weeks.

By associating self-relaxation exercises with pleasurable and rewarding activities you reward yourself for practicing relaxation. You make use of another powerful conditioning principle, conditioning through reinforcement, to facilitate the mastery of self-relaxation. But more than this, you begin the process of exploring the rewards and potentials of self-relaxation. It is only through such personal experimentation that you can discover what the various exercises of Relaxation Dynamics have to offer.

First, try to think of some pleasant activities you would like self-relaxation to precede or follow. For the time being, put all criticism aside. Let yourself be creative. Think of as many activities as possible. Put them all down—the good ideas as well as the bad, the reasonable and the not so reasonable. Have some fun and see how many you can think of.

Pleasant Activities That Could Be Done
Before or After Self-Relaxation

1. _____
2. _____
3. _____
4. _____
5. _____
6. _____

7. _____

8. _____

9. _____

10. _____

11. _____

12. _____

13. _____

14. _____

15. _____

16. _____

17. _____

18. _____

19. _____

20. _____

Now, which of these are realistic? Which would you like to do before or after a brief session of self-relaxation? Place a check next to your choices.

You now are ready for some trial runs. Do no more than one trial run a day. You may use shortened versions (5 to 10 minutes) of self-relaxation exercises. After each trial run, report your results on the following Trial Run Report form.

Trial Run Report

Date and time _____

Describe the relaxation exercises used.

Describe the pleasurable activity done before or after the exercises.

Describe the results.

Worksheet 18

SETTING UP A QUIETING SEQUENCE

If you are practicing a form of mental relaxation (somatic focusing, thematic imagery, contemplation, or meditation), it is a good idea to precede each session with a physical quieting sequence. A quieting sequence consists of a set of squeezing, stretching, and/or breathing exercises designed to calm potentially distracting sources of tension and to focus the mind on the mental relaxation exercise to be practiced.

You may select any combination of physical exercises for your quieting sequence. The sequence should be from 5 to 10 minutes long and should contain 1 to 10 specific exercises. It is often a good idea to try out and compare several quieting sequences before picking the one you want.

Here are the physical exercises presented in Relaxation Dynamics:

Isometric Squeeze
1. Hand Squeeze
2. Arm Squeeze
3. Arm and Side Squeeze
4. Back Squeeze
5. Shoulder Squeeze
6. Back of Neck Squeeze
7. Face Squeeze
8. Front of Neck Squeeze
9. Stomach and Chest
    Squeeze
10. Leg Squeeze
11. Foot Squeeze

Yogaform Stretching
12. Hand Stretch
13. Arm Stretch
14. Arm and Side Stretch
15. Back Stretch
16. Shoulder Stretch
17. Back of Neck Stretch
18. Face Stretch
19. Front of Neck Stretch
20. Stomach and Chest
    Stretch
21. Leg Stretch
22. Foot Stretch

Integrative Breathing
23. Deep Breathing
24. Arm Swing Breathing
25. Body Arch Breathing
26. Breathing and Bowing
27. Bowing and Stretching
28. Stomach Squeeze
      Breathing
29. Active Diaphragmatic
      Breathing
30. Inhaling Through Nose
31. Exhaling Through Lips
32. Focused Breathing
33. Thinking the Word *One*
34. Thinking a Relaxing Word
35. Scanning

Which of these do you want to try out in a quieting sequence? (If you are not in the Complete 14-Week Training Program, you may not have learned every exercise. If so, select only from those you have learned.) On the following page is a form for recording experimental quieting sequences. Invent as many as you wish. Try each out with a mental relaxation exercise, then decide which you want to continue using as your main quieting sequence before every session of mental relaxation. List the one you choose on the final form.

Experimental Quieting Sequence

Exercise # _____

Exercise # _____

Exercise # _____

Exercise # _____

Exercise # _____

Exercise # _____

Exercise # _____

Exercise # _____

Exercise # _____

Exercise # _____

My Quieting Sequence
*(To be practiced before somatic focusing, thematic imagery,
contemplation, or meditation)*

Exercise # _____

Exercise # _____

Exercise # _____

Exercise # _____

Exercise # _____

Exercise # _____

Exercise # _____

Exercise # _____

Exercise # _____

Exercise # _____

Worksheet 19

SETTING UP PERSONALIZED RELAXATION SEQUENCES

You have now learned several approaches to self-relaxation and discovered that different exercises have different effects. Some work for you better than others. In this worksheet exercise you develop your own self-relaxation program, one that you can use for the rest of your life. The first step in constructing your program is deciding how you want to use self-relaxation.

Choosing Your Relaxation Goals

If you plan to continue practicing a relaxation sequence, what do you want to use it for? Check those that apply.

_____ To wake up at the start of the day

_____ To recover from tension at the end of the day

_____ To prepare for sleep

_____ To prepare for a stressful activity

_____ To prepare for work

_____ To prepare for study

_____ To prepare for sports

_____ To recover from a stressful activity

_____ To recover from work

_____ To recover from study

_____ To recover from sports

_____ To improve creativity and problem-solving

_____ To do for fun

_____ To foster personal growth and exploration

_____ To prepare or warmup for meditation or prayer

_____ To prepare for a pleasurable or rewarding activity (reading, music, sex, etc.)

_____ To relax briefly (less than 5 minutes) at any time in the day

_____ Other: _____

Now, look back at the goal(s) you have checked. Write your main goal(s) here (write as few or as many as you want):

Goal 1: _____

Goal 2: _____

Goal 3: _____

Goal 4: _____

Goal 5: _____

Now, consider all the exercises you have learned. Which might be best for the goals you have selected? How might you combine exercises or parts of exercises? On the Personalized Relaxation Sequence form that follows, write down your relaxation goal at the top of the page. List the exercises you think might work best for this goal, and then decide how you will arrange and combine these exercises. If you have several different relaxation goals, do one form for each. For example, if you want to develop a sequence to help you get to sleep and a sequence to help prepare you for studying, treat these as separate goals and fill out a different form for each. For purposes of reference, a list of all Relaxation Dynamics exercises is presented here.

Physical Exercises

Isometric Squeeze
1. Hand Squeeze
2. Arm Squeeze
3. Arm and Side Squeeze
4. Back Squeeze
5. Shoulder Squeeze
6. Back of Neck Squeeze
7. Face Squeeze
8. Front of Neck Squeeze
9. Stomach and Chest Squeeze
10. Leg Squeeze
11. Foot Squeeze

Yogaform Stretching
12. Hand Stretch
13. Arm Stretch
14. Arm and Side Stretch
15. Back Stretch
16. Shoulder Stretch
17. Back of Neck Stretch
18. Face Stretch
19. Front of Neck Stretch
20. Stomach and Chest Stretch
21. Leg Stretch
22. Foot Stretch

Integrative Breathing
23. Deep Breathing
24. Arm Swing Breathing
25. Body Arch Breathing
26. Breathing and Bowing
27. Bowing and Stretching
28. Stomach Squeeze Breathing
29. Active Diaphragmatic Breathing
30. Inhaling Through Nose
31. Exhaling Through Lips
32. Focused Breathing
33. Thinking the Word *One*
34. Thinking a Relaxing Word
35. Scanning

Unrestrictive Mental Exercises

Somatic Focusing (Beginning Exercises)
36. Breathing
37. Mental Isometric Relaxation
38. Mental Massage
39. Warmth and Heaviness

Somatic Focusing (Advanced Exercises)
40. Solar Plexis
41. Erect Spine
42. Heart
43. Base of Throat
44. Visual Phenomena
45. Somatic Deepening Suggestions

Thematic Imagery
46. Pleasure
47. Escape
48. Reminiscence
49. Mastery
50. Expression
51. Intuition
52. Sensation
53. Thematic Deepening Suggestions
54. Generalized "Three R" Thoughts

Restrictive Mental Exercises

Contemplation
55. Contemplation on Personal Strengths
56. Contemplation on Relaxation

Meditation
57. Centered Focus Meditation
58. Open Focus Meditation

Personalized Relaxation Sequence

Goal _____

List those exercises that seem best for meeting this goal.

_____
_____
_____
_____
_____
_____
_____
_____
_____
_____
_____
_____
_____
_____

Describe how you would order and combine these exercises.

1. _____
2. _____
3. _____
4. _____
5. _____
6. _____
7. _____
8. _____
9. _____
10. _____
11. _____
12. _____
13. _____
14. _____
15. _____

Worksheet 19

Evaluating Your Personalized Relaxation Sequences

You are now ready to test out your constructed sequences. Take care not to attempt more than one trial a day. Each time you try a sequence, describe the results using the Sequence Trial Report on the following page. (Make extra copies of this form so you can run several trials.)

Sequence Trial Report

Date and time _____

Describe the relaxation goal or situation.

Describe the personalized relaxation sequence.

What are the strengths and weaknesses of this sequence?

How might you improve upon it?

References

Beiman, I., Israel, E., & Johnson, S. A. (1978). During training and posttraining effects of live and taped extended progressive relaxation, self-relaxation, and electromyogram biofeedback. *Journal of Consulting and Clinical Psychology, 46,* 314–321.

Beiman, I. H., Johnson, S. A., Puente, A. E., Majestic, H. W., & Graham, L. E. (1984). The relationship of client characteristics to outcome for transcendental meditation, behavior therapy, and self-relaxation. In D. H. Shapiro & R. N. Walsh (Eds.), *Meditation: Classic and contemporary perspectives.* New York: Aldine.

Benson, H. (1975). *The relaxation response.* New York: William Morrow.

Bernstein, D., & Borkovec, T. (1973). *Progressive relaxation training: A manual for the helping professions.* Champaign, IL: Research Press.

Borkovec, T. D. (1976). Physiological and cognitive processes in the regulation of anxiety. In G. E. Schwartz & D. Shapiro (Eds.), *Consciousness and self-regulation: Advances in research* (Vol. 1). New York: Plenum.

Boswell, P. C., & Murray, G. J. (1979). Effects of meditation on psychological and physiological measures of anxiety. *Journal of Consulting and Clinical Psychology, 47,* 606–607.

Bower, K. S. (1976). *Hypnosis for the seriously curious.* Monterey, CA: Brooks/Cole.

Budzynski, T. H. (Author). (1974). *Relaxation training program* [Cassette recording]. New York: BMA Audio Cassettes.

Cannon, W. B. (1932). *Wisdom of the body.* New York: Norton.

Carrington, P. (1977). *Freedom in meditation.* New York: Anchor/Doubleday.

Carrington, P. (1978). *Clinical standardized meditation instructor's manual and self-regulating course.* Kendall Park, NJ: Pace Systems.

Carrington, P. (1984). Modern forms of meditation. In R. L. Woolfolk & P. M. Lehrer (Eds.), *Principles and practice of stress management.* New York: Guilford.

Cattell, R. B., Eber, H. W., & Tatsouka, M. M. (1970). *Handbook for the Sixteen Personality Factor Questionnaire.* Champaign, IL: Institute for Personality and Ability Testing.

Charlesworth, E. A., & Nathan, R. G. (1982). *Stress management.* Houston: Biobehavioral Publications.

Cohen, S. (1980). Aftereffects of stress on human performance and social behavior: A review of research and theory. *Psychological Bulletin, 88,* 82–108.

Curtis, J. W. (1984). *Motivation to continue meditating and the ability to sustain nonanalytic attention.* Unpublished master's thesis, Roosevelt University, Chicago.

Davidson, R. J., Goleman, D. J., & Schwartz, G. E. (1976). Attentional and affective concomitants of meditation: A cross-sectional study. *Journal of Abnormal Psychology, 85,* 235–238.

Davidson, R. J., & Schwartz, G. E. (1976). Psychobiology of relaxation and related states: A multiprocess theory. In D. I. Mostofsky (Ed.), *Behavior control and the modification of physiological activity.* Englewood Cliffs, NJ: Prentice-Hall.

Davidson, R. J., & Schwartz, G. E. (1984). Matching relaxation therapies to types of anxiety: A patterning approach. In D. H. Shapiro & R. N. Walsh (Eds.), *Meditation: Classic and contemporary perspectives.* New York: Aldine.

Deikman, A. J. (1982). *The observing self.* Boston: Beacon Press.

Di Nardo, P. A., & Raymond, J. B. (1979). Locus of control and attention during meditation. *Journal of Consulting and Clinical Psychology, 47,* 1136–1137.

Eliade, M. (1969). *Patanjali and yoga.* New York: Funk & Wagnalls.

Ellis, A. (1975). What people can do for themselves to cope with stress. In C. C. Cooper & R. Payne (Eds.), *Stress at work.* New York: Wiley.

Ellis, A. (1984). The place of meditation in cognitive-behavior therapy and rational-emotive therapy. In D. Shapiro and R. Walsh (Eds.), *Meditation: Classic and contemporary perspectives.* New York: Aldine.

Ellis, A., & Harper, R. (1979). *A new guide to rational living.* New Jersey: Prentice-Hall.

Engel, B. T., Glasgow, M. S., & Gaarder, K. R. (1983). Behavioral treatment of high blood pressure III. Follow-up results and treatment recommendations. *Psychosomatic Medicine, 45,* 23–29.

Fehmi, L., & Fritz, G. (1980, Spring). Open focus. *Somatics,* pp. 24–30.

Fenwick, P. B., Donaldson, S., Gillis, C., Bushman, J., Fenton, G. W., Perry, I., Tilsley, C., & Serafinowicz, H. (1977). Metabolic and EEG changes during transcendental meditation: An explanation. *Biological Psychology, 5,* 101–118.

Friedman, M., & Rosenman, R. H. (1974). *Type A behavior and your heart.* New York: Knopf.

Fritz, G., & Fehmi, L. (1982). *The open focus handbook: The self-regulation of attention in biofeedback training and everyday activities.* Princeton, NJ: Biofeedback Computers.

Funderburk, J. (1977). *Science studies yoga.* Glenview, IL: Himalayan Institute.

Gendlin, E. (1981). *Focusing.* New York: Bantam.

Glasgow, M. S., Gaarder, K. R., & Engel, B. T. (1982). Behavioral treatment of high blood pressure II. Acute and sustained effects of relaxation and systolic blood pressure biofeedback. *Psychosomatic Medicine, 44,* 155–170.

Glass, C. D. (1977). *Behavior patterns, stress, and coronary disease.* Hillsdale, NJ: Erlbaum.

Goleman, D. (1977). *The varieties of meditative experience.* New York: Dutton.

Guyton, A. (1976). *Textbook of medical physiology.* Philadelphia: Saunders.

Heide, F. J., & Borkovec, T. D. (1984). Relaxation-induced anxiety: Mechanisms and theoretical implications. *Behaviour Research and Therapy, 22,* 1–12.

Iyengar, B. K. S. (1965). *Light on yoga.* New York: Schocken Books.

Iyengar, B. K. S. (1981). *Light on pranayama.* New York: Crossroad.

Izard, C. E. (1977). *Human emotions.* New York: Plenum.

Jacobson, E. (1938). *Progressive relaxation* (2nd ed.). Chicago: University of Chicago Press.

Jakubowski, P., & Lange, A. J. (1978). *The assertive option.* Champaign, IL: Research Press.

Jencks, B. (1977). *Your body: Biofeedback at its best.* Chicago: Nelson-Hall.

Kanellakos, D. P., & Lukas, J. S. (Eds.). (1974). *The psychobiology of Transcendental Meditation.* Menlo Park, CA: Benjamin.

Kapleau, P. (1965). *The three pillars of Zen.* Boston: Beacon Press.

Krishnamurti, J. J. (1956). *Commentaries on living.* New York: Harper.

Kriyananda (1967). *Yoga postures for self-awareness.* San Francisco: Ananda Publications.

Kroger, W. S., & Fezler, W. D. (1976). *Hypnosis and behavior modification: Imagery conditioning.* Philadelphia: Lippincott.

Lazarus, R. S., & Folkman, S. (1984). *Stress, appraisal, and coping.* New York: Springer.

Lefcourt, H. M. (1976). *Locus of control: Current trends in theory and research.* Hillsdale, NJ: Erlbaum.

Lehrer, P. M., & Woolfolk, R. L. (1984). Are stress reduction techniques interchangeable, or do they have specific effects?: A review of the comparative empirical literature. In R. L. Woolfolk & P. M. Lehrer (Eds.), *Principles and practice of stress management.* New York: Guilford.

LeShan, L. (1974). *How to meditate.* New York: Bantam.

Luthe, W. (1963). Autogenic training: Method, research and application in medicine. *American Journal of Psychotherapy, 17,* 174–195.

Luthe, W. (1965). *Autogenic training.* New York: Grune & Stratton.

Luthe, W. (1977). *Stress and self-regulation: Introduction to the methods of autogenic therapy.* Pointe-Claire, Quebec: International Institute of Stress.

Marlatt, C. A., Pagano, R. R., Rose, R. M., & Marques, J. K. (1984). Effects of meditation and relaxation training upon alcohol use in male social drinkers. In D. H. Shapiro & R. N. Walsh (Eds.), *Meditation: Classic and contemporary perspectives.* New York: Aldine.

Masters, R., & Houston, J. (1972). *Mind games.* New York: Viking.

McCaffery, M. (1979). *Nursing management of the patient with pain* (2nd ed.). Philadelphia: Lippincott.

Meichenbaum, D. H. (1971). Examination of model characteristics in reducing avoidance behavior. *Journal of Personality and Social Psychology, 17,* 298–307.

Meichenbaum, D. H. (1977). *Cognitive-behavior modification: An integrative approach.* New York: Plenum.

Meichenbaum, D. H., & Jaremko, M. E. (Eds.). (1982). *Stress prevention and management: A cognitive-behavioral approach.* New York: Plenum.

Michaels, R. R., Huber, M. J., & McCann, D. S. (1976). Evaluation of transcendental meditation as a method of reducing stress. *Science, 192,* 1242–1244.

Naranjo, C., & Ornstein, R. (1971). *On the psychology of meditation.* New York: Viking.

Norris, P. A., & Fahrion, S. L. (1984). Autogenic biofeedback in psychophysiological therapy and stress management. In R. L. Woolfolk & P. M. Lehrer (Eds.), *Principles and practice of stress management.* New York: Guilford.

Novaco, R. W. (1978). Anger and coping with stress: Cognitive-behavioral interventions. In J. P. Foreyt & D. P. Rathjen (Eds.), *Cognitive behavior therapy: Research and application.* New York: Plenum.

Ornstein, R. (1972). *The psychology of consciousness.* San Francisco: W. F. Freeman.

Patel, C. (1984). Yogic therapy. In R. L. Woolfolk & P. M. Lehrer (Eds.), *Principles and practice of stress management.* New York: Guilford.

Paul, G. L. (1966). *Insight vs. desensitization in psychotherapy.* Stanford: Stanford University Press.

Pelletier, K. R. (1977). *Mind as healer, mind as slayer.* New York: Dell.

Puente, A. E., & Beiman, I. (1980). The effects of behavior therapy, self-relaxation, and transcendental meditation on cardiovascular stress response. *Journal of Clinical Psychology, 36,* 291–295.

Quick, J. C., & Quick, J. D. (1984). *Organizational stress and preventive management.* New York: McGraw-Hill.

Rama, Ballentine, R., & Ajaya. (1976). *Yoga and psychotherapy: The evolution of consciousness.* Glenview, IL: Himalayan Institute.

Rama, Ballentine, R., & Hymes, A. (1979). *Science of breath.* Honesdale, PA: Himalayan Institute.

Reyher, J. (1964). Brain mechanisms, intrapsychic processes and behavior: A theory of hypnosis and psychopathology. *American Journal of Clinical Hypnosis, 7,* 107–119.

Rivers, S. M., & Spanos, N. P. (1981). Personal variables predicting voluntary participation in and attrition from a meditation program. *Psychological Reports, 49,* 795–801.

Rosen, G. M. (1977). *The relaxation book.* Englewood Cliffs, NJ: Prentice-Hall.

Rotter, J. B. (1966). Generalized expectancies for internal versus external control of reinforcement. *Psychological Monographs, 80* (1, Whole No. 609).

Samuels, M., & Samuels, N. (1975). *Seeing with the mind's eye: History, techniques, and uses of visualization.* New York: Random House.

Schwartz, G. E., Davidson, R. J., & Goleman, D. T. (1978). Patterning of cognitive and somatic processes in the self-regulation of anxiety: Effects of meditation versus exercise. *Psychosomatic Medicine, 40,* 321–328.

Selye, H. (1976). *The stress of life* (2d ed.). New York: McGraw-Hill.

Shapiro, D. H. (1980). *Meditation: Self-regulation strategy and altered state of consciousness.* New York: Aldine.

Shapiro, D. H., & Walsh, R. N. (Eds.). (1984). *Meditation: Classic and contemporary perspectives.* New York: Aldine.

Simonton, C., Matthews-Simonton, S., & Creighton, J. (1978). *Getting well again.* Los Angeles: J. P. Tarcher.

Smith, J. C. (1976). Psychotherapeutic effects of transcendental meditation with controls for expectation of relief and daily sitting. *Journal of Consulting and Clinical Psychology, 44,* 630–637.

Smith, J. C. (1977). Yoga and stress. In Ajaya (Ed.), *Meditational therapy.* Glenview, IL: Himalayan Institute.

Smith, J. C. (1978). Personality correlates of continuation and outcome in meditation and erect sitting control treatments. *Journal of Consulting and Clinical Psychology, 46,* 272–279.

Smith, J. C. (1980). *Manual for Stress Inventory 6.* (Available from Dr. J. C. Smith, Roosevelt University, 430 S. Michigan, Chicago, IL 60605)

Smith, J. C. (1982). *Manual for Stress Inventory 7.* (Available from Dr. J. C. Smith, Roosevelt University, 430 S. Michigan, Chicago, IL 60605)

Smith, J. C. (1984). Self-reported reactions associated with nine approaches to relaxation training. (Available from Dr. J. C. Smith, Roosevelt University, 430 S. Michigan, Chicago, IL 60605)

Smith, J. C. (in press). *Meditation: A new way.* Champaign, IL: Research Press.

Smith, J. C., & Seidel, J. M. (1982). The factor structure of self-reported physical stress reactions. *Biofeedback and Self-Regulation, 7,* 35-47.

Smith, J. C., & Sheridan, M. (1983). Type A (coronary-prone) behavior and self-reported physical and cognitive reactions to actual life stressors. *Perceptual and Motor Skills, 56,* 545–546.

Smith, J. C., & Siebert, J. R. (1984). Self-reported physical stress reactions: First-
and second-order factors. *Biofeedback and Self-Regulation, 9,* 215–227.

Stoyva, J., & Anderson, C. (1982). A coping/rest model of relaxation and stress
management. In L. Goldberger & S. Breznitz (Eds.), *Handbook of stress:
Theoretical and clinical aspects.* New York: Free Press/Macmillan.

Stroebel, C. F. (Author). (1983). *Quieting reflex training for adults* [Cassette
recording]. New York: BMA Audio Cassettes.

Tellegen, A., & Atkinson, G. (1974). Openness to absorbing and self-altering
experiences ("absorption"), a trait related to hypnotic susceptibility. *Journal
of Abnormal Psychology, 83,* 268–277.

Travis, T. A., Kondo, C. Y., & Knott, J. R. (1976). Heart rate, muscle tension, and
alpha production of transcendental meditators and relaxation controls. *Biofeedback and Self-Regulation, 1,* 387–394.

Turk, D. C., Meichenbaum, D., & Genest, M. (1983). *Pain and behavioral medicine.* New York: Guilford.

Vahia, N. S., Doongaji, D. R., Jeste, D. V., Ravindranath, S., Kapoor, S. M., & Ardhap-
urkar, I. (1973). Psychophysiologic therapy based on the concepts of Patanjali. *American Journal of Psychotherapy, 27,* 557–565.

Van Nuys, D. (1971). A novel technique for studying attention during meditation.
Journal of Transpersonal Psychology, 3, 125–134.

Van Nuys, D. (1973). Meditation, attention, and hypnotic susceptibility: A cor-
relational study. *International Journal of Clinical and Experimental Hypnosis, 21,* 59–69.

Wallis, C. (1983, June 6). Stress: Can we cope? *Time,* pp. 48–54.

Wolpe, J. (1958). *Psychotherapy by reciprocal inhibition.* Stanford: Stanford
University Press.

Woolfolk, R. L., & Lehrer, P. M. (1984). *Principles and practice of stress management.* New York: Guilford.

Index

351

Wallis, C., 29
Walsh, R. N., 21, 262, 270
Wolpe, J., 7, 62, 265
Woolfolk, R. L., 6, 21, 29, 52, 242, 243,
    255, 261, 262, 263, 264
Worksheets, description of, 47–49

Yoga
    description of, 83
    order of exercises in, 244, 245
    and somatic focusing, 13
    and yogaform stretching, 10, 83–84,
      265
Yogaform stretching
    demonstration of, 10–11, 84–85
    exercises, 85–86

and focusing and passivity, 84–85
in Grand Tour, 10–11
vs. isometric squeeze relaxation, 84–
    85
rationale, 83–85
script, 88–111
vs. traditional yoga, 83–84
yoga, as basis for, 83–84, 265
Yoga Therapy, 245

Zen
    as centered focus meditation, 186, 269
    order of exercises in, 244, 245
    and somatic focusing, 13, 134, 266,
      267

About the Author

Photo by James E. Lee, Jr.

Jonathan C. Smith received his BA from Oberlin College and his PhD in psychology from Michigan State University. He is currently a clinical psychologist, Associate Professor of Psychology at Chicago's Roosevelt University, and Director of the Roosevelt University Stress Institute. Dr. Smith is a practicing psychotherapist specializing in stress management, and has continuing interests in research, writing, and program development. In addition he has conducted hundreds of workshops for universities, hospitals, government agencies, and businesses.

Dr. Smith's work on stress and relaxation is well-known by both scientists and practitioners. His articles have appeared in the *Journal of Consulting and Clinical Psychology, Psychological Bulletin, Biofeedback and Self-Regulation,* and *Perceptual and Motor Skills,* and have been reprinted in a variety of major clinical textbooks. In addition Dr. Smith has developed a number of successful training programs over the years. While serving for 4 years as Chairman of the Psychology Department at Roosevelt University, Dr. Smith developed a graduate program in health and community psychology and overhauled existing graduate programs in clinical and general psychology. He resigned as Chairman to establish the Roosevelt University Stress Institute and work on several books on relaxation, meditation, and stress management.

357